iOS App Development for Non-Programmers
Book 2: Flying With Objective-C

Kevin J McNeish

iOS App Development for Non-Programmers
Book 2: Flying With Objective-C

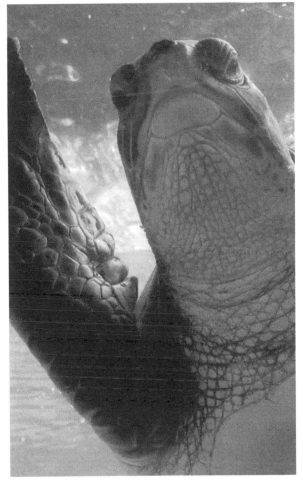

Author
Kevin J McNeish

Technical Editor
Greg Lee

Photography
Sharlene M McNeish

Copy Editor
Benjamin J Miller

© 2013 Oak Leaf
Enterprises, Inc.
1716 Union Mills Rd.
Troy, VA 22974
434-979-2417

http://iOSAppsForNonProgrammers.com

ISBN 978-0-9882327-1-6

Contents

Dedicated to Steve Jobs

The night it was announced Steve Jobs had passed away, by coincidence my wife and I already had tickets to San Francisco for early the next morning because I was scheduled to speak at a Silicon Valley Code Camp.

After arriving in San Francisco, we drove to Cupertino to make some sense of the loss of a great visionary. The flags at Apple were flying at half mast and many others had gathered to honor him with candles, flowers, posters and apples.

We drove to the home where Steve created the first Apple computer, then on to the last place he called home in Palo Alto where many others gathered to pay respects and where his silver Mercedes (famously without license plates) still sat in front of his house.

It was there I purposed to write this book series and do for *iOS* App development what Steve had done for users of iOS devices—make App development accessible to the masses of non-programmers, teaching them to create Apps that surprise and amaze their users.

Foreword

This book is the second in a series designed to teach non-programmers to create *iOS* Apps. Many books designed for beginning iOS App developers assume *way* too much. This book series intends to rectify that by assuming you know *nothing* about programming.

Learning Objective-C is the most difficult step for non-programmers in the iOS App development learning curve. It gets easier after this.

Each chapter, each exercise, and each code sample has been reviewed by people like yourself—with little or no experience (mostly "no experience") in writing code, or creating Apps. I rewrote many sections of the book multiple times, added diagrams, and improved code samples until all of our "beta readers" completely understood each key concept.

Once you master the concepts in this book, you will be able to move forward and learn other technologies such as Xcode, how to create a great user experience, and how to make use of the many tools available in Apple's Software Developer Kit. All of these topics are covered in other books in our *iOS App Development for Non-Programmers* series, with you, the non-programmer, in mind.

So, buckle up again, and let's get started.

Introduction

When I first started writing iOS Apps, coding in Objective-C was somewhat painful—like stuck-in-a-checkout-line-behind-the-old-woman-writing-a-personal-check painful. She's still stuck in the 1980s while everyone else uses debit cards. But then Apple made some major improvements to the language that moved Objective-C into the 21st century. Objective-C still has room for improvement, but you will find it is far more in line with modern programming languages, thanks to Apple's enhancements.

Mastering Objective-C is one of your biggest learning curves—especially if you have never written code before. While you can create prototype applications without writing any code, you need to write code to do anything meaningful.

Why You Should Use Objective-C

If you have developed software using more modern languages such as Java and C#, there are definitely some pain points when moving to Objective-C, but you should still invest the time and energy learning Objective-C to develop Apps that run on iOS devices.

Why?

Although some tools allow you to write in other languages, the vast majority of code samples available on the Internet are written in Objective-C—and believe me, since Apple provides so little in the way of code samples, you will spend significant time scouring the web for sample code.

So, you need to learn Objective-C if for no other reason than to understand the code samples—and, if you write your App in Objective-C, you don't have to translate the sample code into some other language, which can become pretty time-consuming.

So Objective-C it is.

Before you can start writing code, you need to understand the fundamentals of Objective-C, which are covered thoroughly in this book.

Chapter 1: The Basics

Welcome! This is the part of the book where you learn how to get yourself and your computer set for App development, get your hands on the code samples that come with this book, and learn some of the basics of iOS App development.

Sections in This Chapter

1. *Getting Set Up*

2. *Downloading the Sample Code*

3. *iOS—The Operating System*

4. *Source Code, Compilers & Machine Code*

5. *The Cocoa Touch Framework*

6. *Designing with Humans in Mind*

Getting Set Up

Before going further in this book, you need to accomplish three primary tasks:

1. Get an Intel-based Mac computer on which you can build iOS Apps

2. Register as an Apple developer (free)

3. Download and install Xcode

Rather than repeating the details of these tasks in each book in this series, I'll refer you to Chapter 1 in our first book in this series, *iOS App Development For Non-Programmers Book 1: Diving In*.

Downloading the Sample Code

We have spent a lot of time putting together relevant samples for you. Follow these steps to download and install this book's sample code on your Mac:

1. In the browser on your Mac, go to this link:

   http://iOSAppsForNonProgrammers.com/SamplesOC.html

2. When you get to the download page, click the **Download Sample Code** link (Figure 1.1).

Sample Code

Click this link to download the sample code for this book:

Download Sample Code

Figure 1.1 Click the Download Sample Code link

3. If Safari is your default web browser, when you click the link, you will see a blue progress indicator in the upper-right corner of the browser (Figure 1.2).

Figure 1.2 The download progress indicator

4. When the blue progress bar completely fills, and then disappears, the download is complete. To view the downloaded file, click the Show downloads button in the upper-right corner of Safari (Figure 1.3).

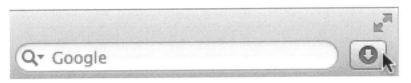

Figure 1.3 Click the Show downloads button.

5. This displays the Downloads popup. Click the small magnifying glass on the right (Figure 1.4).

Figure 1.4 Click the magnifying glass to see the samples.

This displays the downloaded **SamplesOC** folder in the Finder (Figure 1.5).

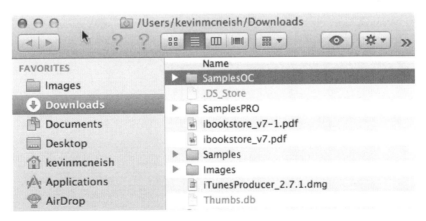

Figure 1.5 The newly downloaded samples

6. Let's make a copy of this folder and save it the **Documents** folder (you can choose a different destination folder if you prefer).

With the **SamplesOC** folder still selected, press the **Command** key (the key to the left of the spacebar), and while holding the key down, press the **C** key (in other words, press **Command+C**). This makes a copy of the folder in memory.

7. Next, on the left side of the Finder window, click the **Documents** folder as shown in Figure 1.6, and then press the **Command+V** keys to add a copy of the **SamplesOC** folder into the **Documents** folder.

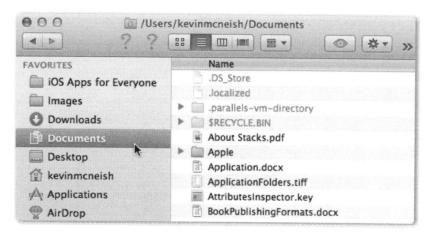

*Figure 1.6 Select the **Documents** folder.*

8. Double-click the **SamplesOC** folder in the right-hand panel of the Finder window and you will see the sample project folders shown in Figure 1.7.

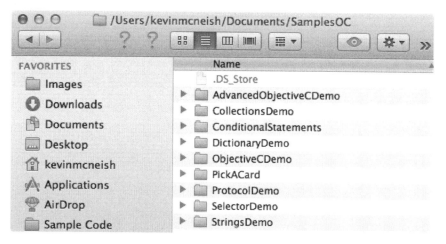

Figure 1.7 The sample project folders

iOS—the Operating System

Apps are not the only software running on an iPhone, iPod Touch or iPad.

They also run an **operating system** called **iOS**, which manages the device hardware and provides the core functionality for all Apps running on the device.

When you first turn on an iPhone, the Apple icon displayed on a black screen greets you. During this startup phase, the operating system gets the iPhone ready to be used. It displays the user's wallpaper and App icons. It also tries to find a carrier signal for the cell phone and a wireless signal for Wi-Fi access.

As Apple releases new versions of the iOS operating system, it continues to improve the core functionality of the device by adding new features, fixing bugs, and even releasing new built-in Apps. With each release of iOS, you can add new functionality to the Apps you create by taking advantage of the new features that it provides.

The type of App that you create is limited only by your imagination. You can use specific hardware and software features of iOS devices for widely different purposes. For example, you can use the microphone to record voice memos or to act as an input for a musical wind instrument (check out the *Ocarina* App for an example of this). You can use the camera not only to take pictures, but also to view details of the world around you as in augmented reality Apps such as the *Yelp* App. You can use Internet access to get the latest weather forecast or to retrieve a list of current political candidates. You can use the GPS to show the user's current location on a map or as an altimeter to show his or her current elevation.

Each time that you install an App on your smart phone, it gets smarter. The newly installed App empowers your phone with a new set of functionality. And now with the advent of *Siri*, the voice-activated assistant introduced in the iPhone 4s, your phone seems even smarter with a personality to go along with its intelligence (unfortunately, there is currently no way to access Siri's functionality from the Apps that you create).

Source Code, Compilers & Machine Code

In this book you will learn to use the Objective-C programming language to write code for your App. Objective-C is a **high-level language**, meaning it is closer to human language than the actual code an iOS device executes when it is running your App. A high-level language makes it easier for you, the App developer, to understand and write code for your App.

Ultimately, an iOS device doesn't understand the Objective-C programming language. Rather, an iOS device understands a **machine code** instruction set consisting of bits of data (ones and zeroes) specific to its **processor**. For example, the iPhone 4 and iPad use the Apple A4 processor, the iPhone 4s and iPad 2 use the newer Apple A5 processor, the new iPad uses the A5x processor, and the iPhone 5 uses the A6 processor.

So, there needs to be an interpretation, or conversion of the Objective-C code that you write into machine code, which an iOS device can actually execute. The tool that performs this magic is known as a **compiler**. As you work through the samples in this book, you will add code to an Xcode project, and then *build* the project. This build process is what takes the Objective-C code that you have written and converts it into machine code as shown in Figure 1.8.

Figure 1.8 The compiler converts source code to machine code.

So, whenever you read about compiling or building a project, now you have a high-level picture of what's going on behind the scenes.

The Cocoa Touch Framework
—Oh, the Things You Can Do!

You need more than just Objective-C to create an App. Everything that you do in your App—such as designing the **user interface** (**UI**), writing the **core logic**, and saving and retrieving **data**—gets its functionality from Apple's **Cocoa Touch Framework**. The Cocoa Touch Framework provides access to important services that allow your App to do great things. Cocoa Touch is actually a set of many smaller frameworks (reusable sets of tools), each focusing on a set of core functionality.

The following table lists some of the most commonly used frameworks and services included in Cocoa Touch as well as a description of the functionality that each service provides for your App.

Scanning through this table should give you some ideas of the features that you can add to your App in order to provide a compelling experience for your users.

We will only be using a few of these Cocoa Touch frameworks in this book, but for extensive coverage of the other key Cocoa Touch frameworks, check other books in this series.

Cocoa Touch Frameworks

Framework	Description
Foundation	Contains the low-level core classes such as collections, strings, and date and time management.
UIKit	Contains all the standard iOS user-interface controls that you need to design a great user experience including buttons, text fields, sliders, activity indicators, and table views for displaying lists of data.
Address Book	Lets you access the contacts stored on a device from your App.

Framework	Description
Cut, Copy and Paste	Allows you to share images, rich text, and HTML between Apps.
Core Location	Allows you to determine the location (latitude and longitude) of the device. You can use this information to display points of interest near the user or even show his or her current altitude.
Gyroscope and Accelerometer	Your App can use the device's gyroscope and accelerometer (iPhone 4 and newer) to sense motion, 3D attitude, and rate of rotation. This is great for games or other Apps that use motion to improve the user experience.
Compass	Another feature that allows you to improve location and map services by providing the user's heading (the direction they are facing) from the device's magnetometer.
Map Kit	Allows you to add maps to your App that the user can zoom and pan. You can also add overlays with your own custom information.
Event Kit	Allows a user to access his or her existing calendar of events and to add new calendar events and alarms.
Core Data	Provides a high-level graphical interface for designing the structure of your App's data. Core Data is designed to manage potentially large amounts of data.

Framework	Description
Multitasking	Allows your App to perform background tasks for better performance and battery life.

iCloud	Lets you store a user's documents and data in a central location on the Internet that can be accessed from any of the user's devices.
System Configuration	Allows you to determine if a Wi-Fi or cell connection is in use and whether a particular host service can be accessed through a connection.
Camera and Photo Library	Allows you to import images from the photo library, take new photos, and create augmented reality Apps using the live camera feed. In iPhone 4 and newer, you can access both front & main cameras.
iPod Media Library	Allows you to play music in the background while your App runs and provides access to the full media library on the device.
Text and Email Messaging	Provides a user interface and underlying components to compose and send text messages and emails from within your App.
Quick Look	Provides your App with an interface for previewing content files your App does not directly support such as iWork or Microsoft Office.
Accessories	Lets you control hardware devices attached to the 30-pin connector at the bottom of iOS devices.

Framework	Description
Multi-Touch Gestures	Allows you to add standard iOS gesture recognition to your App for gestures such as tap, double-tap, swipe, pinch, rotate, and pan.
Store Kit	Allows you to set up the purchase of content and services from within your App such as unlocking additional App features or new levels in a game.
iAd	Lets you embed ads into your App that users can click to learn more about a particular product. By implementing iAd, you're basically putting an empty billboard into your App onto which Apple fills ad space. iAd allows you to generate more revenue from your App!

Designing With Humans in Mind

I know you're itching to put fingers to keyboard and get on with the fun of creating Apps, but you should absolutely read Apple's *iOS Human Interface Guidelines* document first. One of the biggest problems in software development is forgetting about end users. If you lose sight of the people who will be using your App, you may create an App that is difficult to comprehend and use.

There is a reason that Apple has taken over the world with iOS devices in contrast with products like Microsoft's Zune that are now acting as expensive paperweights. It's because Apple has designed its devices and Apps with humans in mind. And not just any humans—they are designed for what Apple likes to call "the 80 percent," or the majority of your users.

Sometimes it's hard to ignore the very vocal 20 percent of users; but if you fold on this point and add complex features to please a smaller percentage of users, your App will not be easily used by the other 80 percent.

I highly recommend you read this document thoroughly and keep it close in mind through the entire adventure of building your Apps.

Chapter 2: Understanding Classes & Objects

The Objective-C programming language is object-oriented. This means that when you write code, you are mostly interacting with objects. This is similar to other object-oriented languages such as Java and C#. Understanding the foundational information in this chapter is key to your success as an iOS App developer.

Sections in This Chapter

8. *NSObject—The Queen Mother*

9. *id—the Object Identifier*

10. *Summary*

User-Interface Objects

When you create iOS Apps, the majority of objects that you work with are user-interface objects. As you can see by looking at the iOS Clock App shown in Figure 2.1, there are many different kinds of user-interface objects.

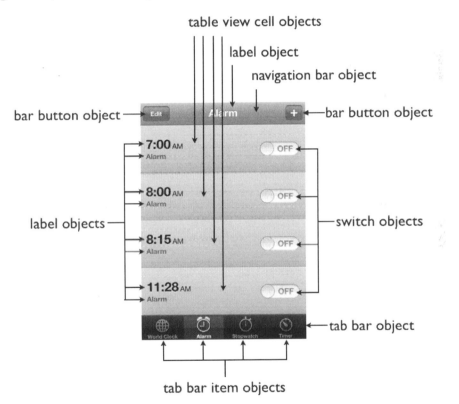

Figure 2.1 User-interface objects in the Clock App

You can interact with some objects by touching, tapping, pinching, and sliding them. Other objects, such as labels, are not interactive; they are only used to display information.

Fortunately, Apple allows you to use, in your own custom Apps, the very same user-interface objects that they have used in the built-in iOS Apps. When you install Xcode on your computer, you also install a library full of user-interface controls as shown in Figure 2.2.

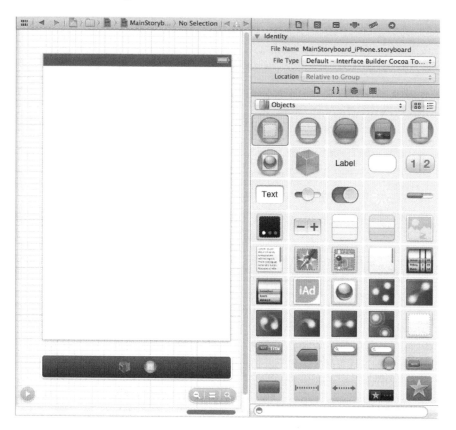

Figure 2.2 User-interface Control Library

Each one of the user-interface icons on the right represents an Objective-C class. A ***class*** is like a blueprint for an ***object***. You create objects from a class. For example, when you drag a Label icon from the list on the right and drop it on the design surface on the left (Figure 2.3), you are creating a label object from the **UILabel** class.

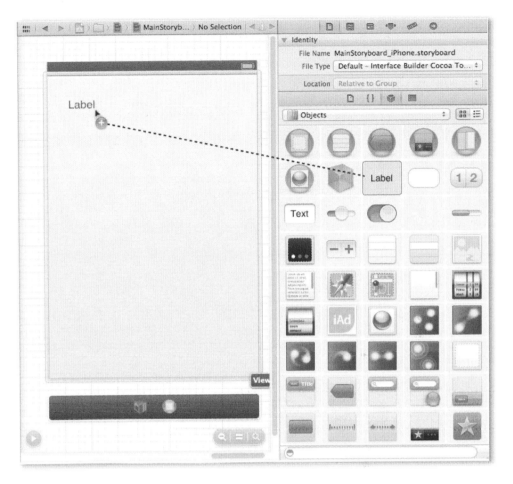

*Figure 2.3 Creating a label object from the **UILabel** class*

You can create many objects from a single class. As shown in Figure 2.4, four text fields have been created from the **UITextField** class by dragging the **Text** field icon and dropping it onto the design surface.

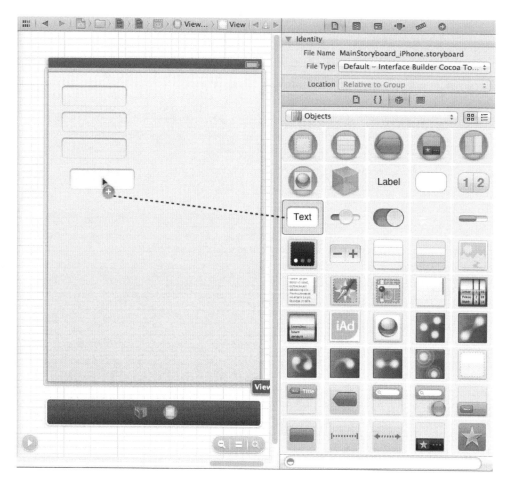

Figure 2.4 Creating multiple objects from a class

To see which class a particular user-interface icon represents, click the class in the library (Figure 2.5).

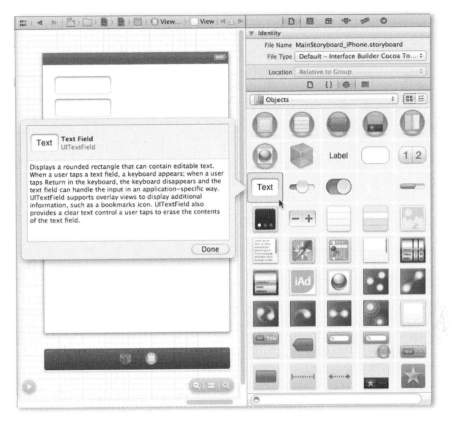

Figure 2.5 Click a user-interface icon to see which class it represents.

Clicking on a user-interface icon pops up a help dialog, which tells you the class that it represents (**UITextField** in this example), as well as a description of the physical ***attributes*** and behavior of objects created from that class. In object-oriented programming, an object created from a class is referred to as an ***instance*** of the class.

Examining Object Attributes

To see the attributes of a user-interface object, you can use Xcode's Attribute Inspector (Figure 2.6). First, click on a user-interface object in the design surface to select it. Then, to bring up the Attributes Inspector, select **View > Utilities > Show Attributes Inspector** from the menu. You can see the Attributes Inspector in the upper-right corner of Figure 2.6. Whenever you select an object in the design surface, you can see its attributes in the Attribute Inspector. Every object has its own set of attributes, so you can change an attribute on one object without affecting any other objects.

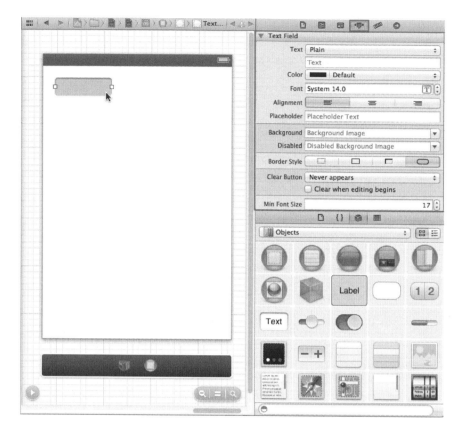

Figure 2.6 Viewing an object's attributes with the Attribute Inspector

As you can see, you can choose from quite a few attributes. Here is a description of some of them:

- **Text** – Specifies the text contained in the text field

- **Background** – Specifies the background color of the text field

- **Alignment** – Specifies if the text is left-, center-, or right-aligned

- **Color** – Specifies the color of the text within the text field

An object's attributes are defined in the class blueprint from which the object was created. Each attribute has a default value, also specified in the class. After an object has been created, you can change the value of its attributes. For example, in Figure 2.7, the selected text field's **Text** has been changed to **www.apple.com**, its **Alignment** has been changed to **Centered**, and its text **Color** has been changed to red.

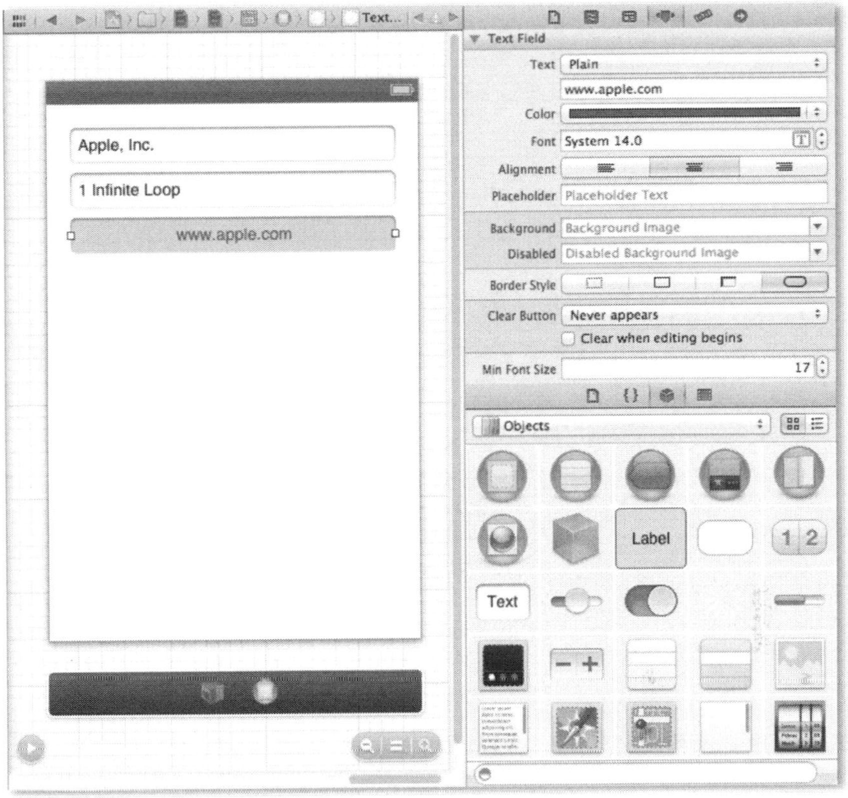

Figure 2.7 Changing the values of an object's attributes

So what does all of this have to do with Objective-C? Apple used Objective-C to create the user-interface classes. All of the classes that you create will also be written in Objective-C, so it's instructive to take a closer look at these classes and see how they work.

Understanding Class Properties

Up to this point, we have been talking about an object's *attributes*. Ultimately, for every attribute you see in the Attribute Inspector, there is a corresponding **property** in the class definition. In fact, Apple could have called it the *Property* Inspector. If you look at Apple's documentation for the **UITextField** class, you see a list of properties such as:

- background
- borderStyle
- clearButtonMode
- clearsOnBeginEditing

17

- font

- placeholder

- text

- textAlignment

- textColor

In this context, attributes and properties are similar. In Xcode, an object has attributes; in Objective-C, the class on which an object is based has properties.

Understanding Class Methods

Not only do user-interface objects have attributes, they also have behavior. For example, when you touch a text field in an iOS App, a keyboard pops up and each letter that you type on the keyboard automatically appears in the text field.

The behavior of an object, or the actions that it can perform, are defined in the class blueprint as **methods**. A method is comprised of one or more (usually more) lines of code grouped together to perform a specific task.

Figure 2.8 shows a formal representation of the **UITextField** class known as a **class diagram**. It lists the properties of **UITextField** as well as a few of its commonly used methods.

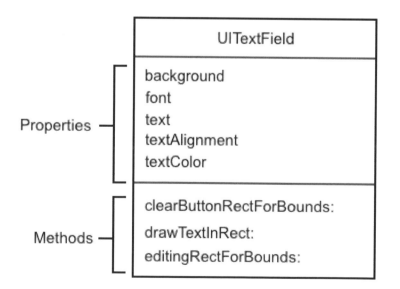

*Figure 2.8 **UITextField** properties and methods*

Each of these methods can be performed individually and has a different effect on the text field. For example, the **drawTextInRect:** method displays the text inside the text field.

All objects created from a single class have the same behavior because the same method code runs for every object created from that class.

Non-Visual Objects

Not all objects can be seen or interacted with as you can with user-interface objects. A good example of a non-visual object is the *View Controller* object shown on the left in Figure 2.9. On the right side is a *view*. A view contains one screen of information on an iOS device.

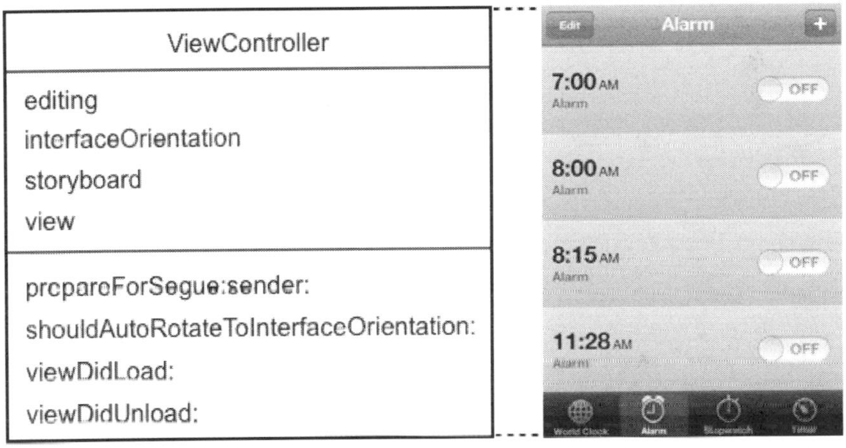

Figure 2.9 The View Controller is a non-visual object.

Every view in an iOS App has a view controller that works behind the scenes in conjunction with the view. It has properties that (among other things):

- Indicate if the user can edit items in the view

- Report the orientation of the user interface (portrait or landscape)

- Allow you to access user-interface elements

It has methods that

- Allow you to navigate to other views

- Specify the interface orientations that the view supports

- Indicate when the associated view is loaded and unloaded from the screen

View controller objects are based on the Cocoa Touch Framework's **UIViewController** class, or one of its subclasses.

Another category of non-visual objects that work behind the scenes is **business objects**. Business objects contain the core business logic of your App. They often represent real-world entities such as a customer, an invoice, a product, or a payment. Figure 2.10 shows a **Calculator** business object that contains the core logic behind the **Calculator** user interface. The **Calculator** business object is created from a custom **Calculator** class (Apple doesn't provide a **Calculator** class in the Cocoa Touch Framework).

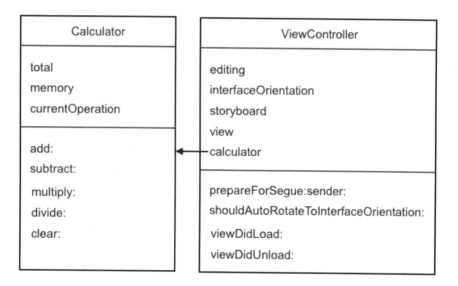

Figure 2.10 The Calculator business object contains business logic.

Typically, Apple's user-interface classes such as labels, text fields, and buttons do everything you need them to—with no extra programming on your part.

In contrast, you have to add properties and methods to view controller classes to do things that are specific to the App that you are building. For example, you need to add code that responds to the touch of a button or the slide of a switch, or that collects information from text fields. When it comes to business objects—such as the Calculator, Invoice, or Customer—you have to do even more coding because you have to create these from scratch, since no class in the Cocoa Touch Framework has the properties and methods that you need.

So, check out the custom **ViewController** code shown in Figure 2.11.

```
@interface DetailViewController ()
@property (strong, nonatomic) UIPopoverController
    *masterPopoverController;

- (void)configureView;
@end

@implementation DetailViewController

@synthesize detailItem =
    _detailItem;
@synthesize detailDescriptionLabel =
    _detailDescriptionLabel;
@synthesize masterPopoverController =
    _masterPopoverController;

#pragma mark - Managing the detail item

- (void)setDetailItem:(id)newDetailItem
{
    if (_detailItem != newDetailItem) {
        _detailItem = newDetailItem;

        // Update the view.
        [self configureView];
    }

    if (self.masterPopoverController != nil) {
        [self.masterPopoverController
         dismissPopoverAnimated:YES];
    }
}
```

Figure 2.11 ViewController code written in Objective-C

What does this code do? How does it work? How do you change existing methods and add new properties and methods to accomplish the tasks that you need to perform in your App?

By the time you finish this book, you will know the answer to all these questions and more. You will have learned Objective-C.

Object-Orientation and Discoverability

Working with an object-oriented language is a great advantage. One reason is

discoverability—a measure of how easy is it to discover, or find the code that you need to perform a particular task.

Apple provides thousands of classes for you to build your Apps. When you need to perform a specific task, your first job is discovering which Cocoa Touch Framework class will help you get the job done. However, once you discover the class you need, it opens up a world of functionality for you because each class contains many related methods.

For example, let's say that you are creating an App having one text field for the user's first name and another text field for his/her last name (Figure 2.12). When the user clicks the **Done** button, you want to display a welcome message that combines the first and last names (for example, "Welcome Steve Jobs"). So, how do you do this?

Figure 2.12 How do you combine first and last names into a single message?

A bit of research will reveal that the Cocoa Touch Framework contains the **NSString** class, which allows you to manipulate a set of characters. It has two methods that allow you to combine strings:

- **stringByAppendingFormat:**

- **stringByAppendingString:**

Just what you were looking for!

Once you learn about the existence of the **NSString** class, the whole world of string manipulation is open to you. In fact, **NSString** has over 140 methods that you can use for manipulating strings.

In **Table 2.1**, the column on the left lists a few of the tasks you can perform with **NSString** and the column on the right lists the associated **NSString** methods that you can use to perform each task.

You don't need to know how all these methods work right now. I just want to give you a sense of the kinds of methods available to you.

You will find object-orientation is "the gift that keeps on giving" as you discover new Cocoa Touch Framework classes and see how each one opens a world of functionality for you.

Table 2.1 Common Tasks and Methods of NSString

Task	Methods
Creating and Initializing Strings	initWithString: initWithFormat:
Combining Strings	stringByAppendingFormat: stringByAppendingString:
Dividing Strings	substringFromIndex: substringToIndex:
Finding Characters and Substrings	rangeOfString: enumerateLinesUsingBlock:
Identifying and Comparing Strings	isEqualToString: hasPrefix: hasSuffix:
Changing Case	lowercaseString: uppercaseString:
Getting Numeric Values	doubleValue: floatValue: intValue: boolValue:

Inheritance

Inheritance, a basic principle of object-oriented programming, is important for you to understand. The term "inheritance" refers to the concept that a class can be based on, or inherit its attributes (properties) and behavior (methods) from another class.

For example, as illustrated in Figure 2.13, the **UITextField** class inherits from the **UIControl** class.

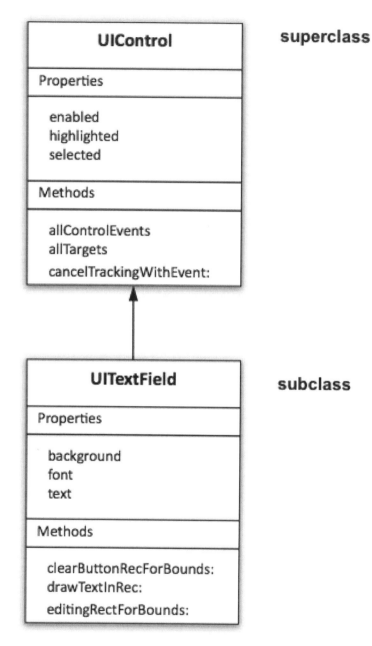

*Figure 2.13 **UITextField** inherits from **UIControl***

Because of this relationship, **UITextField** inherits the **UIControl** class's **enabled**, **highlighted**, and **selected** properties as well as all of its methods. In this relationship, **UIControl** is referred to as a ***superclass*** of **UITextField**. In turn, **UITextField** is referred to as a ***subclass*** of **UIControl**.

Class inheritance can go much further than just one level. For example, if you trace **UITextField's** heritage to the top level, it looks as shown in Figure 2.14.

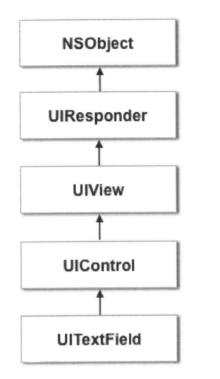

*Figure 2.14 **UITextField** full inheritance chain*

UITextField inherits from **UIControl**, which inherits from **UIView**, and so on, all the way up to **NSObject**, which sits at the top of the inheritance chain. As you walk the inheritance chain the other way, from top to bottom, each class adds new properties and methods, which are inherited by the class below it.

In Objective-C, a class can have only one superclass but can have zero, one, or many subclasses (known as zero-to-many). For example, **UIControl** has several subclasses, three of which are shown in Figure 2.15.

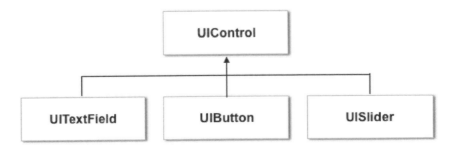

Figure 2.15 Classes can have zero-to-many subclasses.

Where will you come across subclasses in your daily App development? For starters, when you create a new iOS project, Xcode automatically adds view controller subclasses to your project. For example, if you create a Master-Detail App, Xcode adds **MasterViewController** and **DetailViewController** classes to your project, as shown in Figure 2.16 (you will learn all about these classes a little later).

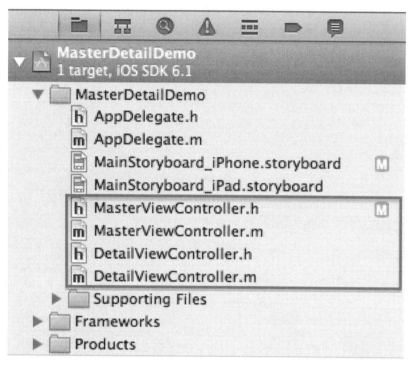

*Figure 2.16 **MasterViewController** and **DetailViewController** classes*

As you can see in Figure 2.17, **MasterViewController** is a subclass of **UITableViewController**, which is in turn a subclass of **UIViewController**. The **DetailViewController** class is a direct subclass of **UIViewController**.

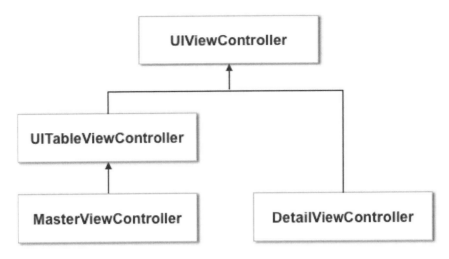

Figure 2.17 View controller class hierarchy

NSObject—The Queen Mother

NSObject is the queen mother of all classes in the Cocoa Touch Framework. Ultimately, the **NSObject** class defines the basic attributes and behavior for Objective-C objects. For the most part, each class found in the Cocoa Touch Framework, as well as the custom classes that you create, can trace its heritage back to the **NSObject** class, just as you saw with **UITextField** in Figure 2.14.

> **Fun Fact:** Many of the classes in the Cocoa Touch Framework start with the prefix "NS," which stands for "NeXTStep," the operating system developed by Steve Jobs' NeXT Computer company. It was later acquired by Apple after they brought the prodigal son Steve back into the fold.

I say "for the most part," because you can define your own root class that isn't a subclass of **NSObject**—but you probably shouldn't and won't.

NSObject has basic properties and methods that are inherited by all subclasses. One example is the **description** method, which returns a string describing the object. By default, **description** returns the name of the class, but you can override this method in a subclass and return something more meaningful. For example, the **description** method of the **NSDate** class returns the current date as a string.

id—the Object Identifier

Since you can declare your own root classes, there has to be another way to refer to any type of object—whether it's derived from **NSObject** or from your own custom root class. That's where the **id** keyword comes into play.

In Objective-C, all objects are of type **id**. The **id** designation provides no information about an object except it *is* an object!

You will see the **id** keyword used in later chapters when you begin creating code that responds to the user touching the user interface.

Summary

In this chapter, you learned the following facts about classes, objects, and inheritance:

- A class is a blueprint from which objects are created.

- A class defines the attributes and behavior of objects created from it.

- Class properties define the attributes of objects and methods define their behavior.

- Inheritance is a key feature of object-oriented programming. It allows a subclass to inherit attributes and behavior from a superclass.

- A class can have zero or more subclasses.

- All classes can trace their heritage back to the **NSObject** class.

- The **id** keyword is used in Objective-C to denote "any object at all."

Chapter 3: Working With Cocoa Touch Classes

Most books start to teach you Objective-C by having you build your own custom classes. For non-programmers, it's like teaching someone to drive by having him or her build a car—it can be a bit overwhelming.

So, I'll teach you to drive first, and then I'll show you how to build your own custom car. Let's start out with a few easy classes to help you get a feel for Objective-C.

Sections in This Chapter

1. *Opening the ObjectiveCDemo Sample Project*

2. *Running the Sample App*

3. *Creating Variables, Setting Property Values*

4. *Setting Property Values*

5. *Summary*

Opening the ObjectiveCDemo Sample Project

If you haven't already done so, it's time to download the sample code for this book. Instructions for downloading the sample code are located in *Chapter 1: Getting Started* under the topic Downloading the Sample Code.

Here are the steps for opening the **ObjectiveCDemo** sample project:

1. Launch the Xcode application on your computer. If you have never launched Xcode before, it's normally found in the Dock on your Mac. All you have to do is click the Xcode icon to launch it as in Figure 3.1.

Figure 3.1 Launching Xcode from the Mac OS X Dock

2. If you don't see Xcode in your Dock, click the **Applications** icon in your Dock, and then select Xcode from the pop-up list of applications (you may have to scroll down to see it).

3. After Xcode launches, you should see the **Welcome to Xcode** window (as long as you haven't unchecked **Show this window when Xcode launches** located at the bottom of the window) as shown in Figure 3.2. If you *don't* see the **Welcome to Xcode** window, in Xcode's **Window** menu select **Welcome to Xcode**.

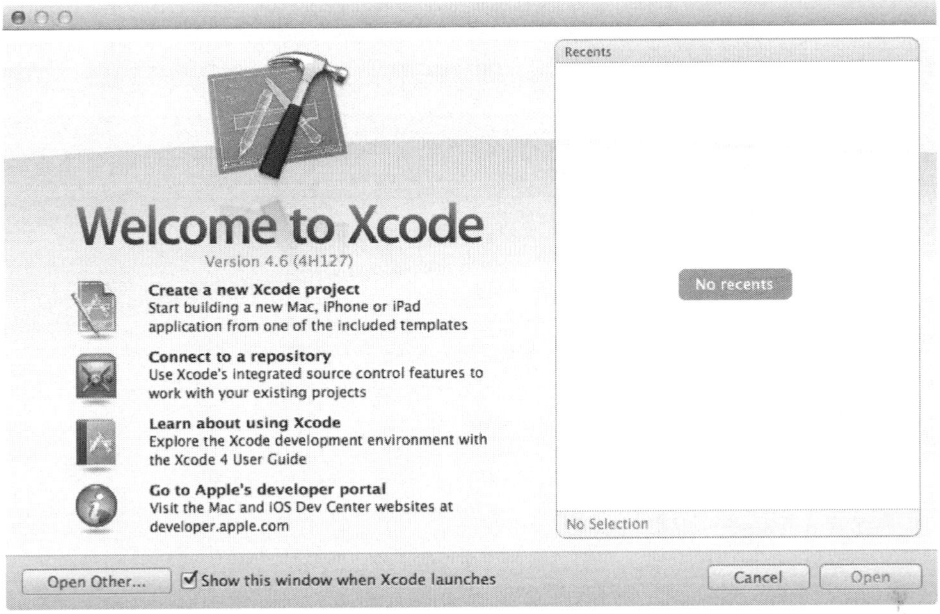

Figure 3.2 The Welcome to Xcode window lets you create new project or open existing project.

4. In the bottom-left corner, click the **Open Other...** button to open the sample project.

5. In the Open window, navigate to the location where you have copied the sample code for this book. If you have used the suggested folder, select the **Documents** folder in the **Favorites** panel, and then double-click the **Samples** folder on the right. Expand the **ObjectiveCDemo** folder (Figure 3.3), select the **ObjectiveCDemo.xcodeproj** file, and click **Open**.

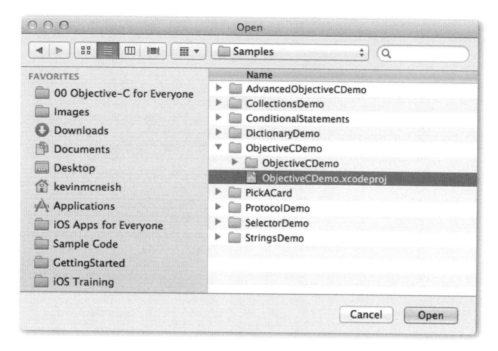

*Figure 3.3 Opening the **ObjectiveCDemo** sample project.*

When you first open the project, it should look like the screen shot shown in Figure 3.4. On the left side of the Xcode window, is the Project Navigator. If you don't see the Project Navigator, press **Command+1** to display it.

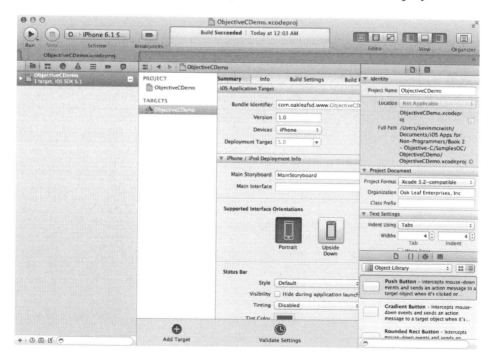

*Figure 3.4 The newly opened **ObjectiveCDemo** project*

> **Note:** Throughout this book, when I mention pressing the **Command** key plus any other key, you should simultaneously hold the **Command** key down and press the other key mentioned (in this case, the number **1**).

The Project Navigator contains the highlighted **ObjectiveCDemo** project item. Click the small white triangle on the left to expand the project item, and then click the gray arrow to the left of the **ObjectiveCDemo** subfolder to expand it. This folder contains the main code files in the project (Figure 3.5).

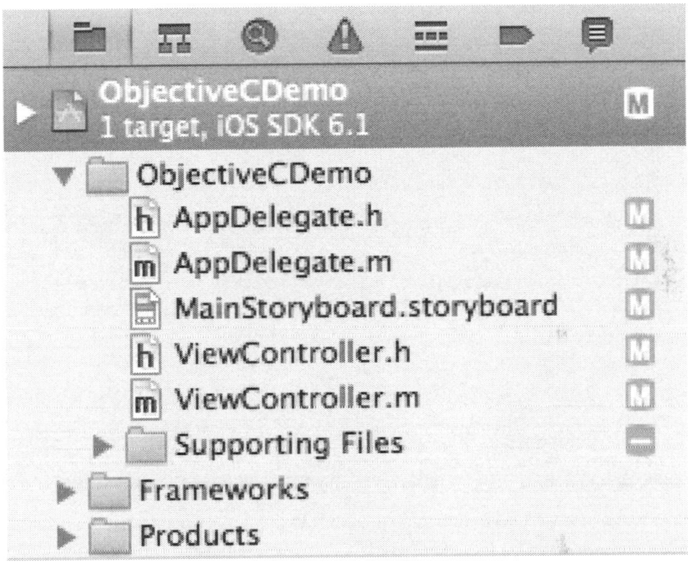

Figure 3.5 The Project Navigator contains a list of files.

Click on the **MainStoryboard.storyboard** file in the Project Navigator to display the App's user interface in Xcode's designer as shown in Figure 3.6. As you can see, it looks like a blank iPhone screen (except for the Label) and even includes a status bar with a green battery icon.

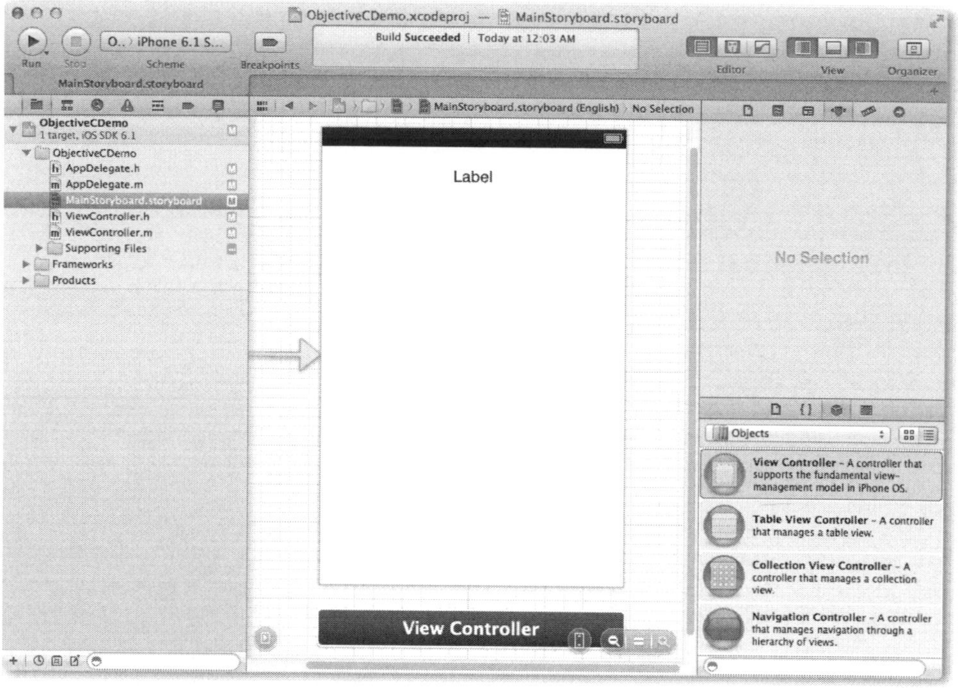

*Figure 3.6 The **ObjectiveCDemo** project's main storyboard*

For now, there are just a few things you need to know about laying out the user interface. First of all, the white rectangular area in the middle of the screen that contains the Label is a *view*. Again, a view displays one screen of information on an iOS device.

Each view usually has a related view controller class that contains code associated with that view. In this case, the view controller class is stored in the two files: **ViewController.h** and **ViewController.m**. These are displayed in the Project Navigator on the left side of the screen in Figure 3.6. You will learn more about these two files in just a bit.

Running the Sample App

To establish a starting point, let's run the project to see what it looks like in the iOS Simulator. First, make sure the **Scheme** control at the top left of the Xcode window is set to the iPhone Simulator (Figure 3.7).

*Figure 3.7 Make sure the **Scheme** control is set to run in the iPhone Simulator.*

Next, click the **Run** button in the upper-left corner of the Xcode window (Figure 3.8).

*Figure 3.8 Click **Run** to run the App in the Simulator.*

After several seconds, the iOS Simulator appears and displays the App as shown in Figure 3.9.

*Figure 3.9 The **ObjectiveCDemo** App in the Simulator*

No surprises here. The screen looks the same as it does in Xcode's design surface.

Creating Variables, Setting Property Values

As a first step to learning Objective-C, you are going to write a few lines of code that will change the text of the label when the App runs in the Simulator. This is something you often need to do in an iOS App, so it's a valuable exercise. Along the way, you will learn about *variables* and *properties*.

1. Go back to Xcode (if you can't see the Xcode window to click on it, you can press **Command+Tab** to get back) and click the **Stop** button in the upper-left corner of Xcode to stop the App from running in the Simulator.

2. Next, you are going to look at one of the project's code files. When viewing code, it's a good idea to turn off Xcode's Assistant Editor in order to provide a larger code editing area in the center of the window. If the Assistant Editor is on, it displays two code windows (either on top of or next to each other) in the center panel of Xcode. Turn it off by clicking the **Show the Standard editor** button, which is the first on the left in the three-button group above the **Editor** label in the top right corner of the Xcode window (Figure 3.10). If this button is already selected (as it is in the figure), then the Assistant Editor is off.

Figure 3.10 Hiding the Assistant Editor

3. In the Project Navigator on the left, select the **ViewController.m** file to display it in the code editor. Near the top of this file is the following declaration:

```
@implementation ViewController
```

This declaration tells you this is the **ViewController** class implementation file.

Notice the following lines of code a little further down in the code file:

```
- (void)viewDidLoad
{
    [super viewDidLoad];
    // Do any additional setup after...
}
```

This section of code is called a *method*. As mentioned earlier, a method groups one or more lines of code that are executed as a unit. An Objective-C class usually has dozens of methods. The left curly brace on the second line indicates the beginning of the code block and the ending curly brace indicates the end of the code block. All method code in your App *must* be placed within the curly braces of a method. Entering code outside these curly braces is one of the most common mistakes for new iOS developers, so definitely watch out for this!

The name of this method is **viewDidLoad**, and it is inherited from the **UIViewController** class. This method is automatically executed at run time when the view is first loaded for display. The **void** return value indicates this method does not return anything. The text in green, called a *comment*, is used to provide an explanation of the code that follows. Comments are not code and are therefore not executed.

4. You are now going to add code that changes the label's text at *run time* (run time is when the App is running in the Simulator or on an iOS device). To do this, click your mouse pointer to the immediate right of the comment, and then press **Enter**. This adds a new empty line directly below the existing code.

> **Note:** Throughout this book, when I ask you to create a new empty line, this is how you do it!

5. Now type the following highlighted lines of code (each line of code is known as a *statement*). Make sure you type all characters in upper or lower case as shown in this code sample because Objective-C is *case sensitive*. This means you must type the uppercase and lowercase letters exactly as shown:

```
- (void)viewDidLoad
{
    [super viewDidLoad];
    // Do any additional setup after...
    NSString *myString = @"Objective-C";
    self.lblDemo.text = myString;
}
```

Creating a Variable

The first line of code that you added creates a ***variable*** named **myString**, which contains a *string object*. Let's dissect that.

A variable is a place in memory where you can store and retrieve information. It's called a variable because you can change the information that you store in it. You can store one piece of information in a variable then store another piece of information in the same variable. Variables declared within a method are called ***local variables***, because they can only be accessed locally, from within the method in which they are declared.

You can name variables anything you want, although something meaningful is best. Also, variable names must be unique within the same scope. This means that you can't have two variables in a method with the same name. However, you can have variables with the same name if they are in different methods.

Although you can change the information stored in a variable, there is a limit on the type of information you can store. In the first line of code that you just added, the first word in the statement, **NSString**, indicates the variable can only store information of the type **NSString**:

```
NSString *myString = @"Objective-C";
```

The **NSString** class is part of the Cocoa Touch Framework and represents a set of characters. So, you can store any set of characters in the **myString** variable, but you can't store other types of information such as an integer, true or false values, and so on. When you declare a variable, you always declare the type of information that it can hold.

The asterisk following the **NSString** declaration indicates that the variable being created holds a pointer, or reference to an object (you will learn more about pointers a little later). In this case, the object is an **NSString** object:

```
NSString *myString = @"Objective-C";
```

The next part of the statement, **myString**, specifies the variable name:

```
NSString *myString = @"Objective-C";
```

The equal (=) sign is the assignment operator (for an extensive list of operators, see Appendix C: Objective-C Operators). It indicates you are storing a value in the **myString** variable:

```
NSString *myString = @"Objective-C";
```

The rest of the line stores the string *literal* "Objective-C" into the new variable. In Objective-C, a literal is a notation representing a fixed value. You declare a string literal by typing an "at" (@) sign prefix, and then listing the string between open and closed double quotes:

```
NSString *myString = @"Objective-C";
```

In Objective-C, you indicate the end of a line of code by typing a semicolon:

```
NSString *myString = @"Objective-C";
```

> **Note:** You can break up a single line of code into multiple physical lines in the code file as follows. A semicolon indicates the end of a single Objective-C statement.
>
> ```
> NSString *myString = @"Objective-C";
> ```

In review:

- **NSString** is the class.

- The asterisk indicates a reference to an object.

- **myString** is the variable name.

- The equal (=) sign is the assignment operator. It takes the value on its right and stores it into the variable or property on its left.

- @"Objective-C" is a string value.

- Storing the string value in the **myString** variable creates a string object.

Setting Property Values

The next statement that you entered takes the string value stored in the **myString** variable (@"Objective-C") and saves it in the Label's **text** property:

```
self.lblDemo.text = myString;
```

For now, all you need to know is:

- **self** refers to the **ViewController** class (the class in which you typed the code).

- **lblDemo** refers to a property on the view controller that references the label.

- **text** is a property on the label that specifies the text displayed in the label.

- The equal (=) sign is the assignment operator. It takes the value on its right and stores it into the property or variable on its left.

- Notice that an asterisk is not used in front of the **myString** variable. You only need to use the asterisk when you first declare the variable.

1. Run the App in the iOS Simulator by clicking the **Run** button in the upper-left corner of Xcode.

Note: If you get the **Stop "ObjectiveCDemo"?** warning, it's because you didn't press the **Stop** button and the App is still running in the Simulator. If you see this dialog, click **Stop** and then restart the App.

2. After several seconds, the iOS Simulator should appear and display the App (Figure 3.11).

Figure 3.11 Your code running in the Simulator

This should be an emotional moment for you. Take a few minutes to soak it in.

OK, let's get back to work!

3. Go back to Xcode and press the **Stop** button.

Summary

Here are some of the key concepts you learned in this chapter:

- A variable is a place in your App's memory where you can store and retrieve information.

- It's called a variable because you can change the information that you store in it.

- Variable names must be unique in the scope in which they are declared.

- You are limited as to the type of information that you store in a variable.

You can only store information of the type specified in the variable declaration.

- To store a value into a property or variable, you use the assignment operator, which is an equal (=) sign. It takes the value on its right and stores it into the property or variable on its left.

- An asterisk in front of a variable name indicates that the variable holds a pointer, or reference to an object.

- You don't need to use an asterisk when referencing the variable later on— only when declaring it.

Chapter 4: Passing Object Messages

You are going to work with many different kinds of objects as you create iOS Apps. So far, you have learned how to store a value in an object property. Now you are ready to learn how to run a method on an object by passing it a message.

Sections in This Chapter

To begin this chapter, you will learn how to call the **stringByAppendingString:** method on the string object that you created in the previous chapter by passing it a message. You may recall that this method of the **NSString** class is used to combine two strings.

Remember, a method groups one or more lines of code that are executed as a unit. To run a specific method, you pass a ***message*** to the object requesting it to run that method as depicted in Figure 4.1. In this example the **stringByAppendingString:** message is passed to the **myString** object, and it returns the appended string.

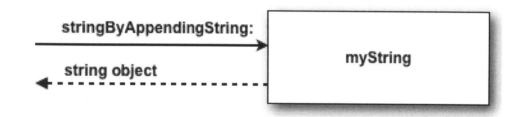

*Figure 4.1 Passing a **stringByAppendingString:** message to the **myString** object*

The Anatomy of a Message Call

The act of sending a message to an object is known as a ***message call***. Figure 4.2 illustrates the anatomy of a message call.

Here are the key things to note:

- A message call begins with a left square bracket, and ends with a right square bracket.

- The object you are sending the message to is known as the ***receiver***.

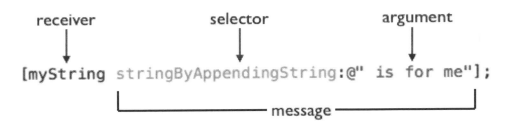

Figure 4.2 The anatomy of a message call

- The message can be broken down into two parts:

    1. The **selector** is the name of the method.

    2. An **argument** is a piece of data sent to a method.

Passing a Message Step by Step

Follow these steps to learn how to pass a message to an object and learn more about the anatomy of a message call:

1. Open the **ObjectiveCDemo** project if it's not already open in Xcode.

2. Assuming you went through the step-by-step instructions in the previous chapter, go back to the lines of code that you added in **ViewController.m**; and in the last line of code, delete the **myString** variable to the right of the equal (=) sign like this:

    ```
    NSString *myString = @"Objective-C";
    self.lblDemo.text = ;
    }
    ```

3. Now type a left square bracket ([ ) to the immediate left of the semicolon:

    ```
    self.lblDemo.text = [;
    }
    ```

    In Objective-C, typing a left square bracket indicates that you are going to pass a message to an object (or, as you will learn later, a class). If you are familiar with more modern C-based languages such as C# and Java, this is the part of Objective-C that seems very foreign.

4. Next, type **myString** again, but pause after typing the first two letters and you should see Xcode's Code Completion display **myString**:

```
        self.lblDemo.text = [myString;
}          Ⓜ NSString * myString
```

Code Completion is Xcode's way of helping you write code. Based on the characters you type, it provides its best guess as to what you need to complete a code statement. Just press **Enter** to have Xcode automatically enter the full text of the word for you.

> **Note:** If the Code Completion pop-up help goes away, then just press the **Escape** key to bring it back. The popup disappears if you click somewhere else in Xcode, wait too long, or **Command+Tab** to another application and back again.

5. In Objective-C, the object that you type immediately after the left square bracket ([ ) is the object to which you are going to pass a message. For this reason, it's known as the receiver. In this case, you are going to pass a message to the **myString** object.

    Press the space bar to insert a space, and then press **Escape**. This brings up a list of all the possible methods that you can call on the **myString** object. Xcode knows **myString** is an **NSString** object because earlier, you declared the **myString** variable type as **NSString**. So, Xcode brings up a list of methods that you can potentially pass in a message to an **NSString** object.

6. The method that you are seeking is named **stringByAppendingString:**. You can narrow the list by typing the first several characters of this method name. When you only have a few choices in the list, use the up/down arrow keys to move to the **stringByAppendingString:** method and press **Enter**. Now you should see a highlight like this:

```
[myString stringByAppendingString:(NSString *);
```

Xcode gives you a clue as to what it expects you to type next. When you pass a message to an object, you first pass the name of the method that you want to call (which you just did) and then any additional information that the method requires. As already mentioned, these additional pieces of data are known as *arguments*. The message includes the name of the method that you want to run as well as any arguments, which are separated by a colon (:) character.

In this case, the **stringByAppendingString:** method expects you to pass a single **NSString** argument. The string that you enter here is passed to the **stringByAppendingString:** method, which appends it to the string stored in the **myString** variable.

7. Now finish the statement by typing the following (there is a space after the first double quote):

```
self.lblDemo.text = [myString
stringByAppendingString:@" is for me"];
```

The **@" is for me"** string argument will be appended to the value in the **myString** variable. The right square bracket is part of a matched set with the left square bracket that marks the beginning and end of the message call. The semicolon marks the end of the statement.

8. Let's run the App to see the effect of this new code in the Simulator. To do this, click the **Run** button in the upper-left corner of Xcode. Now the top of your App should look like Figure 4.3 (the last code statement shown in this figure is broken into two lines for space considerations).

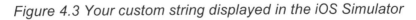

```
- (void)viewDidLoad
{
    [super viewDidLoad];
    // Do any additional setup after loading the view,
    NSString *myString = @"Objective-C";
    self.lblDemo.text =
        [myString stringByAppendingString:@" is for me"];
}
```

Figure 4.3 Your custom string displayed in the iOS Simulator

9. Go back to Xcode and click the **Stop** button.

Congratulations on completing your first message call!

Arguments and Parameters

You often see the words ***argument*** and ***parameter*** used interchangeably, however there is a subtle difference. As you learned in the previous section, an argument is a piece of data that you pass to a method. A *parameter* is a part of the method declaration that dictates the argument(s) to be passed to the method. In short, arguments appear in message calls, parameters appear in method declarations.

Figuring Out How to Pass a Message

As you write code for your App, you are going to call many methods on many Cocoa Touch Framework objects. You will be using a wide variety of classes and objects, and you need them to perform specific tasks for you. Maybe you need to send a text message, find the user's current location, or get the current user's high score in a game. It's one thing to figure out *which* class and method to call, it's another hurdle to figure out *how* to call that method. Many students in my iOS classes have expressed difficulty in figuring out how to call a method, so I'd like to demystify this process for you.

First of all, you need to know that in Objective-C, there are two main types of methods—**instance methods** and **class methods**. Instance methods are called on instances of an object—meaning, you create an object from a class, and then pass a message to the object. In contrast, class methods belong to the class itself, meaning that you pass the message to the class directly, without creating an instance of the class.

Calling Instance Methods

Let's start by looking at some instance methods in the **NSString** class. Afterwards, we will look at how to call class methods.

1. Go back to Xcode and at the bottom of the **viewDidLoad** method (right before the ending curly brace), add a new empty line. Next, type the following directly below the code you previously added (the last character is the lowercase letter "l"):

   ```
       [myString l
   }
   ```

   As soon as you type this, Xcode displays all the methods of the **NSString** class that begin with the letter "l" as shown in Figure 4.4. This popup is a great place to learn how to pass a message.

M	NSString * lastPathComponent
M	NSUInteger **length**
M	NSUInteger lengthOfBytesUsingEncoding:(NSStringEncoding)
M	NSRange lineRangeForRange:(NSRange)
M	NSArray * linguisticTagsInRange:(NSRange) scheme:(NSStr
M	NSComparisonResult localizedCaseInsensitiveCompare:(NSString *)
M	NSComparisonResult localizedCompare:(NSString *)
M	NSComparisonResult localizedStandardCompare:(NSString *)
M	long long longLongValue

Figure 4.4 NSString methods that begin with "l"

Remember, the variable **myString** contains an object that is an instance of the **NSString** class. You created the object earlier by storing a string into the variable. So, all the methods in the pop-up list are *instance* methods.

The pop-up list contents provide clues on how to call each method:

- On the far left is an "M" indicating each item is a method.

- The next column to the right specifies the type of value returned from each method. For example, the **length** method returns an **NSUInteger** value. **NSUInteger** is a Cocoa Touch class that represents an unsigned integer—a whole number that has no positive or negative sign, such as 1, 10, and 365.

- The last column specifies the method name along with any arguments that you need to pass. For example, the **length** method accepts no arguments.

2. When you highlight a particular method in the popup, a description of that method appears at the bottom of the popup as shown in Figure 4.5.

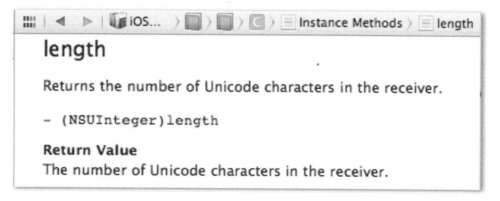

```
M          NSString * lastPathComponent
M          NSUInteger length
M          NSUInteger lengthOfBytesUsingEncoding:(NSStringEncoding)
M          NSRange lineRangeForRange:(NSRange)
M          NSArray * linguisticTagsInRange:(NSRange) scheme:(NSStr
M NSComparisonResult localizedCaseInsensitiveCompare:(NSString *)
M NSComparisonResult localizedCompare:(NSString *)
M NSComparisonResult localizedStandardCompare:(NSString *)
```
Returns the number of Unicode characters in the receiver. More...

Figure 4.5 The method description

3. Click the **More...** link to bring up Xcode's Organizer dialog that describes what the method does as shown partially in Figure 4.6.

```
▦  ◄  ►  📱 iOS...  ›  ▢  ›  ▢  ›  ⓒ  ›  ▤ Instance Methods  ›  ▤ length
```

length

Returns the number of Unicode characters in the receiver.

- (NSUInteger)length

Return Value
The number of Unicode characters in the receiver.

Figure 4.6 Help for the length method

So, in this example, the pop-up help says the **length** method "returns the number of Unicode characters in the receiver." Although technically accurate, this isn't the clearest description for someone new to Objective-C. It actually means that, when you pass the **length** message to a string object (the receiver of the message), the string object returns the number of characters, or length, of its string as an **NSUInteger**.

4. Delete the partial line of code that you just typed:

```
NSString *myString = @"Objective-C";
self.lblDemo.text = [myString
    stringByAppendingString:@" is for me"];
[myString
```

To make it easy for you, I have created **Table 4.1**, which you can use to figure out how to call a method. Each time you come across a new instance method, read the pop-up documentation in Xcode first, as you just did, to see what the method does. Then refer to the steps outlined in **Table 4.1** to figure out how to call it.

Table 4.1 Steps for Calling an Instance Method

1. Create the receiver object (the object you are passing the message to).

2. If there is a return value:

    - Create a variable to hold the return value (you can name it whatever you want).

    - Type " = " to store the return value in the variable.

3. Type a left square bracket to start the message.

4. Type the name of the variable that holds the receiver object.

5. Type a space, and then, the name of the method to be called.

6. If there are any arguments

    - Type a colon, then the first argument value.

    - Do the same for any additional arguments.

7. Type a right square bracket to end the message.

8. Type a semicolon to end the statement.

Let's see how that process works now with the **length** method. Follow these instructions, which mirror each step in **Table 4.1**:

1. You already have a line of code that creates the receiver object:

   ```
   NSString *myString = @"Objective-C";
   ```

   So, the first step is complete.

2. The **length** method returns an **NSUInteger**, so create a variable to hold the value, and then type the assignment operator " = " as shown below (with a space before and after the equal sign):

   ```
   NSString *myString = @"Objective-C";
   self.lblDemo.text = [myString
   ```

```
      stringByAppendingString:@" is for me"];
NSUInteger stringLength =
```

3. Type a left square bracket to start the message call:

```
NSUInteger stringLength = [
```

4. Type the name of the variable that holds the receiver object (the **myString** variable you created earlier):

```
NSUinteger stringLength = [myString
```

5. Type a space and the name of the method to be called:

```
NSUInteger stringLength = [myString length
```

6. There are no arguments, so you do nothing in this step.

7. Type a right square bracket to end the message call:

```
NSUInteger stringLength = [myString length]
```

8. Type a semicolon to end the statement:

```
NSUInteger stringLength = [myString length];
```

That's it. You have completed a call to an instance method! At this point, we won't run this code because I just want you to get a feel for calling methods in a variety of ways. If you were to run this code, the **myString** object's **length** method would return the number of characters in the **myString** object. Since there are 11 characters in the word "Objective-C", it would store the integer 11 in the **stringLength** variable.

To prevent panic: You may have noticed the yellow exclamation mark in the gutter to the left of the code window. This warning icon added by Xcode lets you know that there is a possible issue with your code. If you click on the icon, it warns you about "Unused variable 'stringLength'":

```
stringLength = [myString length];
         ⚠ Unused variable 'stringLength'
```

You are getting this warning because this line of code creates a variable, but you haven't done anything with the variable yet. This is obviously not OK in a real App but is fine when you are creating example code.

To review, as shown in Figure 4.7, this line of code passes a **length** message to the **myString** object. The **length** method executes and returns the length of the string in the **myString** object.

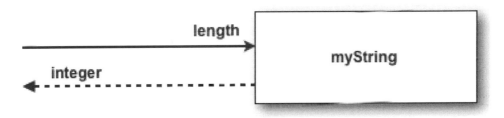

Figure 4.7 The **length** message is passed to the **myString** object, which returns its length as an integer.

Calling Methods With Arguments

Now let's try to call a method that takes arguments. This time, rather than looking at the pop-up help in Xcode to learn about a method, let's look at the Cocoa Touch Framework documentation instead.

You can get documentation for a method in a few ways —directly in Xcode's Organizer window as we did in the previous section and online help as we're doing here. I want you to get comfortable with both approaches, since you will use both in real-world programming.

1. Google **NSString Class Reference**. Usually, the first result is the one you want (the link is to **developer.apple.com/library/...**). Click the link and the help topic should look like Figure 4.8.

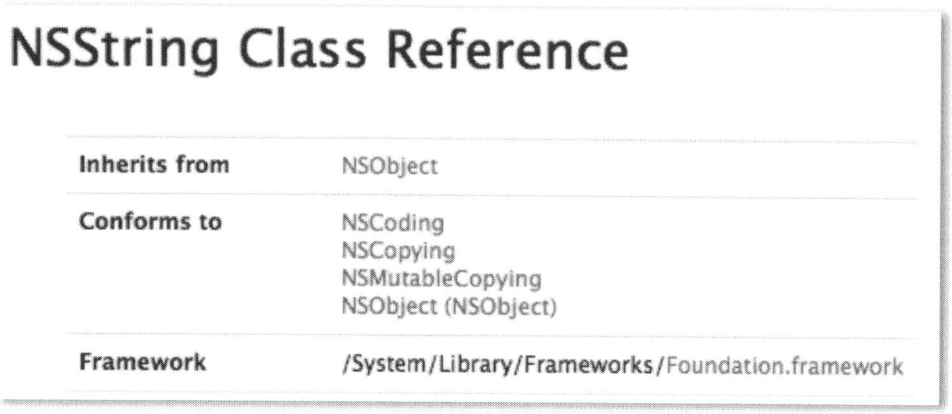

NSString Class Reference

Inherits from	NSObject
Conforms to	NSCoding NSCopying NSMutableCopying NSObject (NSObject)
Framework	/System/Library/Frameworks/Foundation.framework

Figure 4.8 NSString Class Reference

Scroll down until you see a section called **Tasks**. There are subsections listed under **Tasks** that group methods by the kinds of things that you can do, such as:

- Creating and Initializing Strings

- Creating and Initializing Strings from a File

- Creating and Initializing Strings from a URL

- And so on...

At the top of the web page, there is a **Jump To...** combo box (Figure 4.9).

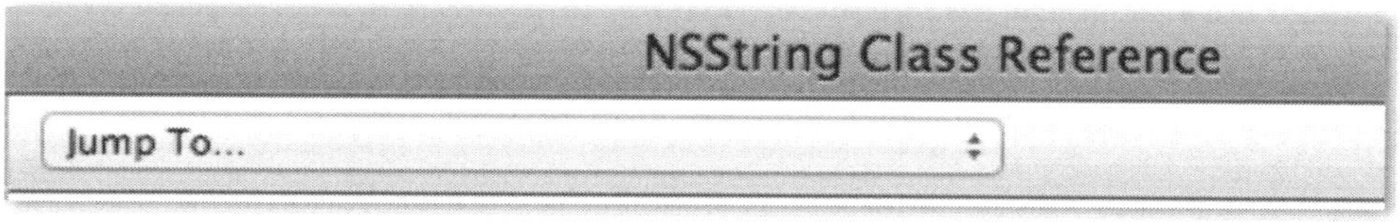

NSString Class Reference

Jump To...

*Figure 4.9 The **Jump To...** combo box takes you to a specific section of the help topic.*

2. Click on this combo box, and look at the list that pops up. It shows all the members of the **NSString** class and the list separates **Class Methods** from **Instance Methods**. Scroll down under **Instance Methods** until you see the **isEqualToString:** method, and then click on it to select it.

Following these steps takes you to the method documentation, where you can see a description that says:

"Returns a Boolean value that indicates whether a given string is equal

to the receiver using a literal Unicode-based comparison."

More simply, the **isEqualToString:** method compares two strings to see if they contain the same characters.

Below the description is a line of code that describes the method. This is known as the ***method signature***:

```
(BOOL)isEqualToString:(NSString *)aString
```

The first thing you should look for is the character at the far left. In this case, it's a minus (-) sign. In Objective-C, the minus sign indicates an instance method (class methods start with a plus (+) sign). Next, you can see this method returns a **BOOL** value which stands for Boolean, which represents a YES or NO value (for a list of other basic data types in Objective-C, check out Appendix B: Basic Data Types). The method also accepts an **NSString** parameter.

Since you know this is an instance method, follow these instructions, which mirror each step in **Table 4.1**:

1. Again, you already have a line of code that creates the receiver object:

    ```
    NSString *myString = @"Objective-C";
    self.lblDemo.text = [myString
        stringByAppendingString:@" is for me"];
    NSUInteger stringLength = [myString length];
    ```

    So, the first step is complete.

2. The **isEqualToString:** method returns a **BOOL** value, so create a new empty line after the three lines of code shown above. In that empty line, create a variable to hold the value; type a space, an equal (=) sign, and then another space:

    ```
    BOOL isStringEqual =
    ```

3. Type a left square bracket to start the message call:

    ```
    BOOL isStringEqual = [
    ```

4. Type the name of the variable that holds the receiver object (the **myString** variable again):

```
BOOL isStringEqual = [myString
```

5. Type a space and the name of the method to be called:

```
BOOL isStringEqual = [myString
    isEqualToString
```

6. There is a single **NSString** parameter, so type a colon and then the following string:

```
BOOL isStringEqual = [myString
    isEqualToString:@"Object-C"
```

7. Type a right square bracket to end the message call:

```
BOOL isStringEqual = [myString
    isEqualToString:@"Object-C"]
```

8. Type a semicolon to end the statement:

```
BOOL isStringEqual = [myString
    isEqualToString:@"Object-C"];
```

In review, as shown in Figure 4.10, you are passing a message to the **myString** object, asking it to run the **isEqualToString:** method on itself. You are passing the value to be compared (in this case, **@"Object-C"**) as an argument. The **myString** object compares this value against its own string (**@"Objective-C"**); and if they are the same, it returns **YES**, but if they are not the same, it returns **NO**.

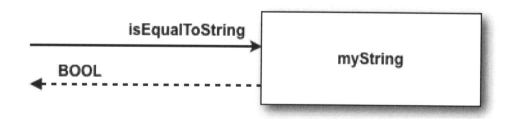

Figure 4.10 The *isEqualToString:* message is passed to the *myString* object, which returns a *BOOL* value.

In our example, the method returns **NO** because the strings are similar, but not exactly the same.

Calling Class Methods

As you have already learned, you can pass messages to objects created from a class, and you can also pass certain messages to the class itself. Methods that belong to a class are called *class methods* and methods that belong to an object, or an instance of a class, are called *instance methods*.

Table 4.2 outlines the steps for calling a class method. As you might imagine, there is one less step when calling a class method because you don't need to create an instance of the class.

1. If there is a return value:

    - Create a variable to hold the return value (you can name it whatever you want).

    - Type " = " to store the return value in the variable.

2. Type a left square bracket to start the message.

3. Type the name of the class you are sending the message to.

4. Type a space and then the name of the method to be called

5. If there are any arguments,

    - Type a colon and then the value for the first argument.

    - Do the same for any additional arguments.

6. Type a right square bracket to end the message.

7. Type a semicolon to end the statement.

Let's use the **NSURL** class to demonstrate how to call a class method. **NSURL** class a variety of methods for working with *URLs* (*uniform resource locators*, or character strings that reference an Internet resource or a local file on the device). Typically, a URL is a web address that points to a resource such as a web site, HTML page, or image—such as **http://www.apple.com.**

In iOS Apps, you work with **NSURL** objects rather than with simple URL strings, so you often need to convert a simple string to an official **NSURL** object. The **NSURL** class has a **URLWithString** method that allows you to do this. You pass the class method a string, and it returns an **NSURL** object.

The **NSURL** Class Reference documentation provides information about the **URLWithString:** method shown in Figure 4.11.

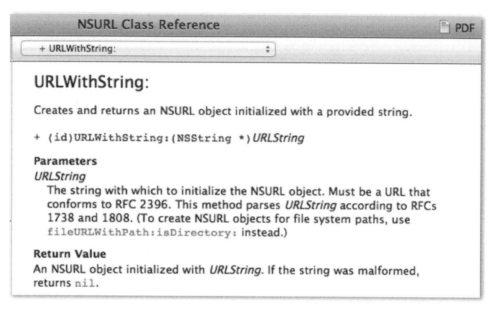

*Figure 4.11 The **NSURL urlWithString:** method*

The description of the **URLWithString** method states:

Creates and returns an NSURL object initialized with a provided string.

The documentation says the method returns a value of type **id**. As you have learned, **id** means "any object." However, if you look further down in the documentation under **Return Value** it says the method returns an **NSURL** object. Any time you know the type of the value returned from a method, you should use it instead of the generic **id** type.

Now look at the method signature. Because the first character is a plus (+) sign, you know immediately that this is a *class* method, so follow these instructions, which mirror each step in **Table 4.2**:

1. First, create a new empty line. Next, create a variable to hold an **NSURL** return value, and then type " = " to store the return value in the variable:

```
NSURL *myURL =
```

2. Type a left square bracket to start the message call:

```
NSURL *myURL = [
```

3. Type the name of the class you are sending the message to:

```
NSURL *myURL = [NSURL
```

4. Type a space, and the name of the method to be called:

```
NSURL *myURL = [NSURL URLWithString
```

5. Because there is one **NSString** argument, type a colon and then enter the following string as an argument:

```
NSURL *myURL = [NSURL URLWithString:
    @"http://www.oakleafsd.com"
```

6. Type a right square bracket to end the message call:

```
NSURL *myURL = [NSURL URLWithString:
    @"http://www.oakleafsd.com"]
```

7. Type a semicolon to end the statement:

```
NSURL *myURL = [NSURL URLWithString:
    @"http://www.oakleafsd.com"];
```

That's it! You have successfully created a line of code that calls a class method. In review, as shown in Figure 4.12, you are passing a message to the **NSURL** class, asking it to run the **URLWithString:** method on itself. You are passing a URL string, which the **URLWithString:** method converts and returns as an **NSURL** object.

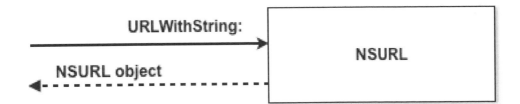

*Figure 4.12 The **URLWithString** message is passed to the **NSURL** class, which returns a URL object.*

You can now refer back to **Table 4.1** for the steps in calling an instance method and to **Table 4.2** for the steps in calling a class method.

Commenting Out Code

You are not going to use the last three statements that you created right now, so you can comment these out to get rid of the warnings. When you comment out the code, it is no longer processed by the compiler as Objective-C commands, so the code no longer executes.

To do this, first select all three lines of code by clicking to the left of the first line, holding the mouse button down, and then dragging your mouse as shown here:

```
NSUInteger stringLength = [myString length];  ⚠
BOOL isStringEqual = [myString isEqualToString:
NSURL *myURL = [NSURL URLWithString:@"http://ww
```

With all three lines of code selected, press **Command**+/ (forward slash) and Xcode places two forward slashes in front of each line, commenting them out:

```
//  NSUInteger stringLength = [myString length];
//  BOOL isStringEqual = [myString isEqualToString:
//  NSURL *myURL = [NSURL URLWithString:@"http://ww
```

If you want to reverse this process and uncomment these lines of code again, you can select them and press **Command**+/ again (let's leave them commented).

Summary

Here are the key points to remember when passing a message to an object:

- To call a method on an object, you pass it a message.

- The object you are sending a message to is known as the *receiver*.

- An *argument* is a piece of data passed to a method.

- A *message* call begins with a left square bracket, followed by the name of the receiver object.

- The message begins with the name of the method, known as the *selector*, followed by any arguments.

- A *parameter* is part of the method declaration that dictates the number and type of arguments that are passed to the method.

Here are the steps for figuring out how to call an instance method:

1. Create the receiver object (the object that you are passing the message to).

2. If there is a return value:

    -   Create a variable to hold the return value (you can name it whatever you want).

    -   Type " = " to store the return value in the variable.

3. Type a left square bracket to start the message call.

4. Type the name of the variable that holds the receiver object.

5. Type a space, and then the name of the method to be called.

6. If there are any arguments:

    -   Type a colon, and then the value for the first argument.

    -   Do the same for any additional arguments.

7. Type a right square bracket to end the message call.

8. Type a semicolon to end the statement.

Here is an example of calling an instance method:

```
NSString *myString = @"Objective-C";

BOOL isStringEqual = [myString
        isEqualToString:@"Object-C"];
```

Here are the steps for figuring out how to call a class method:

1. If there is a return value:

    -   Create a variable to hold the return value (you can name it whatever you want).

    -   Type " = " to store the return value in the variable.

2. Type a left square bracket to start the message call.

3. Type the name of the class that you are sending the message to.

4. Type a space, and then the name of the method to be called.

5. If there are any arguments:

   • Type a colon, and then the first argument value.

   • Do the same for any additional arguments.

6. Type a right square bracket to end the message call.

7. Type a semicolon to end the statement.

Here is an example of calling a class method:

```
NSURL *myURL = [NSURL URLWithString:
        @"http://www.oakleafsd.com"];
```

Exercise 4.1

In this exercise, you will use what you have learned in this chapter about figuring out how to call a method.

1. The **NSString** class has a method named **stringByReplacingOccurrencesOfString:withString:**, which is documented this way in the **NSString** Class Reference:

---

stringByReplacingOccurrencesOfString:withString:

Returns a new string in which all occurrences of a target string in the receiver are replaced by another given string.

```
- (NSString *)stringByReplacingOccurrencesOfString:(NSString
*)target withString:(NSString *)replacement
```

Parameters
target
   The string to replace.

replacement
   The string with which to replace *target*.

Return Value
A new string in which all occurrences of *target* in the receiver are replaced by *replacement*.

---

2. In the ObjectiveCDemo project, you currently have the following string in the **viewDidLoad** method of the **ViewController.m** class file:

```
self.lblDemo.text = [myString
stringByAppendingString:@" is for me"];
```

3. Add another line of code below this line that uses **stringByReplacingOccurrencesOfString:withString:** to replace the string "me" with the string "us". Store the resulting value back into the **lblDemo** object's **text** property.

4. You should then be able to run the App in the Simulator and see the text has changed.

Solution Movie 4.1

To see a video providing the solution for this exercise, go to the following link in your web browser.

http://www.iOSAppsForNonProgrammers.com/B2M41.html

Chapter 5: Creating Objects From Classes

As you have already learned, objects are created from class "blueprints" that define the object's attributes and behavior. In this chapter you will learn how to create objects from Apple's Cocoa Touch Framework classes.

Along the way, you are also going to learn a little more about properties and be introduced to functions, constants, and enumerations.

Sections in This Chapter

1. *alloc and init Methods*

2. *alloc and init Step by Step*

3. *Multiple init Methods*

4. *More About Properties*

5. *Introducing Functions*

6. *Introducing Constants and Enumerations*

7. *Adding the Text Field to the View*

8. *Summary*

9. *Exercise 5.1*

10. *Solution Movie 5.1*

In the previous chapter, you created a string object by storing a string into a variable like this:

```
NSString *myString = @"Objective-C";
```

This doesn't look much like creating an object from a class, does it? In fact, this is not the usual way to create an object. Normally, you send a message to a class, asking it to create an object. This is where the **alloc** and **init** methods come into the picture. You are going to be creating *many* objects from classes as you write your Apps, so this is an important skill to learn early on.

In *Chapter 2: Understanding Classes and Objects*, you learned that you can create an instance of a text field class visually by dragging a text field class icon from the library to the design surface (Figure 2.4). In this chapter, you will see that you can also create a text field object by writing code. This is something that you often need to do in your Apps, so it's a good skill to master.

alloc and init Methods

Normally, you use the **alloc** and **init** methods to create and initialize a new object. Each method performs a different task in the object creation process.

The alloc method

This is the method that actually creates the object. You pass an **alloc** message to the class, which tells the class to create a new object from its blueprint. The class *allocates*, or sets aside memory for the new object. Since **alloc** is a message sent to a class, that means it is a *class method*.

After the object is created, **alloc** sets all of the object's instance variables to zero (or **nil** for pointers), and it returns a reference to the new object. In Figure 5.1 an **alloc** message is passed to the **UITextField** class, which returns a new text field object.

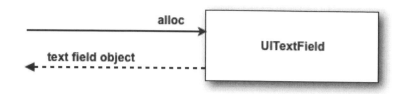

Figure 5.1 Passing an alloc message to the UITextField class

The init method

The **init** method *initializes* selected variables on the object to something other than zero or nil. You pass the **init** message to the object after it is created, so that means it is an *instance method*. In Figure 5.2, an **init** message is passed to a text field object, which returns a reference to itself.

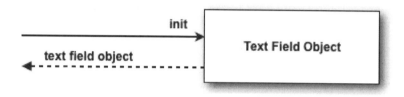

*Figure 5.2 Passing an **init** message to a text field object*

For example, think about how a real-world calculator works. When you turn the calculator on, it displays the total from when the calculator was last used. If you want to replicate this behavior in an App, you can create a **Calculator** class that has a **total** instance variable. By default, when you call **alloc** to create a Calculator object from the **Calculator** class, the **total** instance variable is set to zero. In the **Calculator init** method, you can set the value of the **total** instance variable to the "last used" value instead.

alloc and init Step by Step

Follow these instructions to learn how to use **alloc** and **init** to create a new object.

1. Open the **ObjectiveCDemo** project in Xcode if it's not already open.

2. In the Project Navigator, go to the **ViewController.m** code file; and in a new empty line under the code that you commented out at the end of the last chapter, add this partial line of code:

```
UITextField *textField = [
```

This time, you are declaring a variable of the class type **UITextField** and you are naming the variable **textField**. You know the variable holds an object reference because of the asterisk (*) immediately before the variable name. The equal (=) sign specifies that you are storing something into the variable. Again, the left square bracket indicates that you are getting ready to pass a message.

3. Now finish the statement with the following code:

    ```
    UITextField *textField =
        [UITextField alloc];
    ```

    This code passes an **alloc** message to the **UITextField** class. Since you are sending a message directly to a class (rather than an instance of the class), this means **alloc** is a class method.

    As already mentioned, when you send an **alloc** message to a class, it creates an object from the class definition or blueprint, allocating space for the object in memory. It also sets all of the object's instance variables to zero or nil. The **alloc** method returns a reference, or a ***pointer*** to the object's location in memory. A pointer is like a book index which points to a specific page where information can be found.

    In the above code, the reference or pointer to the **UITextField** object returned from the **alloc** method is stored in the **textField** variable.

4. Now press **Enter**, and below the code you just entered, add the second statement shown here:

    ```
    UITextField *textField =
        [UITextField  alloc];
    textField = [textField init];
    ```

    You should remember that, as soon as you type a left square bracket, you are passing a message. In this case, the message receiver object is **textField** and **init** is the method called on the object.

    Remember, the **init** method initializes selected instance variables to values other than zero. Like the **alloc** method, the **init** method also returns a reference to the object. This line of code stores the reference to the initialized object back into the **textField** variable.

5. I had you enter these two lines of code separately to make clear how they work; but normally, the **alloc** and **init** messages are passed in a statement

like this:

```
UITextField *textField =
    [[UITextField alloc] init];
```

What's happening in this line of code? When you are trying to read a line of code, you should start looking at the right side of the assignment operator (=), and first look at the code that is nested the deepest (kind of like an equation in math class).

- The **[UITextField alloc]** message is nested inside the message to the init method, which means it runs first. The **alloc** method returns a reference to the newly created object.

- Next, an **init** message is sent to the newly created object, which returns a reference to the initialized object.

- The assignment operator (=) stores a reference to the text field object in the **textField** variable.

6. Go ahead and replace the two statements that you typed earlier and with the one statement above.

This is the usual way you create objects. Calling **alloc** / **init** returns a brand new initialized object for you.

Multiple init Methods

Often, a class has more than one **init** method to choose from. To see an example of this:

1. Place your cursor immediately before the final right square bracket in the line of code you just added, like this:

```
[[UITextField alloc] init];
```

2. Now press the **Escape** key. You will see a list of three initialization methods to choose from. You used the first **init** method in the code that you just entered, but you can also choose **initWithCoder** or **initWithFrame** to pass additional arguments:

```
[[UITextField alloc] init];
```

```
M  id init
M  id initWithCoder:(NSCoder *)
M  id initWithFrame:(CGRect)

Implemented by subclasses to initialize a
new object (the receiver) immediately
after memory for it has been … More…
```

Typically, the extra arguments that you pass are used to provide additional initialization data. Apple's Cocoa Touch Framework documentation provides details for each argument. As you enter code in subsequent sections of this chapter, you will use a variety of initialization methods other than the standard **init**.

More About Properties

As you have already learned, not only do classes have methods, but they also have properties. Follow these instructions to set the text field's **placeholder** property.

1. Move your cursor to the end of the line of code that you just created, press **Enter** to create a new empty line, and type **textField** followed by a period. This brings up a list of properties for the **textField** object as shown in Figure 5.3 (if you're using an older version of Xcode, you may need to press **Escape** to see this list).

```
textField.tag
P     NSArray * subviews
M          Class superclass
P        UIView * superview
P         NSInteger tag
P       NSString * text
P  UITextAlignment textAlignment
P        UIColor * textColor
P        UIView * textInputView

An integer that you can use to identify view objects in your
application. More…
```

Figure 5.3 Code Completion provides a list of object properties.

When accessing object properties, you don't have to use square brackets as you do with methods (although you can if you want to). Instead, you can use **dot notation**, which is what you see here. You just type a period after the object name, and then type the name of the property.

2. Choose the **placeholder** property from the list (press **Escape** to display the list if it has disappeared). To do this, you can use the scroll bar on the far right of the popup, use the up/down arrow keys, or just start typing the name of the property to narrow down the list. In either case, when the **placeholder** property is selected in the list, press **Enter** to have Xcode complete the name for you. Afterwards, finish the line of code as shown here:

```
textField.placeholder = @"First Name";
```

This line of code stores the string "First Name" in the **textField** object's **placeholder** property. When you run the App later on, you will see what the **placeholder** property does for you.

Note: You may hear of great Internet battles debating whether using dot notation will be the end of civilization as we know it, or if it will bring peace to all nations. Ultimately, there are interesting arguments on both sides of the debate.

Personally, I like the way dot notation draws a contrast between an object's state, or its properties, and an object's behavior as implemented in its methods. It's a syntax used in more modern languages such as Java and C# and one that I find to be a nice addition to Objective-C.

Introducing Functions

Now you are going to use what you have learned so far to write code that adds the text field to the user interface at run time. On the way, you are going to learn about Objective-C *functions*.

Normally, you add a text field to a user interface in Xcode by dragging a text field from the Object Library and positioning and sizing it on the design surface. When you are adding a text field in code, you specify its size and position by means of its **frame** property. A *frame* is a rectangle that specifies the text field's position on the user interface (in x and y coordinates) as well as its width and height.

1. Create a new line of code by pressing **Enter** after the code that you just entered, and then type the following:

```
textField.frame = CGRectMake
```

2. Typing this brings up a Code Completion list. Select the first item in the Code Completion list and then press **Enter**; then, you should see the following:

```
CGRectMake( CGFloat x , CGFloat y , CGFloat width ,...
```

3. The code that you typed so far assigns a value to the text field's **frame** property. But what about the code to the right of the equal sign? This is something new. **CGRectMake** is a *function*, not a method. A function is a lot like a method; it groups together one or more lines of code that perform a specific task. However, *unlike* a method, a function is not attached to an object or a class. It's stand-alone, or "free floating."

> **Note**: Objective-C is not fully object-oriented. Sometimes, rather than passing a message to an object, you call a function instead!

4. Notice that Xcode's Code Completion guides you to enter x and y coordinates as well as a width and a height.

   - To enter the **x** coordinate (which specifies how far the text field is placed from the left side of the view), enter the number **20**.

   - To enter the **y** coordinate (which indicates how far down to place the text field from the top of the view), press **Tab** and enter **50**.

   - Press **Tab** again and enter **280** for the **width**.

   - Press **Tab** again and enter **31** for the **height**.

   - Finally, add a semicolon to end the statement.

   The complete line of code should look like this:

```
textField.frame =
    CGRectMake(20, 50, 280, 31);
```

   I have chosen numbers that I know will place the text field in a good location, and with an appropriate size on the iPhone.

> **Note:** When using functions such as **CGRectMake** to specify coordinates and size, the numbers represent points rather than actual pixels on the screen. One point is not necessarily equal to one pixel. It's a relative number whose actual size is not important. At run time, the point size is translated to the correct number of pixels based on the device's screen resolution. This allows you to write code that works on any iOS device without worrying about its screen resolution.

Introducing Constants and Enumerations

By default, a text field added to the user interface in code doesn't have a border, so you need to add another line of code that sets the border style. To do this:

1. Add a new empty line, and then type the following partial line of code:

    ```
    textField.border
    ```

    As soon as you type this, Code Completion displays the popup shown in Figure 5.4.

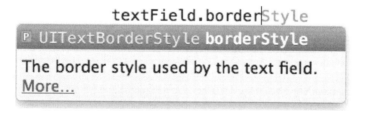

*Figure 5.4 Code completion for the **borderStyle** property*

The fact that you typed a period after the variable name indicates you are referencing a property. Code Completion suggests you are looking for the **borderStyle** property, which you are. Before continuing, notice the pop-up indicating that the property is of type **UITextBorderStyle**. This is worth noting because it is an indicator of the type of value that you are expected to store in this property.

2. Press **Enter** to select the **borderStyle** property, and then continue typing the following partial code:

    ```
    textField.borderStyle = UITextB
    ```

    This displays the popup list of choices shown in Figure 5.5. Notice that all

72

of the choices in the list have **UITextBorderStyle** listed on the left. This is the property type specified in the pop-up in the previous step. Each item in the list is a different kind of border style that you can specify for the text field. Each of these four options is a ***constant*** that is predefined in the Cocoa Touch Framework.

```
textField.borderStyle = UITextBorderStyleBezel
   K UITextBorderStyle UITextBorderStyleBezel
   K UITextBorderStyle UITextBorderStyleLine
   K UITextBorderStyle UITextBorderStyleNone
   K UITextBorderStyle UITextBorderStyleRoundedRect
```

Displays a bezel-style border for the text field. This style is typically used for standard data-entry fields. More...

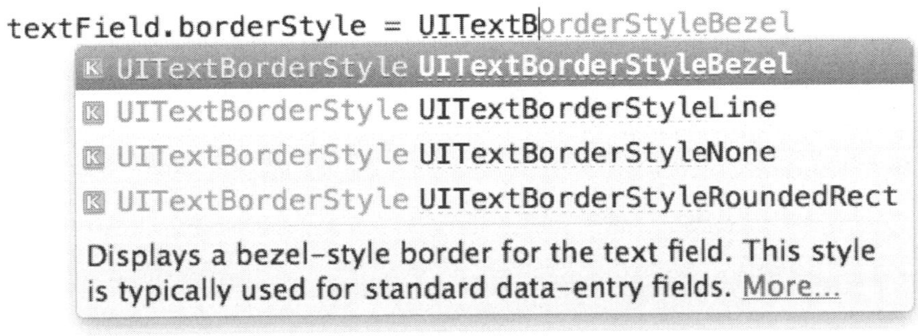

Figure 5.5 **UITextBorderStyle** *options*

In contrast with variables, constants are just that—constant. They don't change. Sometimes constants are stand-alone, but, as in this case, they are often grouped together with other related constants known as an ***enumeration***. This means that you can select any one of these styles when setting the **borderStyle** property of a text field.

3. Select **UITextBorderStyleRoundedRect**, and make sure you add a semicolon at the end:

```
textField.borderStyle =
    UITextBorderStyleRoundedRect;
```

Because there are many different constants and enumerations in the Cocoa Touch Framework, this is a great introduction to the concept. You will learn more about constants and enumerations in in *Chapter 15: Comments, Constants and Enumerations*.

Adding the Text Field to the View

Now you're ready to write code that adds the text field to the view.

1. Add the following line of code immediately after the border style code you just entered:

```
[self.view addSubview:textField];
```

This code begins with a square bracket, so you know it's a message call. In this case, the receiver object is **self.view**, where **self** refers to the view controller and **view** refers to a property that references the view on which you want to add the text field. The method being called on the view is **addSubView:**, and the argument being passed is the new **textField** object.

Effectively, this message tells the view, "Add this text field to yourself."

All iOS user-interface controls are subclasses of the **UIView** class, and are therefore a kind of view. That's why the method **addSubview:** is used here.

2. Before running the App, take a look at the code that you have entered so far. It should look like this:

```
UITextField *textField =
    [[UITextField alloc] init];
textField.placeholder = @"First Name";
textField.frame =
    CGRectMake(20, 50, 280, 31);
textField.borderStyle =
    UITextBorderStyleRoundedRect;
[self.view addSubview:textField];
```

In review, the first line of code creates a new text field object from the **UITextField** class. After that, the code sets the **placeholder** property, the **frame** property (for size and position), and the **borderStyle** property. The last line of code adds the text field to the view. Adding a user-interface control to the view using code is also known as adding it *programmatically*.

3. Now run the App by pressing the **Run** button in Xcode. You should see the text field displayed below the label (Figure 5.6).

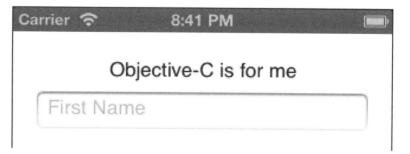

Figure 5.6 A text field added to the view using code

As you can see, the **placeholder** text is displayed in light gray. It's a clue to the user as to the information that he or she is expected to enter. As soon as the user types the first character, the **placeholder** text disappears. If you click in the text field, a keyboard pops up in the Simulator. You can use the Simulator keyboard or your computer keyboard to enter a value in the text field.

4. Take a moment again to feel the thrill of success.

5. Press the **Stop** button to stop execution of the App.

Now that you have learned some of the basics for using Apple's Cocoa Touch classes, it's time to create your own classes in the next chapter.

Summary

In this chapter, you learned the following important information about creating objects, calling functions, and using constants and enumerations:

- You normally use the **alloc** and **init** methods to create an object from a class.

- The **alloc** method creates the object, allocating space for it in memory.

- The **init** method initializes important variables.

- An object may have more than one **init** method that takes additional arguments. Typically, the extra arguments that you pass are used to provide additional initialization data.

- You can access properties by using dot notation.

- A function is a lot like a method. It groups together one or more lines of code that perform a specific task. However, unlike a method, a function is *not* attached to an object or a class.

- Constants are values that do not change.

- An enumeration is a group of related constants.

- You can create user-interface controls in code and then add them to a view by using the view's **addSubView:** method. This is known as adding a control *programmatically*.

Exercise 5.1

In this exercise you will create a new label object from the **UILabel** class and add it to the view using code, as you did with the text field object earlier in this chapter. When you're finished, your App should look like Figure 5.7 (if you don't do the extra credit).

Figure 5.7 The label added programmatically to the view

Here are the basic steps you need to take:

1. Create a new label object from the **UILabel** class.

2. Set the **text** property of the label to "Exercise 5.1."

3. Add the label to the view at the following coordinates and the specified size:

   - x = 20, y = 100

   - width = 280, height = 21

4. Note that labels don't have a **borderStyle** property.

5. Add the label to the view using code.

6. For extra credit, center the text of the label horizontally so it's in the middle of the view rather than aligned to the left.

Hint: Google "UILabel center text horizontally". The results you find on www.StackOverflow.com are usually best because participants get to vote for the best answer (the best answer has a green check mark next to it).

Solution Movie 5.1

To see a video providing the solution for this exercise, go to the following link in your web browser.

http://www.iOSAppsForNonProgrammers.com/B2M51.html

Chapter 6: Creating Your Own Custom Classes

So far, everything you have done has used Cocoa Touch Framework classes. You have learned to:

- Create objects from a class
- Set an object property
- Call an object method
- Call a class method

Now it's time to learn how to create your own classes.

Sections in This Chapter

In this chapter, you are going to create a new **Calculator** business class from scratch. The **Calculator** class will perform addition, subtraction, multiplication, and division. This is a non-visual class that can be used behind the scenes to perform important functionality. After creating the class, you will write test code that creates a Calculator object from the **Calculator** class and call its methods from within an App.

Creating the Calculator Class

1. Open the **ObjectiveCDemo** sample project.

2. Go to the Project Navigator on the left side of Xcode and select the **ObjectiveCDemo** folder (Figure 6.1).

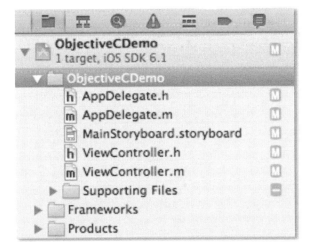

Figure 6.1 New files are added to the selected folder.

This is important because when you add a new file, it is added beneath the folder that you have selected in the Project Navigator.

3. Next, from the **File** menu, select **New > File...** (or just press **Command+N**). This launches the New File dialog (Figure 6.2).

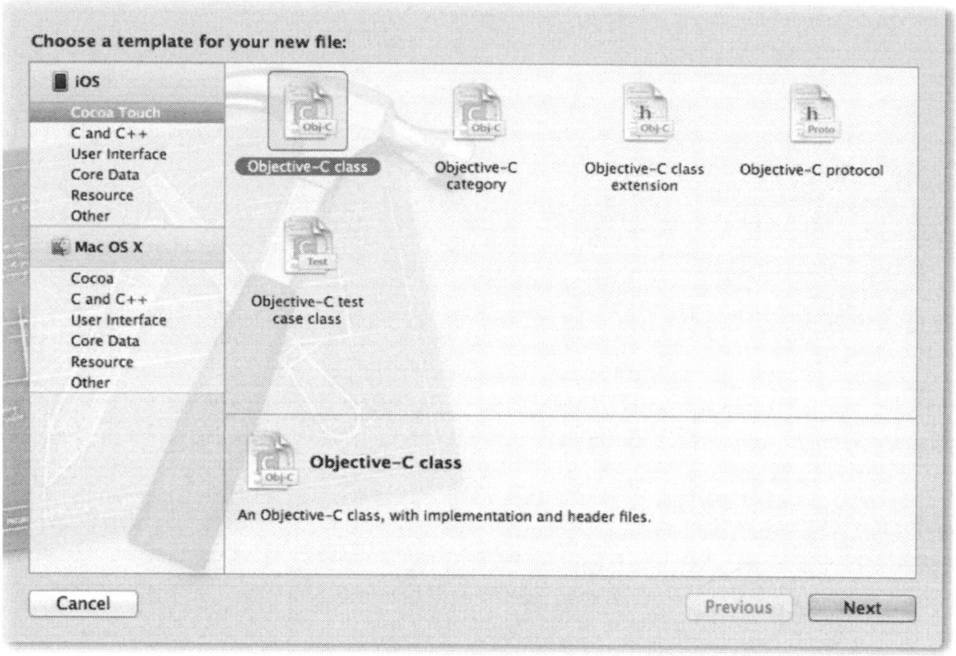

Figure 6.2 Make sure you select items in the iOS section.

On the left side of the dialog, two sections are listed—**iOS** and **Mac OS X**. Both these options are available because you can use Xcode to create both iOS and Mac OS X desktop applications. However, when creating iOS Apps, make sure that you select items under the **iOS** section.

So, under **iOS**, select **Cocoa Touch** to display the associated file templates. On the right side of the dialog, select the **Objective-C class** template and then click **Next**.

4. In the next page of the dialog (Figure 6.3) in the **Class** box, enter **Calculator** as the name of the class you want to create. In the **Subclass of** combo box, enter **NSObject** as the class you want to subclass from (the superclass), and then click **Next**.

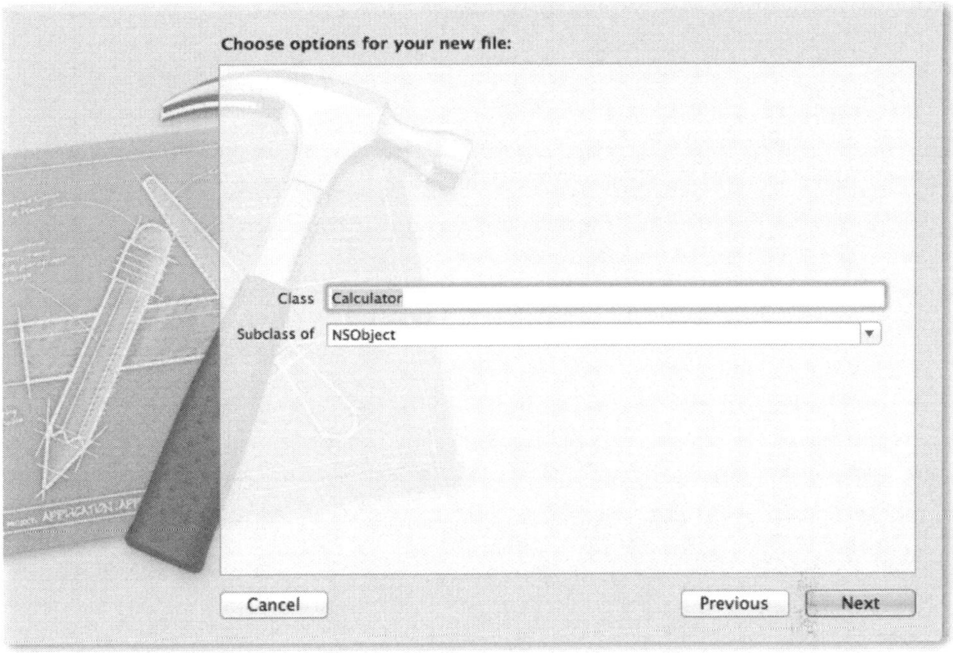

Figure 6.3 In the New Class dialog, specify the new name and its superclass.

Class names always begin with an uppercase letter, and then the first letter of each word in a compound word is capitalized—for example, **InvoiceDetail** and **PatientHistory**. This is known as ***Pascal case***. Also, class names should be singular, so you would have a **Customer** class, *not* a **Customers** class.

5. The next page of the dialog allows you to specify where you want to store the new file on your computer. The location defaults to your project's main folder, which is a good choice. Click **Create** to accept this default as shown in Figure 6.4.

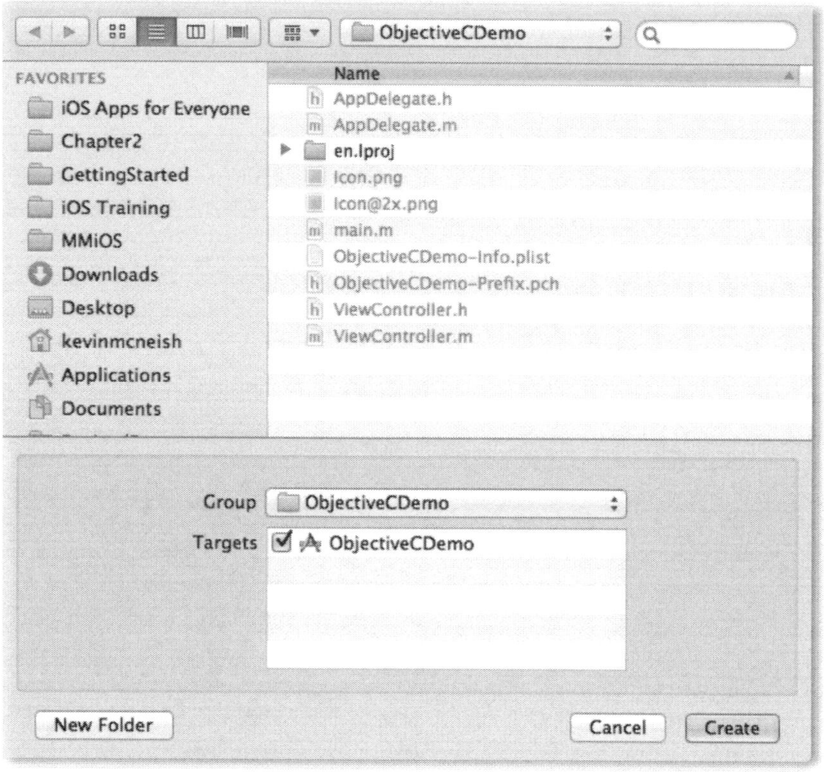

Figure 6.4 Saving classes in the main project folder

Afterwards, the Project Navigator contains two new files—**Calculator.h** and **Calculator.m** (Figure 6.5).

Figure 6.5 Objective-C classes are comprised of two files.

> **Note:** When you add new files to a project, they are added below the last item in the currently selected folder. If you want them to appear in a different order in the list, you can simply drag and drop them to another location in the list of files.

So why were two files added to the project when you only added one class? In Objective-C, a single class definition is declared in two separate files.

The first file, **Calculator.h**, is a public *class header file* (also known simply as *header file*). The header file declares the class's *public interface* to other classes. It's called a public interface because it describes the properties and methods that can be accessed by other classes. This public interface is what allows Xcode to pop up a list of available properties and methods in its Code Completion list.

Calculator.m, is a *class implementation file* (also known simply as *implementation file*). It implements, or contains the actual code for, the properties and methods declared in the public interface. It also declares private variables and methods.

6. Select the **Calculator.h** file in the Project Navigator. The code within looks like this:

```
#import <Foundation/Foundation.h>

@interface Calculator : NSObject

@end
```

Here are some important points to note:

- Directly below the comments, at the top of the file, is the **#import** statement, which is described in *Chapter 7: Referencing Classes*.

- The actual class interface definition begins with the **@interface** directive and ends with the **@end** directive.

- The header file declares the class name—in this case, **Calculator**.

- The header file declares the class heritage—in this case, **NSObject** is the superclass.

- In the header file, you declare public properties and methods. "Public" means that someone can create an object from your class, call these methods, and access these properties.

7. Select the **Calculator.m** class implementation file in the Project Navigator to see its contents:

```
#import "Calculator.h"

@implementation Calculator

@end
```

Here are some important points to note:

*   Directly below the comments, at the top of the file, is the **#import** directive, which is described in *Chapter 7: Referencing Classes*.

*   The actual class implementation begins with the **@implementation** directive and ends with the **@end** directive.

*   The implementation file is used to add the actual code to public methods as well as to declare private methods.

*   The implementation file is used to synthesize public properties (more on this later) and to declare private class-level variables.

Declaring Methods

You have already learned how to pass messages to an object created from a Cocoa Touch class. Now, you will learn how to declare methods in your own class. Let's cover a few ground rules first.

In Objective-C, you declare methods in the class header (.h) file. Method names are *camel cased*, meaning the first letter is always in lower case, and the first letter of each word in a compound word is uppercased (like a camel's head and its humps). For example, the method names **areYouOld** and **amIOld** are both camel cased.

When declaring a method in the class header file, follow these steps:

1. Type a minus (-) sign if you are defining an instance method (a method that belongs to instances of the class) or a plus (+) sign if declaring a class method (a method that belongs to the class itself).

2. Specify the method return type, enclosed in parentheses.

3. Specify the method name and any parameters.

Declaring a Method with No Parameters

Let's start by looking at a method that has no parameters. If you were able to access the source code for the **NSString** Cocoa Touch Framework class, you would see the method declaration for its **lowercaseString** method looks like this:

```
- (NSString *)lowercaseString;
```

From this declaration, you can determine:

1. It's an instance method because it begins with a minus sign.

2. The method returns an **NSString** value.

3. The method name is **lowercaseString**.

Declaring a Method with Parameters

When you declare a method that accepts parameters, each parameter:

1. Starts with a parameter description (optional)

2. Followed by a colon

3. Followed by the type of the parameter in parentheses

4. Finished with the parameter name

For example, if you were to look at the source code for the **stringByAppendingString:** method of the **NSString** class, it would look like this:

```
- (NSString *)stringByAppendingString:
        (NSString *)aString;
```

From this, you can see:

1. It's an *instance* method because it begins with a minus (-) sign.

2. The method returns an **NSString** value.

3. The name of the method is **stringByAppendingString:** (notice the inclusion of the colon in the method name).

4. It has a single parameter whose type is **NSString** and name is **aString**.

Here is an example of a method with multiple parameters (the method declaration is broken into three lines of code to make it easier to read):

```
- (NSString*)stringByReplacingOccurencesOfString:
        (NSString *)target
        withString:(NSString *)replacement;
```

From this, you can see:

1. It's an *instance* method because it begins with a minus (-) sign.

2. The method returns an **NSString** value.

3. **stringByReplacingOccurrencesOfString:withString:** is the name of the method.

4. It has two parameters. The first parameter type is **NSString** and its name is **target**. The second parameter type is also **NSString**. Its description (discussed below) is **withString**, and its name is **replacement**.

This is the first time you have seen a parameter declaration that includes a description. Although a description is optional, it's *very* common (and highly recommended) to use descriptions for method parameters in the Cocoa Touch Framework. Since it's optional, what are the benefits? Parameter descriptions help document what a method does because the *description* is included as part of the method name.

In Objective-C, a method name includes all keywords including colons and argument descriptions but does *not* include the argument name, return type, or parameter types. Method names should combine with the argument descriptions in such a way that the method's name naturally describes the arguments.

The **stringByReplacingOccurrencesOfString:withString:** method is a great example of this. The **withString:** parameter description helps you to understand the string that you pass as an argument is used to replace characters in the original string.

Note that you can't put descriptive text before the first parameter—instead, the method name is used for that.

Adding Methods to the Calculator Class

Now that you know the basic ground rules of declaring methods, it's time to create some methods of your own. You will start by making the **Calculator** class functional by adding methods that clear the running total, add, subtract, multiply, and divide.

1. If it's not already open, in Xcode, open the **ObjectiveCDemo** project.

2. In the Project Navigator, select the **Calculator.h** header file.

    The first thing that you're going to do is to add a method declaration. Remember: the reason that you declare a method in the class header file is because doing so makes the method visible to anyone who wants to use your class. It lets the rest of the world know all the things that your class can do.

3. Create a new empty line and enter this highlighted method declaration before the **@end** directive:

```
@interface Calculator : NSObject

// Clears the calculator's running total
- (void) clear;

@end
```

The code that you just entered declares a method that returns nothing (**void** is used to indicate this) and the method's name is **clear**. The purpose of this method is to clear the **Calculator's** total. It's a best practice to place a comment above a method declaration in the header (.h) file. This makes it easy for others looking at your code (or for you, six months later) to quickly identify what this method does.

Creating Instance Variables

The next thing that you are going to do is to declare a class-level variable (also known as an *instance variable* or *ivar*) named **total** to the **Calculator** class implementation file. You need this instance variable because all the methods that you add to the class need to act on the **total** value—by adding to it, subtracting from it, multiplying it, and so on. Therefore, the variable needs to be defined at the class level so all methods have access to it. Although you have created local variables inside of methods before, this is the first time that you have created a class-level variable; so I'll provide detailed instructions.

1. In the Project Navigator, select the **Calculator.m** file. Add the following instance variable declaration:

```
@implementation Calculator
{
    double total;
}
@end
```

Notice the instance variable is declared between curly braces.

2. This variable's type is **double** and its name is **total**. The **double** data type represents floating point numbers. For those of you who aren't math majors, a floating point number gets its name from the decimal point that can "float," or be placed anywhere in a number (for example, 1.234, or 12.34 or 123.4). So, a **double** value is perfect for use in the **total** variable.

Note: It used to be that you could only declare instance variables in the class header file. That's why most of code samples you see declare instance variables in the header file rather than the implementation file. Although you *can* still declare them in the header file, it's better to declare them in the implementation file. Instance variables are not public, so don't belong in the public header file. So flex your newfound freedom and declare your instance variables in the class implementation file!

Instance Variable Visibility

An instance variable's **visibility** refers to the ability of other classes to "see" or access the variable. In Objective-C there are three levels of visibility:

*   **public** – Any class can access the instance variable.

*   **protected** – The class in which the instance variable is declared can access it, as well as subclasses of the class in which it is declared.

- **private** – The class in which the instance variable is declared is the only class that can access it—subclasses cannot access it. Make an instance variable private if you don't want other classes changing the value of the instance variable.

You should *not* use the **public** accessibility option. If you want other classes to access your class's data, you should provide a property instead (more on that later). This keeps your class implementation *encapsulated*, hiding its "inner workings". This prevents other classes from knowing too much about how your class works, limiting the interdependencies between classes.

Instance variables declared in the class header file are **protected** by default. Instance variables declared in the class implementation file are **private** by default.

Objective-C has the **@protected** declaration to indicate the instance variables that follow it to are protected, and the **@private** declaration to indicate the instance variable that follow it arc private. However, these declarations can only be used in the class header file. For example:

```
@interface Calculator : NSObject {


@protected
        double memory1;
        double memory2;
@private
        double privateMemory;
}
```

In this code sample, the class has declared two **protected** instance variables—**memory1** and **memory2**, and a **private** instance variable named **privateMemory**. So, bottom line, if you want to declare a **protected** instance variable, you still need to do that in the class header file.

Creating Method Implementations

You have already declared the **clear** method in the **Calculator** class's header (.h) file. Now you need to finish the job by creating an implementation of the method in the class's implementation (.m) file. If you declare a public method in the class header (.h) file, you must create an implementation of that method in the class implementation (.m) file.

A method implementation has the exact same return value, name, and parameters as the method declaration in the header (.h). It contains the actual code that is executed when your App runs in the iOS Simulator or on an iOS device.

To add an implementation for the **clear** method in the **Calculator.m** file:

1. Add the following method implementation after the **total** instance variable declaration, and before the **@end** directive:

```
#import "Calculator.h"

@implementation Calculator
{
    double total;
}
- (void) clear
{
        total = 0.00;
}

@end
```

The implementation code for the clear method is pretty simple—just one line of code that stores **0.00** into the class-level **total** instance variable that you declared earlier. That's it! Notice that the code is contained between opening and closing curly braces.

Figure 6.6 provides an overview of what you have done so far. You declared the **clear** method in the public header (.h) file, and implemented it in the (.m) file. You also added the **total** instance variable to the implementation file. Instance variables and properties are usually declared at the top of the implementation files, and methods are declared below that.

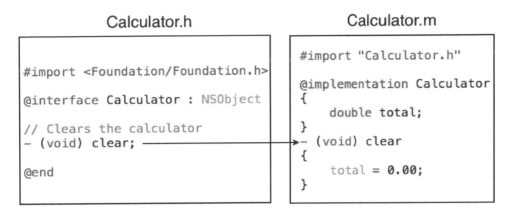

Figure 6.6 Calculator header and implementation files

2. Now let's add a few more methods. As before, you first add the method declarations to the class header file, so in the Project Navigator, select the **Calculator.h** header file. Next, add the following method declarations *after* the declaration of the **clear** method and *before* the @end directive:

```
@interface Calculator : NSObject

// Clears the calculator's running total
- (void) clear;

// Adds the specified value to the total
- (double) addToTotal:(double)value;

// Subtracts the specified value from the total
- (double) subtractFromTotal:(double)value;

// Multiplies the specified value times the total
- (double) multiplyTimesTotal:(double)value;

// Divides the specified value into the total
- (double) divideIntoTotal:(double)value;

@end
```

These methods add new functionality to the **Calculator** class for adding, subtracting, multiplying and dividing values against the running total. Notice the camel casing of each method name. Each method returns a **double** value. Each method has a **double** parameter that accepts the value being added, subtracted, multiplied, or divided into the running total.

Notice that each method declaration has a comment, so anyone reading your public header file can easily determine what each method does.

3. Now you're ready to add the implementations for the methods that you just declared. Go to the Project Navigator and select the **Calculator.m** class implementation file. Add the following method implementations *after* the **clear** method implementation and *before* the **@end** directive (Note that there is a space before and after the +=, -=, *=, and /= operators):

```
- (void) clear
{
    total = 0.00;
}

- (double) addToTotal:(double)value
{
    total += value;
    return total;
}

- (double) subtractFromTotal:(double)value
{
    total -= value;
    return total;
}

- (double) multiplyTimesTotal:(double)value
{
    total *= value;
    return total;
}

- (double) divideIntoTotal:(double)value
{
    total /= value;
    return total;
}

@end
```

Each of these methods has a **value** parameter of type **double**, which is used to act on the running total.

This is the first time you have seen the +=, -=, *= and /= operators. These are **compound assignment operators**. Each of these operators is shorthand for performing two operations. For example, the += operator adds the **value** parameter to the **total** variable, and then stores the result back into the **total** variable. As I'm sure you can guess, -= performs subtraction, *= performs multiplication, and /= performs division, and each stores the resulting value back into the variable. After performing the operation, the methods return the new running total.

4. This is a great time to make sure that your project has no errors or warnings. Press **Command+B** to build the project and make sure that there are no errors or warnings before moving on.

All the methods that you have created in the **Calculator** are public methods accessible by anyone who creates an instance of the **Calculator** class. There are times when you should make a method private to the class, so no other code outside the class can see it. You will learn how to do this in *Chapter 16: Advanced Objective-C* under the section Creating "Private" Methods With Class Extensions.

Summary

In this chapter, you learned how to create your own custom classes. Here are the main points to remember:

- Class names are Pascal cased with the first character uppercased and the first letter of each word in a compound word uppercased.

- Class names should be singular.

- A class definition is spread across two files—a header (.h) file and an implementation (.m) file.

- A class header (.h) file declares the class's *public interface* to other classes. It's called a *public* interface because it describes the properties and methods that can be accessed by other classes.

- The class interface definition in the header file begins with the **@interface** directive and ends with the **@end** directive.

- The header file declares the class name and the superclass.

- To declare a method in the class header (.h) file:

1. Type either a minus (-) sign if you are defining an instance method (a method that belongs to instances of the class) or a plus (+) sign if declaring a class method (a method that belongs to the class itself).

2. Specify the method return type, enclosed in parentheses.

3. Specify the method name and any parameters. For example:

```
- (double) addToTotal:(double)value;
```

- A class implementation (.m) file *implements*, or contains the actual code for, the properties and methods declared in the public interface. It also declares private variables and methods.

- If you declare a public method in the class header (.h) file, you *must* create an implementation of that method in the class implementation (.m) file.

- The class implementation begins with the **@implementation** directive and ends with the **@end** directive.

- A method implementation has the exact same return value, name, and parameters as the method declaration in the header (.h). It contains the actual code that is executed when your App runs in the iOS Simulator or on an iOS device.

- Variables declared at the class level are known as instance variables, or ivars. These variables should be declared in the class implementation (.m) file, below the **@implementation** directive. For example:

```
@implementation Calculator
{
    double total;
}
@end
```

Exercise 6.1

In this exercise, you will create a custom **AskJeeves** class with an **amIOld:** instance method.

1. Create a new class called **AskJeeves** (in honor of the Ask.com web site) based on **NSObject**.

2. In the **AskJeeves.h** header file, declare a new instance method called **amIOld:** that accepts an integer parameter called **age** and that returns a **BOOL** value.

3. In the **AskJeeves.m** implementation file, implement the method and return **YES** if the age is over 100, otherwise, return **NO**. This single line of code does the trick:

```
return age > 100;
```

Solution Movie 6.1

To see a video providing the solution for this exercise, go to the following link in your web browser.

http://www.iOSAppsForNonProgrammers.com/B2M61.html

Chapter 7: Referencing Classes

Now that you have created your custom Calculator class in the previous chapter, you're ready to create an instance of it and test it. However, in order to use this new class, you must first learn how to *reference* it. It's not difficult to do, but there are some best practices you need to learn as outlined in this chapter.

Sections in This Chapter

1. *Creating an Instance Variable for Your Custom Class*

2. *Using the @class Directive*

3. *Importing a Class Header*

4. *Importing Superclass Header Files*

5. *Import in the Header or Implementation File?*

6. *When to Use @class Vs. #import*

7. *Understanding Prefix Header Files*

Creating an Instance Variable for Your Custom Class

Up to this point, each time that you have created an object from a class, you have stored the newly created object in a local variable—a variable you declared in a method. If you were to create a local variable to hold a reference to the calculator object, it would look like Figure 7.1.

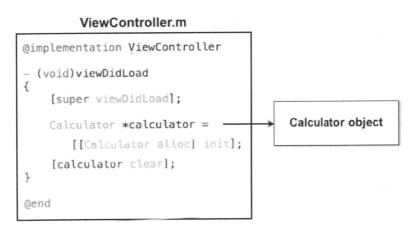

ViewController.m

```
@implementation ViewController

- (void)viewDidLoad
{
    [super viewDidLoad];

    Calculator *calculator =
        [[Calculator alloc] init];
    [calculator clear];
}

@end
```

Calculator object

Figure 7.1 Local variable referencing the Calculator

This works great as long as you only need to use the Calculator object in one method of the view controller. If you need to access the Calculator object from multiple methods in the **ViewController** class, you can create a class-level instance variable from which the Calculator can be referenced (Figure 7.2).

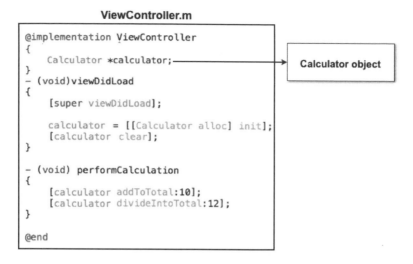

Figure 7.2 An instance variable referencing the Calculator

The main thing to notice is that the Calculator object gets created in the **viewDidLoad** method, but it can also be accessed from the **performCalculation** method because it is stored in a class-level instance variable.

Follow these steps to create the **calculator** instance variable to reference the Calculator object.

1. If it's not already open, in Xcode, open the **ObjectiveCDemo** project.

2. Go to the Project Navigator and click on the **ViewController.m** implementation file. Then, click to the immediate right of the following line of code:

```
@implementation ViewController
```

3. Next, press **Enter** to add a new empty line, and then add the following line of code, which declares an instance variable whose type is **Calculator** (upper-case "C") and name is **calculator** (lower case "c"):

```
@implementation ViewController

Calculator *calculator;

@synthesize lblDemo;
```

4. A few seconds after typing this line of code, an error icon appears. If you click on the error icon, you see the message "Unknown type name

'Calculator'":

```
@implementation HomeViewController
{
    Calculator *calculator;   ❶ Unknown type name 'Calculator'
```

Why are you getting this error? Xcode is telling you that it doesn't know about the type, or class **Calculator**. Why not? The **Calculator** class definition files are included in the project as shown in Figure 7.3 where the files are highlighted in a red box.

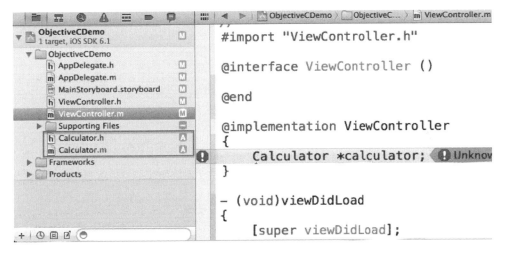

Figure 7.3 Including class files in the same project isn't enough when referencing another class.

In Objective-C, it's not enough to simply have class definition files listed in the same project. Whenever you reference another class, you must include a declaration that provides additional information about that class.

There are two ways you can do this. The first is to use the **@class** directive, and the second is to **import** the class header file. Each of these options provides a different level of detail about the class that you are referencing and are appropriate under different circumstances.

Let's take a side trip in order to thoroughly understand how to reference classes in your App before we get down to the business of testing the **Calculator** class in the next chapter.

Using the @class Directive

The **@class** directive provides minimal information about a class. In fact, it only indicates that the class you are referencing *is* a class! In Objective-C, the use of the **@class** directive is known as a ***forward declaration***. Follow these steps to see how it works:

1. If it's not already open, in Xcode, open the **ObjectiveCDemo** project.

2. Add a new empty line below the **#import** statement near the top of the **ViewController.m** file, and then add the following statement:

```
#import "ViewController.h"
@class Calculator;
```
As soon as you add the **@class** directive, the error icon disappears and the type of the variable, **Calculator**, becomes color-coded. This occurs because you have told Xcode that **Calculator** is a class by using the **@class** directive. Again, this is bare minimum information. All Xcode knows at this point is that **Calculator** is a class. It doesn't know any of its properties or methods.

3. Now let's create an instance of the **Calculator** class. This is the first time that you have created an object from a custom class. It works exactly the same as creating an object from a Cocoa Touch class. You call **alloc** and **init** and it returns a new, initialized Calculator object.

   To do this, in the **ViewController.m** file near the top of the **viewDidLoad** method, add a new empty line below the call to **[super viewDidLoad]**, and then add the following code, which creates a new instance of the **Calculator** class:

```
- (void)viewDidLoad
{
    [super viewDidLoad];
    calculator = [[Calculator alloc] init];
```

Again, you can see that Xcode displays an error for this line of code. If you click the error icon, you see the message "Receiver 'Calculator' for class message is a forward declaration":

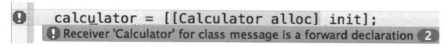

```
calculator = [[Calculator alloc] init];
```
❗ Receiver 'Calculator' for class message is a forward declaration ❷

What does this mean? It means that Xcode recognizes **Calculator** as a class because of the **@class Calculator** directive, but it needs more information to create an instance of the class. You would also get an error if you tried to send a message to an instance of the **Calculator** class because, again, Xcode doesn't have enough information about the class to know which methods it implements.

This is where you need to import a class header.

Importing a Class Header

The second way to provide information about a class is to import its header file. Remember that, because the header file contains important information about the properties, methods, and heritage of a class, it provides much more information than the simple **@class** directive.

Importing the header file for the Calculator class gives the **ViewController** class enough information to create a variable of the type **Calculator** and to create an instance of the **Calculator**. To import the class header:

1. Go to the top of the **ViewController.m** file, remove the **@class** directive and replace it with the following **#import** directive:

    ```
    #import "ViewController.h"
    #import "Calculator.h"
    ```

    As soon as you do this, the error associated with creating an instance of the **Calculator** class disappears!

2. Take a look at the **#import "ViewController.h"** directive listed directly above the **#import** directive that you just added. This **import** statement is automatically added when you create a new class in Xcode. Why is this needed? Because not only does a class need to import the header file of any class that it uses, but it must also import its *own* header file.

3. To see another example of importing a header file, select the **Calculator.h** header file in the Project Navigator. Notice that it imports the **Foundation.h** header file. This import statement is also automatically added when you create a class:

    ```
    #import <Foundation/Foundation.h>

    @interface Calculator : NSObject
    ```

    Why does this header file need to be imported? Because **Calculator** is a subclass of **NSObject**, and the **NSObject** class header file is found in the **Foundation.h** header file. Why isn't this header file called **NSObject.h**? Unlike the header files that you have seen so far, this and other Cocoa

Touch header files contain a reference to the header files of many classes. This makes your life easier, so you only have to import one "super" header file rather than one header file for each class that you use in a particular Cocoa Touch framework.

Notice that you use angle brackets (< >) to import a header file for a class that is part of the Cocoa Touch Framework, as in this example. In contrast, you use double quotes (" ") to import a header file that is defined in your project.

Importing Superclass Header Files

Whenever you specify a superclass in a class header file, you need to import the header file of the superclass.

In the following example, **BusinessObject** is the superclass of **Customer**, so the **Customer** class must import the **BusinessObject.h** header file:

```
#import <Foundation/Foundation.h>
#import "BusinessObject.h"

@interface Customer : BusinessObject
```

This is important to know when you create your own custom classes that are not a subclass of a foundation class such as **NSObject**.

Import in the Header or Implementation File?

If you have been following closely in this chapter, you may have noticed that the **#import** statement can be used in either the header (.h) file or the implementation (.m) file. So where should you use it? Here's a good rule of thumb:

• When you specify a superclass, import the superclass header file in the subclass's *header* file.

• When you are referencing a class from within your implementation file, import the class header in your class *implementation* file.

When to Use @class Vs. #import

So, you may be asking yourself, "If **#import** does everything **@class** does and more, why not just use **#import** all the time?" The answer is found in Apple's own documentation:

> *The @class directive minimizes the amount of code seen by the compiler and linker, and is, therefore, the simplest way to give a forward declaration of a class name. Being simple, it avoids potential problems that may come with importing files that import still other files.*

So, use the **@class** directive when you *can*, and use **#import** when you *must*.

Understanding Prefix Header Files

When you create a new project in Xcode, a prefix header file is automatically added to your project. When you build your project, the compiler automatically adds the content of the prefix header file to every source code file in your project. This is a powerful tool that makes it easy to add **import** statements, in one place, so that you don't have to add them manually to each and every source code file in your project.

Let's see this file in the sample **ObjectiveCDemo** project. In the Project Navigator, click the gray triangle to the left of the **Supporting Files** folder to expand it, and then select the **ObjectiveCDemo-Prefix.pch** file. You should see the following code:

```
//
// Prefix header for all source files of
//

#import <Availability.h>

#ifndef __IPHONE_5_0
#warning "This project uses features only
#endif

#ifdef __OBJC__
    #import <UIKit/UIKit.h>
    #import <Foundation/Foundation.h>
#endif
```

As you can see, a few **import** statements are listed here. The two statements at the bottom import header files for classes commonly used in iOS Apps. The first, **UIKit**, references classes used to create your App's user interface. The second, **Foundation**, imports commonly used core classes including **NSObject**.

So, here's a burning question: If the **import** statements in the prefix header file are automatically added to the top of each source code file, and the prefix header file import the **Foundation.h** file, why do you need the **Foundation.h** file automatically imported at the top of each new class that you create?

For example:

```
#import <Foundation/Foundation.h>
#import "BusinessObject.h"

@interface Customer : BusinessObject

@end
```

The answer is "You don't." It is "belt and suspenders" code. That said, it doesn't *hurt* to have it imported, but it's not necessary since the **import** statement is already included in the prefix header file.

Summary

Here are some important points to remember when referencing classes:

- If you only need to reference an object from a single method, you can store a reference to the object in a local variable. If you need to reference the object from multiple methods, you can store it in a class-level instance variable.

- In Objective-C, it's not enough to have class definition files listed in the same project. When you reference another class, you must include an **@class** or **#import** directive that provides information about that class.

- The **@class** directive provides minimal information about a class. In fact, the only thing that it indicates is that the class referenced is a class! In Objective-C, the use of the **@class** directive is known as a *forward declaration*. For example:

```
@class Calculator;
```

- Another way to provide information about a class is to **import** its header file. The header file contains important information about the properties, methods, and heritage of a class and, thus provides much more information than the simple **@class** directive.

- You use angle brackets (< >) to import a header file for a class that is part of the Cocoa Touch Framework. You use double quotes (" ") to import a header file for a class that is defined in your project. For example:

```
#import <Foundation/Foundation.h>
#import "BusinessObject.h"
```

- Importing a class header file allows you either to create a variable of that class type or to create an instance of that class.

- A class must import its own header file.

- A class must import its superclass header file.

- When you specify a superclass, import the superclass header file in the subclass's header file. When you are referencing a class from within your implementation file, import the class header in your class implementation file.

- Use the **@class** directive when you can, and use **#import** when you must.

- Prefix header files are powerful tools that make it easy to add **import** statements in one place, so that you don't have to add them manually to each and every source code file in your project.

Chapter 8: Testing the Calculator

Whenever you create a new class, or add a new method to an existing class, it's a best practice to step through the code you have written in Xcode to make sure everything is working properly. In this chapter, you will learn some of the basic skills necessary to test your code using Xcode's debugging tools. In addition, stepping through the code will help you better understand how Objective-C works.

Sections in This Chapter

1. *Testing Techniques*

2. *Adding the Test Code*

3. *Setting Breakpoints*

4. *Stepping Through Code in the Debugger*

5. *Deleting and Disabling Breakpoints*

6. *Summary*

Testing Techniques

Now that you have created the **Calculator** class and learned how to reference it from a view controller, it's time to learn how to test it. Admittedly, the **Calculator** class is very basic, but it provides a good example of how you can use the debugging tools in Xcode to test your code after you have written it.

When you really dig into App development, there is something more extensive called ***unit testing*** that you can implement to more fully test your code, but that's beyond the scope of this book (it's covered fully later in this book series. With unit testing, you create classes in a separate project that contain code that tests your App.

For now, the techniques used in this chapter suffice to show you how to examine your code at run time and solidify your understanding of how Objective-C works along the way.

Adding the Test Code

To begin our informal **Calculator** class test, you are going to add some temporary code to the view controller in the **ObjectiveCDemo** project.

1. If it's not already open, in Xcode, open the **ObjectiveCDemo** project.

2. In the Project Navigator, select the **ViewController.m** implementation file, and then add the following lines of code directly below the code that creates an instance of the **Calculator** class (note there is a space after each reference to **calculator**):

```
calculator = [[Calculator alloc] init];

double sum =
    [calculator addToTotal:10];
double difference =
    [calculator subtractFromTotal:6];
double result =
    [calculator multiplyTimesTotal:3];
double quotient =
    [calculator divideIntoTotal:4];
[calculator clear];

NSLog(@"Sum: %f", sum);
NSLog(@"Difference: %f", difference);
```

```
NSLog(@"Result: %f", result);
NSLog(@"Quotient: %f", quotient);
```

In the above code, after creating an instance of the **Calculator** class, there are several messages passed to the Calculator object, and the result is stored in a local variable each time.

After that, there are four statements that use the **NSLog** function. **NSLog** is a Cocoa Touch function that displays a message to Xcode's Console panel in the Debug area, as you will see, when you run the code in the Simulator in just a bit. It's a great tool for debugging your App and is often used to display the value of local variables.

The first argument passed to **NSLog** is a text string. At the end of each text string are the characters **%f**. This set of characters is a *format specifier*. In this case, it tells **NSLog** how to format the second argument (**sum**, **difference**, **result**, and **quotient**). The **f** in the format specifier tells **NSLog** that the second argument is a **double**, or float number (for more information on format specifiers, check out *Chapter 14: Working With Strings* in the section Converting Values to NSString With Format Specifiers).

Setting Breakpoints

To get a closer look at how the code works, you need to temporarily pause execution of the App when the Calculator test code is executed in the Simulator. To do this, you can add a ***breakpoint*** in the code. For now just know need to know that a breakpoint allows you to temporarily pause an App and examine the value of variables, properties, and so on.

1. To set a breakpoint, click in the gutter to the immediate left of the code that creates an instance of the **Calculator** class. Then, add another breakpoint by clicking in the gutter next to the call to **[calculator clear]**. This adds the visual breakpoint indicators shown in Figure 8.1.

```
calculator = [[Calculator alloc] init];

double sum = [calculator addToTotal:10];
double difference =
[calculator subtractFromTotal:6];
double result =
[calculator multiplyTimesTotal:3];
double quotient =
[calculator divideIntoTotal:4];
[calculator clear];

NSLog(@"Sum: %f", sum);
NSLog(@"Difference: %f", difference);
NSLog(@"Result: %f", result);
NSLog(@"Quotient: %f", quotient);
```

Figure 8.1 Setting breakpoints to test the Calculator

2. Unfortunately, at times, Xcode has some debugging "issues," so just to be safe, you should add a few more breakpoints to make sure Xcode steps through the code that I want you to see. To do this, in the Project Navigator, select the **Calculator.m** file. Next, add breakpoints by clicking in the gutter to the left of each line of code as shown in Figure 8.2.

```
- (void) clear
{
    total = 0.00;
}
- (double) addToTotal:(double)value
{
    total += value;
    return total;
}

- (double) subtractFromTotal:(double)value
{
    total -= value;
    return total;
}

- (double) multiplyTimesTotal:(double)value
{
    total *= value;
    return total;
}

- (double) divideIntoTotal:(double)value
{
    total /= value;
    return total;
}
```

Figure 8.2 Set extra breakpoints in the Calculator class.

Stepping Through Code in the Debugger

1. Now, run the App in the Simulator by clicking the **Run** button in the upper-left corner of Xcode. After several seconds, the iOS Simulator starts and Xcode displays the message in Figure 8.3 to indicate that it has paused execution at the breakpoint.

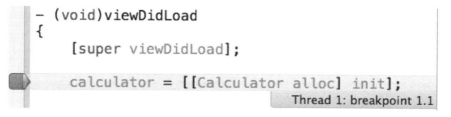

Figure 8.3 Execution is paused at the first breakpoint.

2. The Debug area should automatically be displayed at the bottom of the Xcode window as shown in Figure 8.4. In the upper-left corner of the

debug area, if **Local** is not selected, click on the control and select **Local Variables** from the pop-up list.

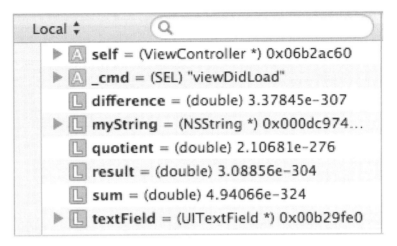

Figure 8.4 The Debug Area showing local variables

The Debug area displays a list of all variables that are *local*, meaning that they are defined in the method currently executing. As you can see, the **difference**, **quotient**, **result**, and **sum** variables are all listed here.

3. You don't see the **calculator** variable in the Debug area because it's not a local variable; it's an instance variable declared at the class level. However, if you hover your mouse pointer over the **calculator** variable in the Code editor, you can see that it is automatically initialized to zero (Figure 8.5). This value is displayed in hexadecimal, a base 16 numeral system often used to represent computer memory addresses (more on that later).

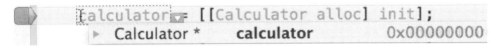

Figure 8.5 The calculator variable is initialized to zero.

4. At the top of the debug area are toolbar buttons that allow you to control App execution (Figure 8.6).

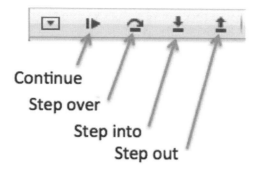

Continue

Step over

Step into

Step out

Figure 8.6 The debug toolbar controls App execution.

- The **Continue** button causes execution to continue to the next breakpoint or, if there is no other breakpoint, resume execution of the App.

- The **Step over** button allows you to step over the current line of code without examining it further.

- The **Step into** button allows you to step into a message call (if any) for the current line of code.

- The **Step out** button allows you to step out of the current method and break on the next line of code outside the method.

If you forget what a button does, just hover your mouse pointer over the button and Xcode displays a popup that describes the button.

5. Click the **Step over** button to step over the code that creates an instance of the Calculator class. Just for fun, hover your mouse pointer over the **calculator** variable. You can see that it's now set to a hexadecimal number that is a pointer. Remember, a pointer points to a particular address, or location in memory where the Calculator object is stored (the number you see will be different from the number shown in Figure 8.7).

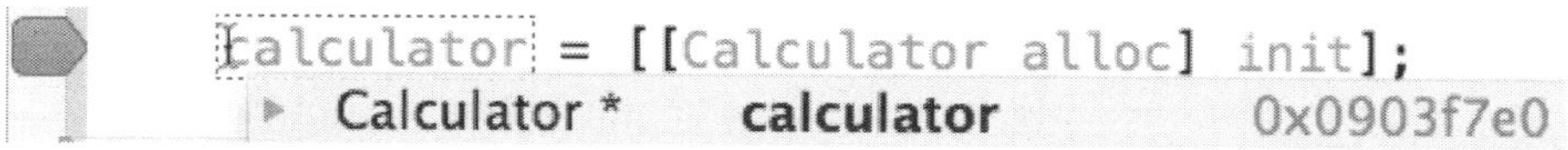

```
calculator = [[Calculator alloc] init];
   ▶ Calculator *     calculator            0x0903f7e0
```

Figure 8.7 The calculator variable contains a pointer.

You will rarely use this piece of information, but the fact that it's non-zero means the Calculator object has been created.

6. Xcode is currently highlighting the next line of code to be executed. Take

note that this code is passing the value 10 to the **addToTotal:** method (Figure 8.8).

7. Click the **Step Into** button to step into the **addToTotal:** method. Xcode should highlight the first line of code in the **addToTotal:** method (Figure 8.9).

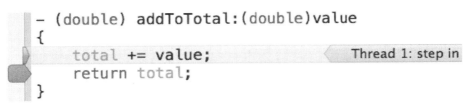

*Figure 8.9 The first line of code in **addToTotal:***

If you hover your mouse pointer over the **value** parameter, Xcode displays a popup that shows the value of the parameter passed. In this case, it's 10 as shown in Figure 8.10.

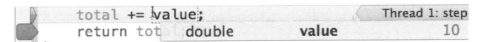

*Figure 8.10 The **value** parameter's value is 10.*

If you hover your mouse pointer over the reference to the **total** instance variable, you should see that it's currently set to zero (Figure 8.11).

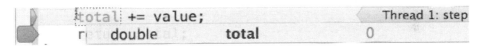

*Figure 8.11 The **total** instance variable is currently zero.*

8. Now click the **Step Over** button in the Debug area toolbar. This executes the line of code that adds the value to the **total** variable, and then, places the highlight bar on the next line of code. If you hover your mouse pointer over the reference to the **total** variable now, it should be set to **10** (Figure 8.12).

*Figure 8.12 The **total** variable is now set to 10.*

The last line of code in the method returns the value stored in the **total** variable. Press the **Step out** button in the Debug area toolbar, and Xcode highlights the same line of code in the **ViewController** class that you saw earlier (Figure 8.13).

```
calculator = [[Calculator alloc] init];

double sum = [calculator addToTotal:10];
```

Figure 8.13 Control passes back to the view controller.

9. This line is highlighted because it's waiting to store the return value of the **addToTotal:** method into the **sum** variable. To make this happen, click **Step over**. Afterwards, hover your mouse pointer over the **sum** variable to see it is set to **10** (Figure 8.14).

```
double sum = [calculator addToTotal:10];
double d   double        sum             10
```

*Figure 8.14 The **sum** variable is now set to 10.*

10. Now press the **Continue** button in the Debug area toolbar. You should hit the breakpoint in the **subtractFromTotal:** method. You can look around at the variables here; or if you prefer, just click **Continue** three more times until execution stops at the **[calculator clear]** message call (Figure 8.15).

```
[calculator divideIntoTotal:4];
[calculator clear];                    Thread 1:
```

*Figure 8.15 Execution is paused on the **clear** message call.*

You can now hover your mouse pointer over the **difference**, **result**, and **quotient** variables to see that the proper value has been stored in each.

11. Next, click the **Continue** button again and you should hit the breakpoint in the **clear** method where the **total** variable is set to **0.00** (Figure 8.16).

```
- (void) clear
{
    total = 0.00;                      Thread 1:
}
```

*Figure 8.16 A breakpoint is hit in the **clear** method.*

12. Now press the **Step out** button, and Xcode places the highlight bar on the code that uses the **NSLog** function to write values to Xcode's Console as shown in Figure 8.17.

```
NSLog(@"Sum: %f", sum);                          Thread
NSLog(@"Difference: %f", difference);
NSLog(@"Result: %f", result);
NSLog(@"Quotient: %f", quotient);
```

*Figure 8.17 Execution pauses on the call to **NSLog**.*

13. Press the Step over button four times, and you will see the output shown
    in the Console panel in Figure 8.18 (if you don't see the Console, in the
    Xcode menu select **View** > **Debug Area** > **Activate Console**).

```
All Output ÷                                        Clear
2012-07-24 21:21:09.385 ObjectiveCDemo[11033:f803] Sum: 10.000000
2012-07-24 21:21:09.936 ObjectiveCDemo[11033:f803] Difference: 4.000000
2012-07-24 21:21:10.443 ObjectiveCDemo[11033:f803] Result: 12.000000
2012-07-24 21:21:10.983 ObjectiveCDemo[11033:f803] Quotient: 3.000000
(lldb)
```

*Figure 8.18 Xcode's Console displays output from the **NSLog** function.*

So there you have it! You have created your first class and tested it in the iOS
Simulator. Go ahead and stop the App from running in the Simulator by
clicking the **Stop** button in the upper left corner of Xcode.

What's great about debugging in Xcode is that, not only can you set
breakpoints and step through code in the Simulator, you can also do the same
when running your App on a real iOS device through Xcode.

Deleting and Disabling Breakpoints

Before moving on, it's a great time to learn how to delete and disable
breakpoints. When you no longer need a particular breakpoint, you can delete
it, which completely removes it from your App's source code. If you want to
keep a break point around, but temporarily deactivate it, you can choose to
disable it.

To delete or disable a single breakpoint, all you have to do is right-click (or
Control+Click) the breakpoint in the gutter to the left of the Code editor
and select **Delete Breakpoint** or **Disable Breakpoint** from the shortcut
menu (Figure 8.19).

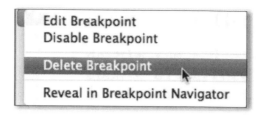

Figure 8.19 Right-click a breakpoint to bring up the menu that lets you disable/enable or delete it.

If you would like to temporarily disable or enable all breakpoints, you can just click the **Breakpoints** button in the toolbar at the top of the Xcode window, which toggles the breakpoints between enabled and disabled. (Figure 8.20).

*Figure 8.20 The **Breakpoints** button enables/disables all App breakpoints.*

Since we will be using the **ObjectiveCDemo** project in the next chapter, let's delete all of the breakpoints that are currently set in the project. The easiest way to do that is to use Xcode's Breakpoint navigator.

1. Go to the Navigation toolbar in the upper-left corner of Xcode and click the **Breakpoint navigator** toolbar button, which displays all the breakpoints in the current project as shown in Figure 8.21.

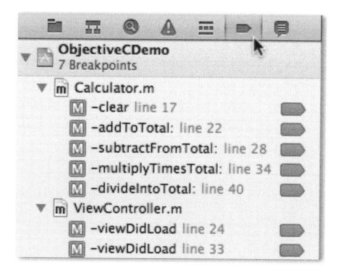

Figure 8.21 The Breakpoint Navigator

2. To delete all breakpoints, right-click the first node labeled **ObjectiveCDemo** and select **Delete Breakpoints** from the shortcut menu (Figure 8.22).

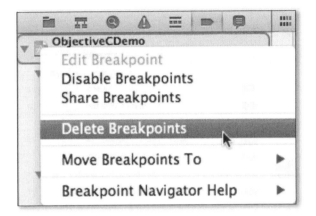

Figure 8.22 This deletes all breakpoints in your App.

3. To redisplay the Project Navigator, simply click the far left button in the Navigator toolbar (Figure 8.23).

Figure 8.23 Click the far left button to redisplay the Project Navigator.

Summary

Setting a breakpoint and stepping through code is something that you will do on a regular basis when creating an iOS App. The process usually works like this:

- You write code, adding a new feature to your App.

- You run the App in the Simulator and find out that it doesn't work properly.

- You set some breakpoints, run the App in the Simulator again, and step through your code, examining variables and property values to see what went wrong.

I recommend being more proactive—each time you create a new method you should set a breakpoint at the top of the method and step through each line of code. It's best to do this immediately after you write the new method, because that's when you remember best how the code is intended to work!

Chapter 9: Declaring Properties

You have already learned that properties describe a class's attributes, or characteristics. Now it's time to learn how to create properties for your own custom classes. In this chapter, you will create a property for the Calculator class and learn how properties differ from instance variables.

Sections in This Chapter

Instance Variable Visibility

As it stands right now, there is no way to check the running total value outside of the **Calculator** class. That's because **total** is declared as a private instance variable. As you have already learned, this means that although the variable can be accessed from methods within the **Calculator** class, it can't be accessed by code external to the class, such as the **ViewController** in Figure 9.1.

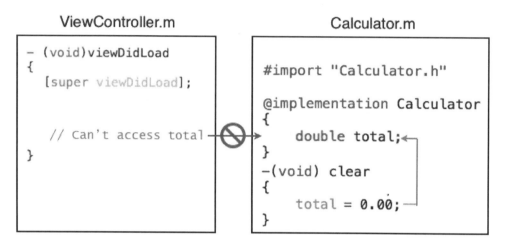

Figure 9.1 The private instance variable **total** cannot be accessed outside the Calculator class.

So, what do you do if you want to provide access to the calculator's **total** to code outside the **Calculator** class? The answer is...create a property.

Property Visibility

Like instance variables, properties can be accessed from methods declared in the same class. However, unlike instance variables, properties are public and can be accessed by code external to the class.

Figure 9.2 shows a **total** property declared in the *public* header file of the **Calculator** class. It can be accessed by the **clear** method that is *internal* to the Calculator class. Since it's public, it can also be accessed from code *external* to the class in the **viewDidLoad** method of the **ViewController** class.

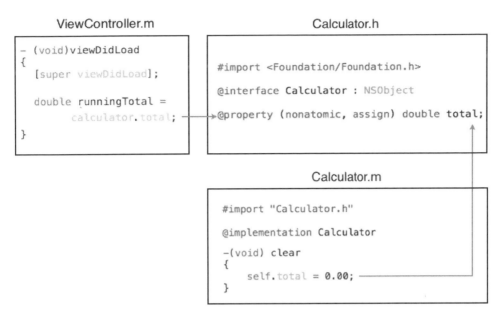

ViewController.m

```
- (void)viewDidLoad
{
  [super viewDidLoad];

  double runningTotal =
       calculator.total;

}
```

Calculator.h

```
#import <Foundation/Foundation.h>

@interface Calculator : NSObject

@property (nonatomic, assign) double total;
```

Calculator.m

```
#import "Calculator.h"

@implementation Calculator

-(void) clear
{
    self.total = 0.00;
}
```

Figure 9.2 Properties are public and can be accessed by code outside of the class in which they are declared.

From a high-level perspective, instance variables and properties are similar. They are both defined at the class level, and they can both hold values. The main difference is their scope, or visibility; instance variables should only be protected or private, and properties are public.

As you are designing your custom iOS classes, you need to ask yourself whether a particular value needs to be accessed outside the class. If it doesn't, make it an instance variable; if it does, make it a property. When you design your classes, you don't want to expose more information to the outside world than is necessary. Hiding information within a class is known in object-oriented programming as **encapsulation**.

Adding a Property to the Calculator

In this section, you will replace the **total** instance variable in the **Calculator** class with a **total** property.

1. If it's not already open, in Xcode, open the **ObjectiveCDemo** project.

2. Declaring a property starts with the class header file, so go to the Project Navigator and select the **Calculator.h** header file.

3. As a matter of style, I prefer to put properties first in the list before any method declarations. Directly after the **@interface** declaration, add a

new property declaration like this:

```
@interface Calculator : NSObject

// Calculator's running total
@property (assign, nonatomic) double total;
```

A property declaration begins with the keyword **@property**. For now, ignore the **assign** and *nonatomic* key words.

The main point to note is how similar this property declaration is to the **total** instance variable declaration. They both declare the type, **double**, and a name, **total**. It's an Objective-C standard to camel case property and instance variable names.

4. In the Project Navigator, select the **Calculator.m** implementation file.

    Just like methods, properties are *declared* in the header (.h) file and *implemented* in the implementation (.m) file. Starting in Xcode 4.4 with the Apple LLVM Compiler 4.0, you no longer need to manually implement the property. However, I recommend that you read the rest of this step since you will encounter a lot of legacy code that implements properties manually.

    If you are using an earlier version of the compiler, you need to add an **@synthesize** directive below the **@implementation** declaration.

    ```
    @implementation Calculator

    @synthesize total = _total;

    double total;
    ```

    This statement implements the **total** property that you declared in the header (.h) file. You will learn more detail about this in the upcoming section, Properties Behind the Scenes, including the reason for the underscore in the **_total** name.

5. Let's leave the **total** instance variable declaration in place for now. Press **Command+B** to build the project. You should have no build errors at this point.

That's it—you have declared your first property!

Accessing the Calculator's Property

Now let's see if you can access this property from outside the **Calculator** class.

1. In the Project Navigator, select the **ViewController.m** file and in the **viewDidLoad** method directly below the call to **[calculator clear]**, type the following:

```
double runningTotal = calculator.t
```

Notice that, as soon as you type the letter "t," Code Completion pops up the suggestion "total" as shown in Figure 9.3.

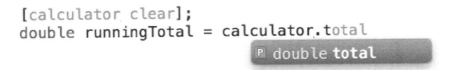

*Figure 9.3 Code Completion indicates that the **total** property is accessible from outside the **Calculator** class.*

This indicates that the new **total** property is accessible outside the **Calculator** class.

2. Go ahead and press **Enter** to accept the Code Completion suggestion, and then type a semicolon to complete the statement:

```
double runningTotal = calculator.total;
```

In review, this line of code gets the value from the Calculator object's **total** property and stores it in a new variable of type **double** named **runningTotal**.

3. At the bottom of the **viewDidLoad** method, add another **NSLog** statement to the end of the list. This outputs the **runningTotal** value to Xcode's Console for debugging purposes:

```
NSLog(@"Sum: %f", sum);
NSLog(@"Difference: %f", difference);
NSLog(@"Result: %f", result);
NSLog(@"Quotient: %f", quotient);
NSLog(@"Running Total: %f", runningTotal);
```

4. As it stands right now, the code in the methods of the **Calculator.m** file
    is not accessing the new **total** property that you just created. Instead, it's
    accessing the **total** class-level variable. Why is that?

    In Objective-C, when you declare a property on a class, any code contained
    in that class must use the **self** keyword to reference the property (for
    example, **self.total**). In the absence of the reference to **self**, the code in
    the Calculator class currently accesses the **total** instance variable rather
    than the **total** property.

    So, to use the new **total** property from within your class, you have to
    locate any code that directly references the **total** instance variable and
    change it to reference the property instead.

    To do this, select the **Calculator.m** file in the Project Navigator and
    change the code to:

```
- (void) clear
{
    self.total = 0.00;
}

- (double) addToTotal:(double)value
{
    self.total += value;
    return self.total;
}

- (double) subtractFromTotal:(double)value
{
    self.total -= value;
    return self.total;
}

- (double) multiplyTimesTotal:(double)value
{
    self.total *= value;
    return self.total;
}

- (double) divideIntoTotal:(double)value
{
    self.total /= value;
    return self.total;
}
```

5. Go back to the **ViewController.m** file and create a breakpoint by clicking in the gutter to the left of the code that gets the value of the **total** property:

```
double runningTotal = calculator.total;
```

6. Afterwards, click the **Run** button to run the App in the Simulator. When the breakpoint is hit, click the **Step Over** button in the Debug area toolbar and then hover your mouse pointer over the **runningTotal** variable. You should see that the value of **runningTotal** is zero because the Calculator's **clear** method was called right before this line of code (Figure 9.4).

```
double runningTotal = calculator.total;
         double          runningTotal          0
```

*Figure 9.4 The value of **runningTotal** is zero.*

7. Press the **Continue** button, and you can see the **runningTotal** value displayed in the Console panel. If the Console panel is not visible, select **View > Debug Area > Activate Console** from Xcode's menu. You have successfully accessed the Calculator object's **total** property!

8. To stop the App from running in the Simulator, click the **Stop** button.

Properties Behind the Scenes

Behind the scenes, properties are actually comprised of a set of two methods and, usually, an instance variable:

1. A **getter** method that gets the value of the property, usually from an instance variable; and

2. A **setter** method that sets the value of the property, usually to the same instance variable.

Collectively, these are known as **accessor methods** because they allow you to access the value of the property.

As mentioned earlier, prior to Xcode 4.4 with the Apple LLVM Compiler 4.0, you had to add an **@synthesize** statement to your class implementation file to implement the accessor methods and instance variable. For example:

```
@synthesize total = _total;
```

If you are using the newer compiler, you no longer need to add this **@synthesize** directive, but in either case, the result is the same. The compiler synthesizes (creates) the items shown in Figure 9.5:

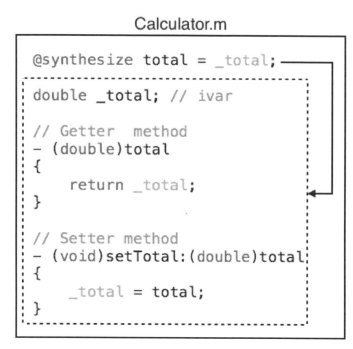

Calculator.m

```
@synthesize total = _total;

double _total; // ivar

// Getter  method
- (double)total
{
    return _total;
}

// Setter method
- (void)setTotal:(double)total
{
    _total = total;
}
```

*Figure 9.5 Either automatically or with a manual **@synthesize** command, the compiler creates an instance variable and getter/setter methods.*

1. An instance variable named **_total**.

2. A getter method named **total** (the same name as the property).

3. A setter method named **setTotal** (a "set" prefix, followed by the name of the property with the first character of the property uppercased).

These items are all created "behind the scenes," because you don't see the instance variable and accessor methods in the source code (thus the dotted line surrounding them in Figure 9.5), but they are in the compiled code, and are very real.

So, when you get the value of a property, the property's getter method is executed. For example, in Figure 9.6, the **ViewController** class has the following line of code that gets the value of the Calculator's **total** property:

```
double runningTotal = calculator.total;
```

When this line of code runs, the **total** property's **total** getter method is executed, which returns the value in the _**total** instance variable.

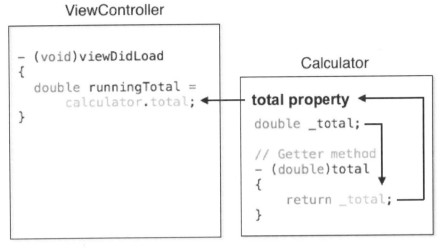

Figure 9.6 Getting a property value executes its getter.

Ultimately, you are still getting the value from the _**total** instance variable in the Calculator object. You are just using the getter method to retrieve it for you, rather than accessing the instance variable directly.

When you set the value of a property, the property's setter method is executed. For example, in Figure 9.7, the **ViewController** class contains the following line of code that sets the value of the Calculator's **total** property to **123.45**:

```
calculator.total = 123.45;
```

When this line of code runs, behind the scenes, the **123.45** value is passed as an argument to the **total** property's **setTotal** setter method. The method then stores the value in the _**total** instance variable.

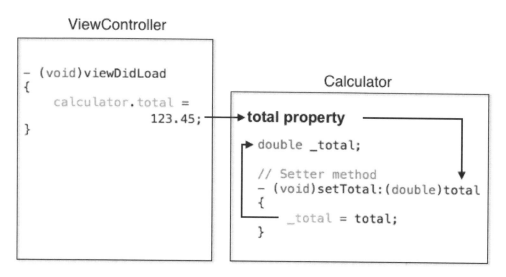

Figure 9.7 Setting a property value executes its setter.

Ultimately, you are setting the value of the **_total** instance variable in the Calculator object. You are just using the setter method to do it.

Since the compiler synthesizes an associated instance variable for a property (whether through a manual **@synthesize** statement or automatically with the newer compiler), you can remove the declaration of the **total** instance variable from the **Calculator** implementation file because it's no longer needed. To do this:

1. In the Project Navigator, select the **Calculator.m** implementation and file and delete the instance variable declaration:

   ```
   @implementation Calculator

   @synthesize total = _total;

   double total;
   ```

2. Press **Command+B** to build the project. You should have no build errors.

Accessing a Property's Instance Variable

Since the property's instance variable is created for you, you can access the **_total** variable directly in code from within the **Calculator** class. For example:

```
- (void) clear
```

```
{
    _total = 0.00;
}
```

Although you *can* access the instance variable directly, you normally *shouldn't* because it can introduce unexpected behavior in your App.

Let's say, for example, that you have code that accesses the **_total** variable in the **Calculator** directly. As the class is currently structured, accessing the variable directly gives you the same result as accessing it indirectly through the property's getter and setter methods. However, what happens if six months from now, you come back to the **Calculator** class and manually create the getter or setter methods, placing additional logic in the new accessor method that does more than just a simple get or set of the value? In every place you access the variable directly, you would bypass the new code in the property accessors.

Would you remember to change all code that references the variable directly to reference the property instead? Ultimately, it's best to follow the rule that whenever you provide accessor methods for an instance variable, you should use the accessor methods within the class itself. The one exception to this rule is discussed in *Chapter 16: Advanced Objective-C* under the section Creating Initializers for Your Custom Classes.

Why Property Instance Variables Have an Underscore Prefix

This reason for naming the instance variable with an underscore prefix (**_total**) is to make it blatantly obvious when you are accessing an instance variable directly, rather than accessing a property—and breaking this rule that we just discussed.

If you see code in your class that accesses an instance variable that has an underscore prefix, it should set off an alarm. Although some developers use an underscore at the beginning of *every* instance variable, I recommend *only* using this naming convention for instance variables associated with a property. Otherwise, your code will be littered with references to instance variables with an underscore prefix, and you won't be alarmed when you accidentally reference a property's instance variable directly.

By the way, if you are using the older compiler and need to manually enter an **@synthesize** statement, you should always provide an instance variable name with an underscore prefix as shown in this chapter. If you don't specify the name of the instance variable, Objective-C will create an instance variable for you—however, *it will be named the same as the property*!

Atomic and Nonatomic Properties

Earlier in this chapter, I promised to talk about the **assign** and **nonatomic** keywords that you used when declaring the **total** property:

```
@property (assign, nonatomic) double total;
```

When you synthesize a property as you did in the previous section, the compiler automatically generates getter and setter methods for you. However, you can change the code that is generated for the getter and setter by using the **nonatomic** keyword.

By default, property accessor methods are *atomic*, meaning they are guaranteed to retrieve or set the correct value in environments that have multiple *threads* of execution. Threading is an advanced topic, which I won't cover in this book (this will be discussed later in this book series). Just know that 99.9% of the time, you don't have to worry about multiple threads of execution and should, therefore, usually specify your properties as **nonatomic**, since this is far more efficient—taking up less memory and improving performance.

Note that there is no *atomic* keyword. If you don't specify that a property is **nonatomic**, it is atomic by default.

Property Setter Options

When declaring a property you can use several optional keywords to change the behavior of the automatically synthesized setter method. Note that you can only use one of these keywords for a given property.

When using a setter keyword, you list the setter along with any atomicity setting within parentheses directly following the **@property** keyword. The following example shows the **assign** keyword in use:

```
@property (assign, nonatomic) double total;
```

Table 9.1 provides a list of setter keywords and a brief description of each. These setter keywords are detailed in the next chapter because they bring us to a larger discussion of object lifetime and memory management.

Table 9.1 Property setter keywords

Keyword	Description
assign	Indicates the setter uses simple assignment to store the property value. This keyword is used for simple data types such as float and BOOL.
strong	Indicates a strong relationship to the object referenced in the property.
weak	Indicates a weak relationship to the object referenced in the property. When the object is released, the property value is automatically set to nil.
copy	Indicates that a copy is made of the object referenced in the property.
retain	Indicates that a retain message is sent to the object stored in the property.

Summary

Here are key points to remember regarding instance variables and properties:

- Like instance variables, properties can be accessed from methods declared in the same class. However, unlike instance variables, properties are public and can be accessed by code external to the class.

- Properties are declared in the class header (.h) file by using the **@property** directive. You usually find properties declared near the top of the file. For example:

```
@interface Calculator : NSObject

// Calculator's running total
@property (assign, nonatomic) double
    total;
```

- Property declarations include the property type and name, and property names should be camel cased

- In the property declaration, you can specify one of the property setter keywords (such as **assign**, **strong**, **weak**, **copy**, or **retain**) to dictate the behavior of the setter method.

- You typically specify a property as **nonatomic**.

- Starting in Xcode 4.4 with the Apple LLVM Compiler 4.0, you no longer need to manually implement properties. However, if you are using an earlier version of the compiler, you need to add a **@synthesize** directive below the **@implementation** declaration. For example:

```
@synthesize total = _total;
```

Whether the compiler synthesizes the property for you, or you manually add the **@synthesize** directive, the result is the same. The compiler creates:

1. An instance variable

2. A getter method with the same name as the property

3. A setter method with a "set" prefix, followed by the name of the property with the first character of the property uppercased.

- When you get a value from a property, a *getter* method executes that usually returns the value of an associated instance variable. When you store a value to a property, a *setter* method executes that usually stores the value to an associated instance variable.

- Don't access the instance variable associated with a property directly unless you are initializing the value.

Exercise 9.1

In this exercise, you will add memory functionality to the Calculator class just like the memory function on a real-world calculator.

1. Add a new property to the **Calculator** class of type **double**, named **memory**.

2. Add a new method to the **Calculator** class named **clearMemory**, which sets the value of the **memory** property to zero.

Solution Movie 9.1

To see a video providing the solution for this exercise, go to the following link in your web browser.

http://www.iOSAppsForNonProgrammers.com/B2M91.html

Chapter 10: Object Lifetime & Memory Management

Starting with the introduction of iOS 5, memory management has become far simpler. Advances in the Objective-C compiler have made it easy for non-programmers to manage memory and produce high quality, stable Apps.

Sections in This Chapter

1. *An Object's Lifetime*

2. *Memory Management: The Way It Was*

3. *Memory Management: The Way It Is*

4. *Memory Management and Local Variables*

5. *Memory Management and Instance Variables*

6. *Memory Management and Properties*

7. *Summary*

An Object's Lifetime

An object "comes to life" when you first create an instance of it from a class definition. Every object you create takes up a different amount of space in memory (Figure 10.1).

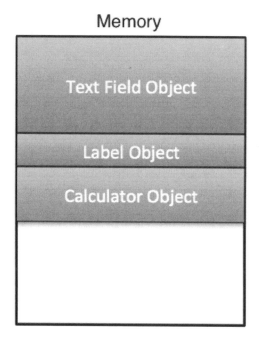

Figure 10.1 Every object you create takes up space in memory.

Each iOS App has a maximum amount of memory allocated to it, so when you are finished using an object, it should be released so that its space taken up in memory can also be released (Figure 10.2).

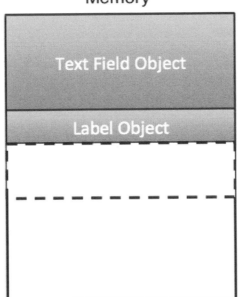

Figure 10.2 Object must be released when no longer in use to free up available memory.

Historically, one of the biggest problems in iOS development is Apps that don't release objects properly. If an App doesn't release objects as it should, the objects eventually take up too much space in memory and the iOS run time reacts by *killing* your App (brutal, I know!). This situation whereby an App continually eats up memory is also known as a **memory leak**.

Memory Management: The Way It Was

Properly releasing unused objects requires memory management. Memory management in Objective-C used to be hard. In the "old days" (before October 2011), when you wanted to keep an object around, you sent it a **retain** message as in Figure 10.3.

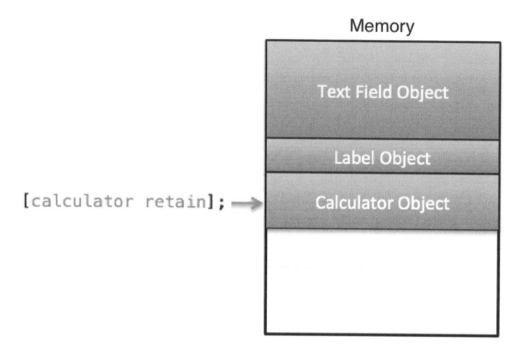

Figure 10.3 Retained objects stay in memory.

Other objects that also wanted to keep this same object around would each send it a **retain** message. Every time an object receives a **retain** message, its internal retain count is incremented (Figure 10.4).

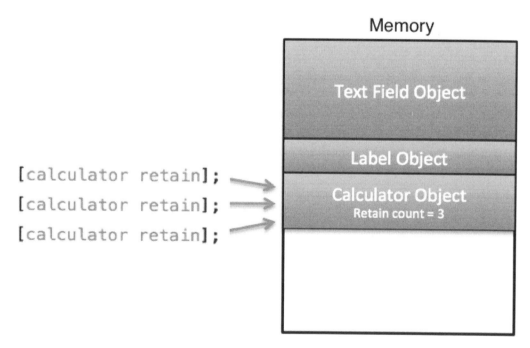

Figure 10.4 Multiple retain messages sent to an object

When you no longer needed an object, you sent it a **release** message, which decrements its retain count (Figure 10.5).

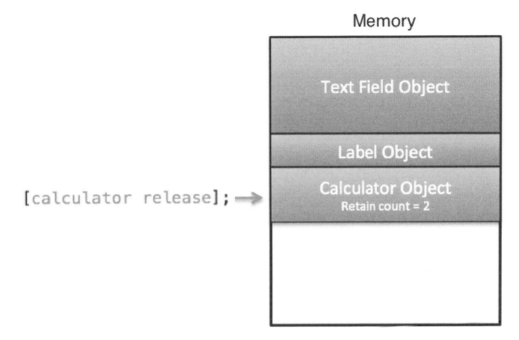

Figure 10.5 A release message decrements an object retain count.

But just because one part of the App doesn't need the object any longer doesn't mean that it isn't needed elsewhere. So, it isn't until an object's retain count is decremented to zero that iOS truly releases the object from memory.

As you might imagine, it took a concerted effort to make sure a class was sent **retain** messages when appropriate and **release** messages when necessary. Forgetting to send an object a **release** message causes its retain count to be something other than zero, the result being that it will never be released. Eventually, this causes a memory leak as more and more memory is consumed.

Memory Management: The Way It Is

Fortunately, starting in iOS 5, Apple introduced the concept of *Automatic Reference Counting*, or *ARC*. With Automatic Reference Counting, the same principles of memory management still apply. Objects must still be sent **retain** and **release** messages. However, rather than manually adding these messages to the code yourself, with ARC, the compiler inserts these **retain** and **release** messages in the compiled code for you!

So, if you no longer send **retain** messages to an object, how do you let the compiler know that you want to keep a particular object around? With ARC, all you need to keep an object alive is to have a variable pointing, or holding a reference, to it.

Whether you realize it or not, you have already seen an example of this. Let's take another look, in case you missed it. If it's not already open, in Xcode, open the **ObjectiveCDemo** project. Next, go to the Project Navigator and select the **ViewController.m** file. Near the top of the file, you can see the **calculator** instance variable you created in *Chapter 7: Referencing Classes:*

```
@implementation ViewController
{
    Calculator *calculator;
}
```

After your App executes the following line of code:

```
calculator = [[Calculator alloc] init];
```

the **calculator** variable contains a pointer to the Calculator object, which keeps it alive (Figure 10.6).

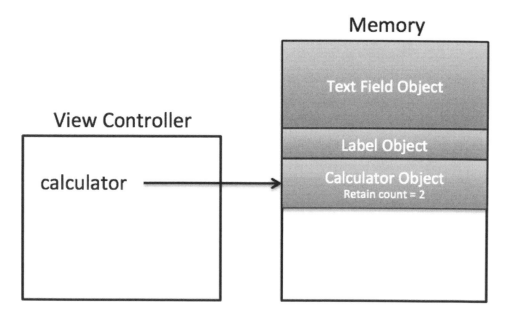

Figure 10.6 The instance variable keeps the object alive!

Memory Management and Local Variables

To understand this concept a little better, rather than using a class-level instance variable, you are going to create a local variable to hold a reference to the Calculator object and then examine how this affects its lifetime.

1. If it's not already open, in Xcode, open the **ObjectiveCDemo** project.

2. Select the **ViewController.m** file in the Project Navigator. Look at the **viewDidLoad** method to see where the Calculator object is first created. This code references the **calculator** instance variable:

    ```
    - (void)viewDidLoad
    {
        [super viewDidLoad];

        calculator = [[Calculator alloc] init];
    ```

3. Change this code to create a new variable that is local to the **viewDidLoad** method like this:

    ```
    Calculator *calculator =
            [[Calculator alloc] init];
    ```

    Notice this local variable is named the same as the calculator class-level instance variable. This works because the new local variable takes precedence over the instance variable, but let's comment out the instance variable just to make the point clear that we are now using the local variable.

4. To do this, place your cursor anywhere in the line that declares the **calculator** instance variable, and then press **Command+/** (forward slash) to comment out the line as shown here:

    ```
    @implementation ViewController
    {
        //Calculator *calculator; <- comment this
    }
    @synthesize lblDemo;

    - (void)viewDidLoad
    {
        [super viewDidLoad];
    ```

As shown in Figure 10.7, when you declare the **calculator** variable within a method, the variable lives until the end of the method. Since the variable keeps the Calculator object alive, when the variable is released at the end of the method, the object is also released.

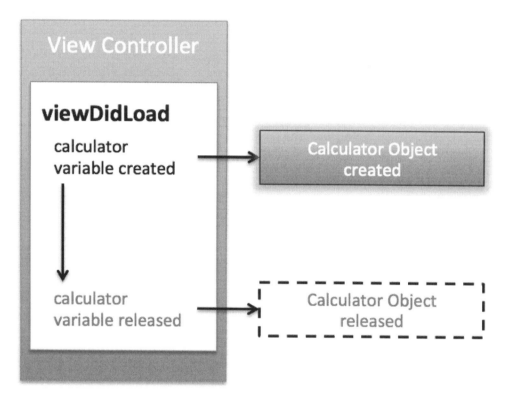

Figure 10.7 Local variables live until the method's end.

To see this demonstrated, you are going to add code to the **Calculator** class that automatically fires when the Calculator object gets released. Then you can see exactly when the Calculator object is released from memory.

Overriding the dealloc Method

Every object in Objective-C has a **dealloc** method, which it inherits from the **NSObject** class. You never send a **dealloc** message directly to an object, but **dealloc** is automatically called on an object by iOS when an object is being released from memory.

All you have to do is implement the **dealloc** method in the **Calculator** class, and add code to the method that makes a call to **NSLog** so we know when the Calculator object is being deallocated.

1. If it's not already open, in Xcode, open the **ObjectiveCDemo** project.

2. Select the **Calculator.m** implementation file in the Project Navigator, and then add the following **dealloc** method directly above the **clear** method:

```
-(void)dealloc
{
        NSLog(@"Deallocating Calculator");
}
- (void) clear
{
    self.total = 0.00;
}
```

3. Remember, when the Calculator object is released at run time, the **dealloc** method fires. So, set a breakpoint in this method so that you can see when the Calculator object is released Figure 10.8.

```
- (void)dealloc
{
    NSLog(@"Deallocating Calculator");
}
```

*Figure 10.8 Set a breakpoint in the **dealloc** method.*

4. In the Project Navigator, select the **ViewController.m** implementation file, and then set a breakpoint on the code that creates an instance of the Calculator (Figure 10.9).

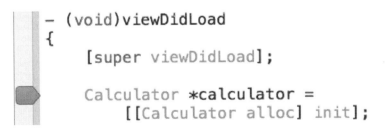

```
- (void)viewDidLoad
{
    [super viewDidLoad];

    Calculator *calculator =
        [[Calculator alloc] init];
```

Figure 10.9 Set a breakpoint on Calendar creation.

5. Next, delete the other breakpoint in the **viewDidLoad** method. Just right-click it and select **Delete Breakpoint** from the shortcut menu as shown in Figure 10.10.

```
double runningTotal = calculator.total;
```
Edit Breakpoint
Disable Breakpoint
                                        sum);
Delete Breakpoint   : %f", difference);
                                     ", result);
Reveal in Breakpoint Navigator   %f", quotient);
        NSLog(@"Running Total: %f", runningTotal);
```

*Figure 10.10 Delete the other breakpoint in **viewDidLoad**.*

# Testing the dealloc Method

Now you're ready to test the **dealloc** method and see when the Calculator object gets released.

1.  Run the project by clicking the **Run** button in the upper-left corner of Xcode. After several seconds, you should hit the first breakpoint (Figure 10.11).

```
Calculator *calculator =
    [[Calculator alloc] init];   Thread 1:
```

*Figure 10.11 The first breakpoint is hit.*

2.  This is the line of code where the Calculator object is first created. Click the **Step over** button in the Debug area to create the Calculator object. You can keep clicking **Step over** as many times as you like; but until you reach the end of the method, the Calculator object is still alive and the **dealloc** method will not fire until then. If you would like to cut to the chase, click the **Step out** button in order to step out of the **viewDidLoad** method.

3.  As mentioned, as soon as you step out of the method, the **calculator** local variable is released; and since there are no other references to the Calculator object, it is also released. At that point its **dealloc** method is executed, and execution stops at the breakpoint that you set (Figure 10.12).
```

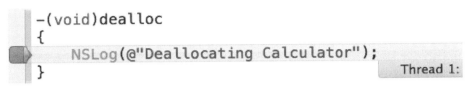

```
-(void)dealloc
{
    NSLog(@"Deallocating Calculator");
}
```

Thread 1:

Figure 10.12 At the end of the method, the calculator local variable is released, and so is the Calculator object.

At this point, you can click the **Stop** button so that you can set up another test case.

Memory Management and Instance Variables

I wanted you first to experience how an object's lifetime works with a *local* variable, since it's easiest to understand. Now let's try an *instance* variable.

Class-level instance variables stay alive as long as the object in which they are declared stays alive. As you can see in Figure 10.13, the calculator variable is declared at the class level, outside any method. Therefore, the Calculator object continues to live as long as the view controller stays alive.

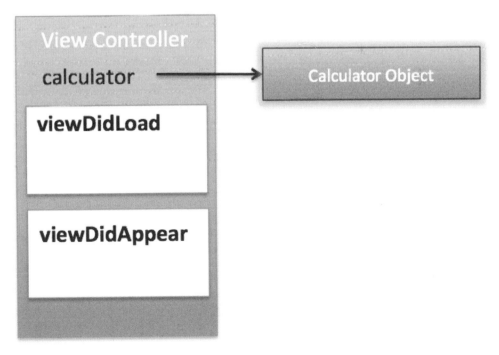

Figure 10.13 Instance variable lifetime

Now let's change the code in the view controller back again to use a class-level variable to store the reference to the Calculator object.

1. In the Project Navigator, select the **ViewController.m** implementation file. Near the top of the file, uncomment the **Calculator** instance variable declaration. To do this, you can simply delete the two forward slashes, or, you can place your cursor anywhere on that line and press **Command+/** to uncomment the line.

```
@implementation ViewController
{
    Calculator *calculator;
}
@synthesize lblDemo;
```

2. Next, go to the **viewDidLoad** method and change the code that creates the Calculator object to store the object in the class-level instance variable again:

```
- (void)viewDidLoad
{
    [super viewDidLoad];

    calculator = [[Calculator alloc] init];
```

3. Keep the breakpoint on this line of code as shown in Figure 10.14.

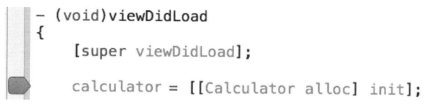

```
- (void)viewDidLoad
{
    [super viewDidLoad];

    calculator = [[Calculator alloc] init];
```

Figure 10.14 Keep the breakpoint on object creation.

4. To demonstrate that the Calculator object continues to live outside the **viewDidLoad** method, you can set a breakpoint in a method that runs after **viewDidLoad** finishes running. One such method is the **viewDidAppear:** method. So, scroll down in the code window, and set a breakpoint in the **viewDidAppear:** method (Figure 10.15).

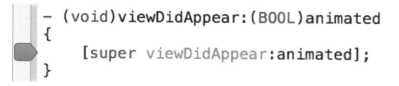

```
- (void)viewDidAppear:(BOOL)animated
{
    [super viewDidAppear:animated];
}
```

*Figure 10.15 Set a breakpoint in **viewDidAppear:**.*

5. Run the project again. After hitting the first breakpoint where the Calculator object gets created, press the **Continue** button in the Debug area toolbar until you hit the breakpoint in **viewDidAppear:** as shown in Figure 10.16.

```
- (void)viewDidAppear:(BOOL)animated
{
    [super viewDidAppear:animated];          Thread 1
}
```

*Figure 10.16 The **viewDidAppear:** breakpoint is hit.*

Since you didn't hit the breakpoint in the Calculator object's **dealloc** method yet, the Calculator is still alive, even after the **viewDidLoad** method has finished executing!

6. Now click the **Continue** button in the Debug area toolbar. You still haven't hit the breakpoint in the Calculator object's **dealloc** method, meaning that the object is still alive.

   It's still alive because the view controller that holds the **calculator** instance variable is still alive. If the view controller object were released, the Calculator object would also be released.

You might expect that clicking the Home button on the iOS Simulator, which closes the App, would cause the view controller to be released, but it doesn't. Go ahead and try it (the Home button is the large, black circular button at the bottom of the Simulator).

Why doesn't it get released? When you press the Home button, the App doesn't actually exit completely. In newer versions of iOS, the App continues to run in the background. As long as the App continues to run, the view controller stays alive, and as long as the view controller stays alive, the **calculator** variable stays alive which, in turn, keeps the Calculator object alive!

Go ahead and press **Stop** in Xcode to stop the App in the Simulator.

Memory Management and Properties

How does memory management work when referencing the Calculator object from a property rather than a variable? Let's add a **calculator** property and see what happens.

First Attempt: Weak Property

Let's start with a **weak** property and see how that works for us.

1. First, change the **ViewController** instance variable **calculator** to a property. To do this, in the Project Navigator, select **ViewController.h** header file and add the following property declaration (you will see an error in Xcode when you add this property; ignore it for now and move on to step 2):

```
@interface ViewController : UIViewController

@property (weak, nonatomic) Calculator
    *calculator;
@property (weak, nonatomic) IBOutlet UILabel
    *lblDemo;
```

You are declaring this property in a way similar to how the **lblDemo** property is already declared.

2. As soon as you type the declaration, you should see an error icon to the left of the property. If you click on the error icon, you see the message shown in Figure 10.17.

```
@property (weak, nonatomic) Calculator *calculator;
 Unknown type name 'Calculator'
```

Figure 10.17 Why are you getting this error?

Can you figure out the problem here? I'll give you a minute.

OK, just as the error says, you haven't yet told the **ViewController** class what "Calculator" is. Remember, there are two options to choose from:

- The **@class** directive or

- The **@import** directive.

3. Since you always want the lightest touch possible, you can use the **@class** directive because the **ViewController** class header file only needs to know that **Calculator** *is* a valid class. It doesn't need to create an instance of it or call its methods. So, add the following **@class** directive at the top of the **ViewController.h** header file:

```
@class Calculator;
```

```
@interface ViewController : UIViewController
```

4. Next, select the **ViewController.m** implementation file in the Project Navigator.

   If you are using Xcode 4.4 with the Apple LLVM Compiler 4.0 you can skip to the next step, because the compiler automatically implements the property for you. If you are using an older version of the compiler, you need to synthesize the getter and setter methods for the **calculator** property manually. To do this, add the following **@synthesize** declaration directly below the **@synthesize lblDemo** declaration:

```
@synthesize lblDemo;
@synthesize calculator = _calculator;
```

5. Since you are creating a **calculator** property, the **calculator** instance variable at the top of the code files is no longer necessary, so let's delete it (as soon as you delete it, you are going to see compiler errors, but move ahead to the next step):

```
@implementation ViewController
{
    Calculator *calculator;
}
@synthesize lblDemo;
@synthesize calculator = _calculator;
```

6. Deleting the **calculator** instance variable introduces several compiler errors into your code. Can you figure out why?

   Remember, when you reference a property, you have to use the **self** keyword. So, you need to change all the calculator references to **self.calculator** (I know these changes may seem psychotic, but it's a great exercise in understanding how to reference instance variables and properties):

```
self.calculator = [[Calculator alloc] init];

double sum =
    [self.calculator addToTotal:10];
double difference =
    [self.calculator subtractFromTotal:6];
double result =
```

```
    [self.calculator multiplyTimesTotal:3];
double quotient =
    [self.calculator divideIntoTotal:4];
[self.calculator clear];
double runningTotal = self.calculator.total;
```

7. Next, add a breakpoint to the line of code that sends the **addToTotal:** message (Figure 10.18).

```
self.calculator = [[Calculator alloc] init];

double sum = [self.calculator addToTotal:10];
double difference = [self.calculator subtractFromTotal:6];
double result = [self.calculator multiplyTimesTotal:3];
double quotient = [self.calculator divideIntoTotal:4];

[self.calculator clear];
double runningTotal = self.calculator.total;
```

*Figure 10.18 Add a breakpoint to the **addToTotal:** message call.*

8. Now you are ready to see how the declaration of a **weak** property works with regard to the Calculator object's lifetime. Click the **Run** button and you will hit the first breakpoint on the line of code that creates the Calculator object (Figure 10.19).

```
- (void)viewDidLoad
{
    [super viewDidLoad];
    self.calculator = [[Calculator alloc] init];
                                          Thread 1: bre
    double sum = [self.calculator addToTotal:10];
```

Figure 10.19 The first breakpoint in the property test.

9. Now click the **Step over** button in the Debug area toolbar to execute this line of code, creating the Calculator object. You should immediately be taken to the Calculator object's **dealloc** method as shown in Figure 10.20.

```
-(void)dealloc
{
    NSLog(@"Deallocating Calculator");
}
                                          Thread 1:
```

Figure 10.20 The object is deallocated too soon!

This probably isn't what you were hoping would happen! The Calculator object was immediately released after it was created—and before you even had a chance to send any messages to it! Let's keep going to see what happens next.

Passing Messages to a Null Object

1. Click the **Continue** button in the Debug area toolbar and you will hit the next breakpoint in the code that calls **addToTotal:** (Figure 10.21).

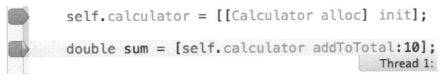

*Figure 10.21 The next breakpoint is hit on **addToTotal:**.*

2. Before doing anything else, think about this: because the Calculator object has already been released, it no longer exists in memory. The current line of code is going to pass an **addToTotal:** message to the Calculator object. Will this cause a run-time error? Find out by clicking the **Step over** button.

3. Interesting—there is no run-time error! However, if you hover your mouse pointer over the **sum** variable, you can see that its value is still zero; therefore, the method didn't actually execute (Figure 10.22).

*Figure 10.22 The sum is zero, so **addToTotal:** never ran!*

What's going on here? This is one of the basic principles of Objective-C at work.

Objective-C allows you to send a message to an object that is null (the Calculator object is null because it's been released). In fact, if you click the **Continue** button in the Debug area, you can see that the Output panel contains a line indicating that the Calculator is deallocated and then lists a log entry showing the result of each message sent to the Calculator object (Figure 10.23).

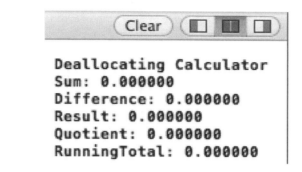

Figure 10.23 Messages passed to a null Calculator object!

As interesting as this is, you actually do want the Calculator to work properly so, ultimately, marking the Calculator property as **weak** is not a good approach because it doesn't allow the Calculator object to live long enough.

IBOutlet Properties

So this begs the question "Why does the **weak** declaration work for the **lblDemo** property that was declared for you?" Take a look at it again:

```
@property (weak, nonatomic) IBOutlet UILabel
        *lblDemo;
```

This property holds a reference to the label that sits at the top of the App's main view as shown in Figure 10.24.

Figure 10.24 A weak property references the label.

Earlier, in the first few chapters of this book, you wrote code that stored strings in the label, and there was no problem at run time. The label stayed alive and displayed the appropriate text strings even though the property referencing it was declared as **weak**.

So, what's going on? This works because, behind the scenes, the view automatically **retains** objects referenced as **IBOutlets**. So, since these user-interface controls are retained by the view, you can declare them as weak because the view keeps them alive for you. Mystery solved!

Second Attempt: Strong Property

Now that you have seen that a **weak calculator** property didn't work well, let's try a **strong** property.

1. If you haven't already done so, click the **Stop** button to stop the App from running. Next, go to the Project Navigator and select the **ViewController.h** file and change the **weak** declaration to **strong**:

```
@property (strong, nonatomic) Calculator
    *calculator;
```

The **strong** keyword indicates a strong relationship between the view controller and the Calculator object. It indicates to the iOS run time that you want the Calculator object to stick around, or be retained.

2. Now click the **Run** button to see how it works at run time. After hitting the first breakpoint where the Calculator object is created, click the **Step over** button twice and then hover your mouse pointer over the **sum** variable. You should see it now contains the value **10** as shown in Figure 10.25.

Figure 10.25 The Calculator works with a strong property.

As you can see, you should declare a property as **strong** when you need the object to stay alive in order to use it later. In fact, the reason the **calculator** instance variable worked in your previous test is because, by default, all object pointer variables are strong!

Go ahead and click the **Stop** button in Xcode.

You now know the basic principles of memory management in iOS!

Summary

Here is an overview of the key points covered in this section on memory management:

- An object "comes to life" when you first create an instance of it from a class definition.

- The "old" way of managing memory required you to:

  1. Send a **retain** message to an object to keep it alive. This increments its retain count.

  2. Send a **release** message to indicate that you no longer need an object. This decrements its retain count.

- When an object's retain count reaches zero, it is physically released from memory.

- Automatic Referencing Counting (ARC) sends the **retain** and **release** messages for you.

- With ARC, all you need to keep an object alive is to have a variable pointing to it.

- Local variables only stay alive in the method in which they are declared. This means that if you create a local variable that references an object, when the method is finished executing, the variable is released, and the object it references is released.

- Class-level instance variables stay alive as long as the object in which they are declared stays alive. Therefore, an object referenced from a class-level instance variable stays alive as long as the object in which it is referenced stays alive.

- When referencing an object from a property, use the **weak** property accessor keyword if you don't need to hold a reference to the object (such as with **IBOutlet** properties that are retained for you). Use the **strong** keyword if you need to keep the object alive.

Chapter 11: Arrays & Other Collections

Now that you have a basic understanding of how classes and objects work, it's time to discuss an easier topic—arrays and other collections. This is a *very* important topic because all the lists of information displayed in your App come from some type of collection. This chapter introduces you to the different collections available to you so you can make smart decisions about which collection to use in different situations.

Sections in This Chapter

1. *What is a Collection?*

2. *Enumerating a Collection*

3. *Examining the CollectionsDemo Sample Project*

4. *NSArray*

5. *NSMutableArray*

6. *NSDictionary*

7. *NSMutableDictionary*

8. *NSSet and NSMutableSet*

9. *Structures*

What is a Collection?

When you hear the word "**collection**," you might think of stamp or coin collections. This is a good metaphor for collections in Objective-C because they provide a way to group one or more related objects together.

All the variables and properties that you have worked with so far have held a single value (such as an integer, Boolean (BOOL), or a single object). In contrast, Cocoa Touch Framework collection classes allow you to group multiple items together into a single collection. The primary collection classes in Objective-C are as follows:

- NSArray

- NSMutableArray

- NSDictionary

- NSMutableDictionary

- NSSet

- NSMutableSet

Often, collections are used in iOS Apps to create lists. For example, you can have a collection of strings used as a list of songs, or an array of images used to display album covers. Note that items in a collection are usually of the same type, but this isn't a restriction. You can put any number of different kinds of items in a collection although you should normally avoid that, since managing such a collection leads to some messy code.

Enumerating a Collection

You can enumerate, or loop through the items in a collection by using one of Objective-C's looping statements as discussed in *Chapter 12: Looping Statements*. You can also enumerate a collection using a more advanced feature known as blocks. For more information, see *Chapter 17: Advanced Messaging* under the section Enhancing Your Code With Blocks.

Examining the CollectionsDemo Sample Project

There's nothing quite like a live sample to help you understand a new topic. The **CollectionsDemo** sample project provides examples of a variety of Objective-C collections.

1. If you have another project open, close it by selecting **File > Close Project** from the Xcode menu.

2. Open the **CollectionsDemo** project by selecting **File > Open...** from the Xcode menu. In the **Open** dialog, navigate to the folder where you have stored this book's sample code. Expand the **CollectionsDemo** folder, select the **CollectionsDemo.xcodeproj** file and then click **Open** as shown in Figure 11.1.

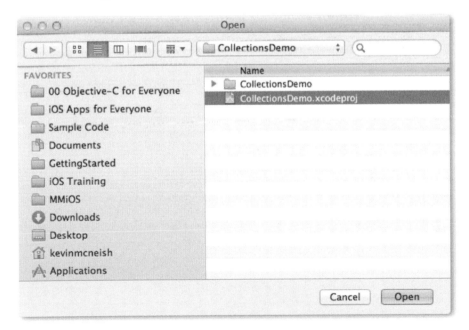

*Figure 11.1 Opening the **CollectionsDemo** project*

3. In the Project Navigator, click the white triangle to the left of the

CollectionsDemo node to expand it, and then click the gray arrow to the left of the **CollectionsDemo** subnode to expand it, and finally select the **MainStoryboard.storyboard** file. You should see the very simple view in Figure 11.2, which contains a label and a *picker view*.

*Figure 11.2 The **CollectionsDemo** project at design time*

4. Click Xcode's **Run** button to see this simple App run in the iOS Simulator. Notice that it looks a little different when you run it. Rather than list California cities in the picker view, it lists several names as shown in Figure 11.3.

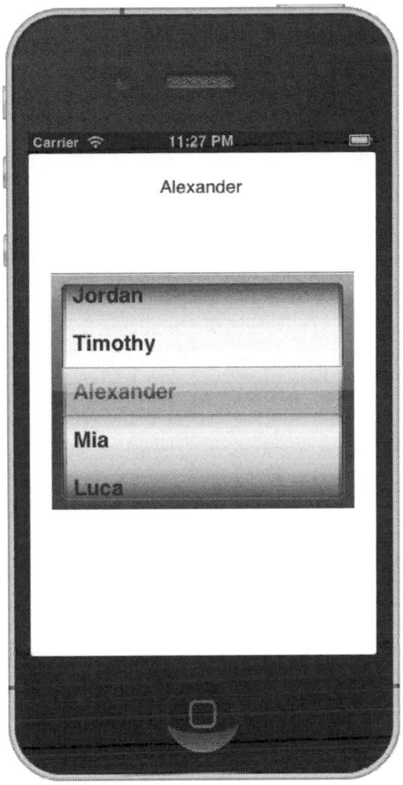

*Figure 11.3 The **CollectionsDemo** project at run time*

5. Where are these names coming from? To find out, go back to Xcode and click the **Stop** button. Select the **ViewController.m** implementation file in the Project Navigator and scroll to the top of the window.

Notice the **@synthesize** statements for properties that reference the label at the top of the view (**lblDemo**) and the picker view (**pckOptions**). There is also an instance variable declaration of type **NSArray** called **names**.

```
@implementation ViewController
{
    NSArray *names;
}
@synthesize lblDemo;
@synthesize pckOptions;
```

The **names** array is used to fill the picker view. Let's take a look at the **NSArray** class to see how it works.

NSArray

The **NSArray** class is one of the most basic kinds of Objective-C collections. You declare an **NSArray** variable just as you would any other variable. Notice that you use an asterisk when declaring the variable, indicating that it's a pointer:

```
NSArray *names;
```

Initializing an NSArray

To initialize an **NSArray** with a set of values, you can use the **initWithObjects:** method. To see this, scroll down just a bit to the **viewDidLoad** method and find the following code, which creates an **NSArray** that contains five strings:

```
names = [[NSArray alloc] initWithObjects:
        @"Jordan",
        @"Timothy",
        @"Alexander",
        @"Mia",
        @"Luca",
        nil];
```

This is the source of the names that you saw in the picker view at run time. Notice the last item in the list is **nil**, indicating the end of the list. If you forget to put a **nil** at the end of the list, you get the compiler warning "Missing sentinel in method dispatch," although I think "Missing nil" would be a bit clearer.

If you are using Xcode 4.4 or later with the Apple LLVM Compiler 4.0 or later, you can create an **NSArray** more easily using the following syntax:

```
NSArray *names = @[@"Jordan",
            @"Timothy",
            @"Alexander",
            @"Mia",
            @"Luca"];
```

The '@ sign' and square brackets is part of the new syntax. Notice you don't have to end the list of objects with a **nil** (in fact, you'll get a compiler error if you do).

This new feature is not limited for use with literals:

```
NSString *name = @"Don";
Calendar *calendar = [[Calendar alloc] init];
NSArray *myArray = @[name, calendar];
```

Note that this new syntax does not work with an **NSMutableArray,** which you will learn about in the next topic.

Getting the Number of Items in an NSArray

To find out how many items are in an **NSArray** you can access its **count** property. Scrolling down a little further to the **pickerView:numberOfRowsInComponent:** method, you can see the **count** property in use. This method tells the picker view how many items to display in its list:

```
- (NSInteger) pickerView:
      (UIPickerView *)pickerView
      numberOfRowsInComponent:
      (NSInteger)component {

      return names.count;
}
```

Referencing Items in the Collection by Index

In Objective-C, collections are zero-based. This means that the first item in the collection is item zero, the second item in the collection is item one, and so on. This takes a little getting used to, since items in the real world are usually numbered starting with "1". (some hotels, use this numbering scheme, by calling the ground floor "zero", and the next floor up "one").

An *index* is a number that references an item by its position in the collection. You can get an item from an **NSArray** by using the **objectAtIndex:** method.

For example, this code retrieves the first item in the array (item 0):

```
NSString *name = [names objectAtIndex:0];
```

This code returns the second item in the array (item 1):

```
NSString *name = [names objectAtIndex:1];
```

and the following code returns the last item in the array:

```
NSString *name =
        [names objectAtIndex:names.count - 1];
```

The above code uses **count − 1** to get the last item in the array. If there are five items numbered zero through four, **count − 1** equates to **5 − 1**, which gives you item four—the last item in the array.

If you are using Xcode 4.5 or later with the Apple LLVM Compiler 4.0 or later *and are compiling with iOS 6 SDK or later*, you can use simpler square bracket syntax to access items in an array. For example:

```
NSString *name = names[0];
```

How the CollectionsDemo App Works

Run the App in the Simulator by pressing the **Run** button in Xcode. Select different items in the list by clicking on them; you should see the label text change to the name that you have selected (Figure 11.4).

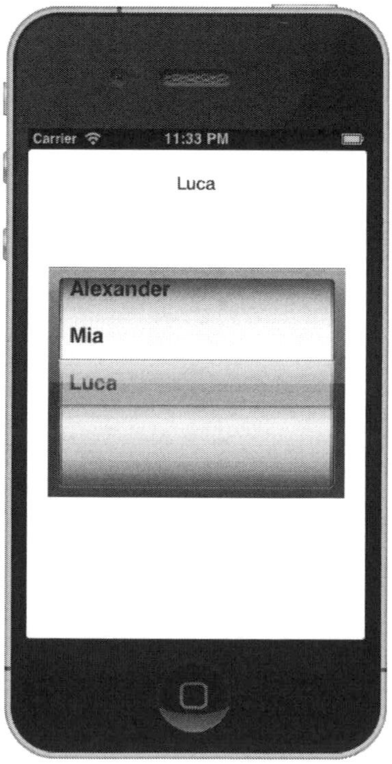

Figure 11.4 Selecting an item sets the text in the label.

Let's find out how this magic works. In Xcode, scroll to the **pickerView:didSelectRow:inComponent** method:

```
- (void)pickerView:(UIPickerView *)
        pickerView didSelectRow:(NSInteger)row
        inComponent:(NSInteger)component
{
        self.lblDemo.text = [names objectAtIndex:row];
}
```

This is the code that sets the text of the label from the currently selected item. Let's look at the order of events when an item is selected in the picker view with the help of the following image:

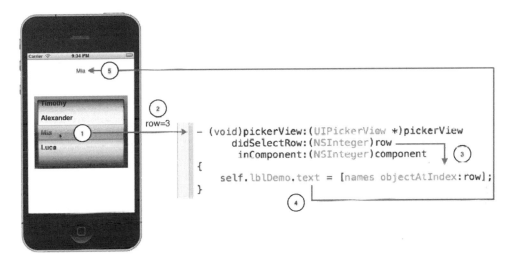

Here's a description of the order of events:

1. An item is selected in the picker view.

2. The **pickerView:didSelectRow:inComponent** method in the view controller is called by the picker view, passing the selected row number (in this case, 3).

3. The **names** array is passed an **objectAtIndex:** message, using the **row** parameter as an argument.

4. The **objectAtIndex:** method returns the string object at index 3 from the **names** array. That string object is stored in the label's **text** property.

5. The name is displayed in the label on the view.

Getting the Index of an Object in an NSArray

One other thing to note about **NSArray** is that you can determine the index of a particular item in the array by using the **indexOfObject:** method. For example:

```
NSUInteger miaIndex =
        [names indexOfObject:@"Mia"];
```

This code returns the number **3**, since "Mia" is the fourth item in the collection.

This discussion is in no way a comprehensive coverage of all that you can do with **NSArray**. For details, check out Apple's *NSArray Class Reference* help topic.

NSMutableArray

The **NSArray** class is extremely useful but has one potential drawback; after you initialize the items in the array, you can't change the array—you can't add an item, remove an item, or change an item. In programming jargon, this is known as being *immutable*.

As you might guess, the opposite of immutable is *mutable*, and so **NSMutableArray** is a close cousin to **NSArray** but has the added benefit of changeability.

Initializing an NSMutableArray

You can initialize an **NSMutableArray** similar to the way that you initialize an **NSArray**:

```
NSMutableArray *names = [[NSMutableArray
        alloc] initWithObjects:
        @"Jordan",
        @"Timothy",
        @"Alexander",
        @"Mia",
        @"Luca",
        nil];
```

Adding and Removing Objects from an NSMutableArray

Since the array is mutable, you can add an object to the array by using the **addObject:** method:

```
[names addObject:@"Kevin"];
```

You can remove objects from an **NSMutableArray** by using the **removeObjectAtIndex:** method:

```
[names removeObjectAtIndex: 2];
```

If the item that you want to remove is last in the list, you can use the **removeLastObject** method:

```
[names removeLastObject];
```

You can also add objects to an **NSMutableArray** at a given index by using the **insertObject:atIndex:** method:

```
[names insertObject:@"Sharlene" atIndex:2];
```

Replacing an Object

You can replace existing objects in the array by using the **replaceObjectAtIndex:withObject:** method:

```
[names replaceObjectAtIndex:2
        withObject:@"Zan"];
```

Again, you can learn even more by checking out Apple's *NSMutableArray Class Reference* help topic.

NSDictionary

Arrays are great for simple collections, but at times you need a little more. It's easy to find a simple string object in an array, but what if you need to find a specific item in a collection of more complex objects? For example, what if you have a collection of Customer objects that are uniquely identified by a Customer ID and you want to search for a particular object by that unique ID? That's where a dictionary can help.

Each item (called an *entry*) in a dictionary has a *key* and a *value*. The key is used to uniquely identify the entry, and the value is the item itself. In the example of a Customer object, the Customer ID is the key, and the Customer object is the value. The **NSDictionary** class provides you with all the basic functionality of a dictionary.

The DictionaryDemo Project

To see a live example of how a dictionary works, let's look at the **DictionaryDemo** project that displays a list of countries in a picker view using an **NSDictionary**. The dictionary is also used to display a two-character country code in the label at the top of the view when the user selects a country from the picker.

1. If you have another project open, close it by selecting **File > Close Project** from the Xcode menu.

2. Open the **DictionaryDemo** project by selecting **File > Open...** from the Xcode menu. In the **Open** dialog, navigate to the folder where you have this book's sample code, expand the **DictionaryDemo** folder. Select the **DictionaryDemo.xcodeproj** file, and then click the **Open** button.

3. Run the project by clicking the **Run** button in Xcode. The App should look like Figure 11.5.

*Figure 11.5 **NSDictionary** in action*

4. Select a country, and notice that the two-character country code is displayed at the top of the view.

5. Go back to Xcode, and then press the **Stop** button.

Let's take a look at the code to see how the dictionary is used to display this information.

Initializing an NSDictionary

In the Project Navigator, select the **ViewController.m** implementation file. Then, in the Code Editor, scroll to the top of the code file. Notice the following instance variables:

```
NSDictionary *countries;
NSArray *keys;
NSArray *values;
```

The first line of code declares an **NSDictionary** variable named **countries**.

The other two lines declare two **NSArray** variables named **keys** and **values**. These arrays are used to initialize the dictionary.

Using the **initWithObjects:forKeys:** method, you can initialize a dictionary with an array of keys and an array of values. Scroll to the **viewDidLoad** method, and notice the following code near the top of the method:

```
keys = [[NSArray alloc] initWithObjects:
          @"Austria",
          @"Bulgaria",
          @"Switzerland",
          @"Germany",
          nil];

values = [[NSArray alloc] initWithObjects:
           @"AT",
           @"BG",
           @"CH",
           @"DE",
           nil];

countries = [[NSDictionary alloc]
      initWithObjects:values forKeys:keys];
```

In this code, the **keys** array is created from a list of country names, and the **values** array is created from corresponding country codes. Afterwards, an **NSDictionary** is created from the two arrays.

If you are using Xcode 4.4 or later with the Apple LLVM Compiler 4.0 or later, you can create an **NSDictionary** more easily by using the following syntax:

```
NSDictionary *countries =
          @{ @"Austria" : @"AT",
          @"Bulgaria" : @"BG",
          @"Switzerland" : @"CH",
          @"Germany": @"DE"};
```

The at "@" sign and curly braces is part of the new syntax. For each entry (each key/value pair is considered a single entry), the key is specified first, followed by a colon, and then the value. A comma separates each entry. Again, you don't have to end the list of entries with a **nil** using this syntax.

Getting the Number of Items in an NSDictionary

You can find how many entries are in a dictionary by checking its **count** property.

Scroll to the **pickerView:numberOfRowsInComponent:** method, and you can see that the **countries** dictionary's **count** property is used to specify how many rows, or items, are in the picker:

```
- (NSInteger) pickerView:
        (UIPickerView *)pickerView
        numberOfRowsInComponent:
        (NSInteger)component {

    return countries.count;
}
```

Returning an Item From the Keys Array

Scroll to the **pickerView:titleForRow:forComponent:** method. Here you can see the code that returns a country name from the **keys** array using **objectAtIndex**:

```
- (NSString *)pickerView:
        (UIPickerView *)pickerView
        titleForRow:(NSInteger)row
        forComponent:(NSInteger)component
{
   return [keys objectAtIndex:row];
}
```

Retrieving a Dictionary Item By Key

To retrieve an entry from a dictionary by its key, use the **objectForKey:** method of **NSDictionary**. Scroll down to the **setLabelTextFromRow:** method to see this code in action:

```
- (void)setLabelTextFromRow:(NSInteger)row
{
    NSString *currentKey =
        [keys objectAtIndex:row];
    self.lblDemo.text =
        [countries objectForKey:currentKey];
```

```
}
```

The first line of code retrieves the key (in this case, a country name) from the **keys** array for the currently selected row in the picker view. It then stores the key in the **currentKey** variable.

The second line of code uses the country name as a key to get the corresponding country code from the **countries** array by using the **objectForKey:** method of **NSDictionary**. It then stores the country code in the **text** property of the label at the top of the view.

Note that as with **NSArray**, an **NSDictionary** is not changeable. Once you create the entries in the dictionary, you can't add, remove, or edit them.

If you are using Xcode 4.5 or later with the Apple LLVM Compiler 4.0 or later *and are compiling with iOS 6 SDK or later*, you can use simpler square bracket syntax to access items in a dictionary. For example:

```
NSString *value = countries[@"Austria"];
```

Using this syntax, you pass the *key* within square brackets and the corresponding *value* is returned to you.

NSMutableDictionary

Are you sensing a pattern? **NSMutableDictionary** is the mutable version of **NSDictionary**.

Initializing an NSMutableDictionary

You initialize an **NSMutableDictionary** in a way similar to how you initialize an **NSDictionary**:

```
NSMutableDictionary *countries =
        [[NSMutableDictionary alloc]
        initWithObjectsAndKeys:
        @"Austria", @"AT",
        @"Bulgaria", @"BG",
        @"Switzerland", @"CH",
        @"Germany", @"DE",
        @"Spain", @"ES",
        @"France", @"FR",
        nil];
```

If you are using Xcode 4.5 or later with the Apple LLVM Compiler 4.0 or later *and are compiling with iOS 6 SDK or later*, you can use square bracket syntax to initialize the dictionary. For example:

```
NSMutableDictionary *countries =
        [@{@"Austria" : @"AT",
        @"Bulgaria" : @"BG",
        @"Switzerland" : @"CH",
        @"Germany": @"DE",
        @"Spain" : @"ES",
        @"France" : @"FR"} mutableCopy];
```

In this code sample, an immutable collection is created, and then a **mutableCopy** message is sent to it to create a mutable version of the collection, which is then stored in the **countries** variable. It's debatable whether the new syntax is an improvement in this case.

Adding and Removing Items From an NSMutableDictionary

To add an entry to the dictionary, you can use the **setObject:forKey:** method:

```
[countries setObject:@"GR" forKey:@"Greece"];
```

To remove an entry from the dictionary, you can use the **removeObjectForKey:** method:

```
[countries removeObjectForKey:@"Bulgaria"];
```

For information on everything **NSMutableDictionary** can do, check out Apple's *NSMutableDictionary Class Reference* help topic.

NSSet and NSMutableSet

I have saved the discussion of **NSSet** and **NSMutableSet** for last because they are the least commonly used collections. That said, they definitely have their place in the Cocoa Touch Framework.

NSSet is a good choice because it's extremely fast at checking for the existence of an object in its collection, but since it stores an unordered set of unique items, it should only be used if:

1. You don't need items listed in a particular order and

2. All the items in the collection are unique,

If you don't need to search for individual items in the collection, you should use **NSArray** instead.

Initializing an NSSet Collection

You can create an **NSSet** collection by using the **initWithObjects:** method:

```
NSSet *set = [[NSSet alloc] initWithObjects:
      @"iPod Touch",
      @"iPhone",
      @"iPad",
      nil];
```

As with all other collections, you use the **count** property to determine how many items are in an **NSSet**.

Getting Items From an NSSet Collection

When it comes to retrieving items from an **NSSet**, you can't retrieve items by index because **NSSet** is unordered, so no particular order and associated index value is guaranteed.

That said, you can use the **containsObject:** method to see if an **NSSet** contains a specific object:

```
BOOL containsObject =
      [set containsObject:@"iPhone"];
```

There is even an **anyObject** method that returns one of the items in the **NSSet**. Note that the item returned is not guaranteed to be random but, as Apple's documentation states, the object returned is "at the set's convenience."

Adding and Removing Items from an NSMutableSet

As you might imagine, **NSMutableSet** is the changeable version of **NSSet**. You can add an item to an **NSMutableSet** by using the **addObject:** method and remove an object by using the **removeObject:** method.

Again, check Apple's documentation for a list of all that you can do with **NSSet** and **NSMutableSet**.

Structures

Although not really a collection, Objective-C ***structures*** allow you to group values together. Structures allow you to group multiple items together as a single unit. For example, SAT college admission scores typically have three numeric scores: writing, mathematics, and critical reading. You could store these in three different integer variables, but since they are related, it's best to store them as a group.

You have actually worked with structures earlier in this book. The **CGRectMake** function returns a **CGRect** rectangle which is a structure containing four floating point members—**x** and **y** coordinates as well as **height** and **width** values.

Declaring a Structure

You can declare a structure that combines the three scores and is called **SATScores**. For example:

```
struct SATScores
{
        int writing;
        int math;
        int reading;
};
```

This code declares a structure named **SATScores** that has three members of type integer named **writing**, **math**, and **reading**. Because you have created a new data type called **SATScores**, you can declare variables to be of this new type. For example:

```
struct SATScores scores;
```

This code declares a variable named **scores** of type **SATScores**. In the same way that you can declare variables of type integer, string, and BOOL, you can also declare variables of type **SATScores**.

Accessing Members of a Structure

You access members of a structure by using dot syntax. For example:

```
scores.math = 515;
scores.reading = 501;
```

```
scores.writing = 493;
```

You can also initialize members of a structure with values separated by commas inside curly braces:

```
struct SATScores scores = {515, 501, 493};
```

Declaring a Structure Using typedef

As the structure is now declared, you always have to use the **struct** keyword when declaring a variable:

```
struct SATScores scores;
```

It would be nice to drop the **struct** keyword because this is extra typing that gets to be an annoyance after a while. It's preferable to write this instead:

```
SATScores scores;
```

To avoid having to use the **struct** keyword when declaring a variable that holds a structure, you can declare a *typedef* for your structure. A **typedef** statement lets you assign a friendly name to your structure. For example, check out the following **typedef** declaration listed after the structure declaration:

```
struct SATScores
    {
        int writing;
        int math;
        int reading;
    };
typedef struct SATScores SATScores;
```

Check out the breakdown of this statement as shown in Figure 11.6.

*Figure 11.6 The anatomy of a **typedef** statement*

It's preferable to write this instead:

```
SATScores scores;
```

To avoid having to use the **struct** keyword when declaring a variable that holds a structure, you can declare a *typedef* for your structure. A **typedef** statement lets you assign a friendly name to your structure. For example, check out the following **typedef** declaration listed after the structure declaration:

```
struct SATScores
      {
          int writing;
          int math;
          int reading;
      };
typedef struct SATScores SATScores;
```

Check out the breakdown of this statement as shown in Figure 11.6.

This allows you to declare a variable that references a structure without using the **struct** keyword:

```
SATScores scores;
```

You can actually simplify the **typedef** statement even further when renaming a **struct**:

```
typedef struct
{
      int writing;
      int math;
      int reading;
} SATScores;
```

This simplified form of the **typedef** statement is what you most commonly see in code samples—and is the best to use in your own code.

If you need a simple way to group several related values, a structure is a good choice. However, if you also need methods to act on a set of values, a class with properties and methods is a better choice.

Summary

Here is an overview of the principles that you learned in this chapter regarding Objective-C collections:

- All Objective-C collections are zero-based, meaning that the items in the collection are numbered starting with zero, rather than one.

- An *index* is a number that references an item by its position in the collection.

- You use the **count** property to get the number of elements of a collection:

```
int itemCount = names.count;
```

NSArray

- The **NSArray** class is one of the most basic kinds of Objective-C collections.

- An **NSArray** collection is *immutable*, which means that, once you declare it, you can't change its members.

- You can use the **initWithObjects:** method to create a new **NSArray**:

```
NSArray *names =
    [[NSArray alloc] initWithObjects:
    @"Jordan",
    @"Timothy",
    @"Alexander",
     nil];
```

- If you are using Xcode 4.4 or later with the Apple LLVM Compiler 4.0 or later, you can create an **NSArray** more easily using the following syntax:

```
NSArray names = @[@"Jordan",
        @"Timothy",
        @"Alexander",
        @"Mia",
        @"Luca"];
```

- You can retrieve an item from a collection by using the **objectAtIndex:** method:

```
NSString *name = [names objectAtIndex:0];
```

- If you are using Xcode 4.5 or later with the Apple LLVM Compiler 4.0 or later *and are compiling with iOS 6 SDK or later*, you can use simpler square bracket syntax to access items in an array:

```
NSString *name = names[0];
```

- You can retrieve the index number of an object by using the **indexOfObject:** method:

```
NSUInteger miaIndex =
    [names indexOfObject:@"Mia"];
```

NSMutableArray

- **NSMutableArray** is the *mutable*, or changeable, version of **NSArray**. You can change, add, or remove items from an **NSMutableArray** after you create it.

- You can use the **initWithObjects:** method to create a new **NSMutableArray**:

```
NSMutableArray *names =
    [[NSMutableArray alloc] initWithObjects:
     @"Alexander",
     @"Mia",
     @"Luca",
     nil];
```

- You can add an item to an **NSMutableArray** by using the **addObject:** method:

```
[names addObject:@"Kevin"];
```

- You can remove an item from an **NSMutableArray** by using the **removeObjectAtIndex:** method:

```
[names removeObjectAtIndex:
    names.count - 1];
```

- You can insert an item into a specific location in an **NSMutableArray** by using **insertObject:atIndex:**

```
[names insertObject:@"Sharlene"
    atIndex:2];
```

NSDictionary

- In an **NSDictionary**, each item (called an *entry*) has a *key* and a *value*. The key is used to uniquely identify the entry, and the value is the item itself.

- An **NSDictionary** is immutable.

- You can initialize a dictionary by using an **NSArray** of keys and an **NSArray** of values:

```
NSArray *keys = [[NSArray alloc]
    initWithObjects:
        @"Austria",
        @"Bulgaria",
        @"Germany",
        nil];

NSArray *values = [[NSArray alloc]
        initWithObjects:
        @"AT",
        @"BG",
        @"DE",
        nil];

NSDictionary *countries =
    [[NSDictionary alloc]
        initWithObjects:values forKeys:keys];
```

- If you are using Xcode 4.4 or later with the Apple LLVM Compiler 4.0 or later, you can create an **NSDictionary** more easily by using this syntax:

```
NSDictionary *countries =
        @{ @"Austria" : @"AT",
        @"Bulgaria" : @"BG",
        @"Switzerland" : @"CH",
        @"Germany": @"DE"};
```

- You can get an item from a dictionary by using the **objectForKey:**

method:

```
NSString *country = [countries
            objectForKey:currentKey];
```

NSMutableDictionary

- **NSMutableDictionary** is the mutable version of **NSDictionary**.

- You initialize an **NSMutableDictionary** in the same way that you initialize an **NSDictionary**.

- To add an entry to the dictionary, you can use the **setObject:forKey:** method:

```
[countries setObject:@"GR"
      forKey:@"Greece"];
```

- To remove an entry from the dictionary, you can use the **removeObjectForKey:** method:

```
[countries
   removeObjectForKey:@"Bulgaria"];
```

NSSet

- **NSSet** stores an unordered set of unique items.

- You create an **NSSet** collection by using the **initWithObjects:** method:

```
NSSet *set = [[NSSet alloc]
    initWithObjects:
        @"iPod Touch",
        @"iPhone",
        @"iPad",
        nil];
```

- You can't retrieve items by index because **NSSet** is unordered, so no particular order and associated index value is guaranteed.

- If you are using Xcode 4.5 or later with the Apple LLVM Compiler 4.0 or later *and are compiling with iOS 6 SDK or later*, you can use simpler square bracket syntax to access items in an array:

```
NSString *value = countries[@"Austria"];
```

- Using this syntax, you pass the *key* within square brackets and the corresponding *value* is returned.

- You can use the **containsObject:** method to see if an **NSSet** contains a specific object:

```
BOOL containsObject =
    [set containsObject:@"iPhone"];
```

NSMutableSet

- **NSMutableSet** is the changeable version of **NSSet**.

- You can add an item to an NSSet by using the addObject: method:

```
[set addObject:@"New iPad"];
```

- You can remove an item from an **NSMutableSet** by using the **removeObject:** method:

```
[set removeObject:@"New iPad"];
```

Structures

- Although not really a collection, Objective-C *structures* allow you to group values together.

- You can declare a structure by using the **typedef** statement to provide a friendly name:

```
typedef struct
{
    int writing;
    int math;
    int reading;
} SATScores;
```

- You access members of a structure by using dot syntax. For example:

```
SATScores scores;
```

```
scores.math = 515;
scores.reading = 501;
scores.writing = 493;
```

- You can initialize members of a structure with values separated by commas inside curly braces:

```
SATScores scores = {515, 501, 493};
```

Exercise 11.1

In this exercise, you change the **CollectionsDemo** project so that it displays a list of days of the week.

1. In the **ViewController.m** implementation file, add a new instance variable of type **NSArray**, named **daysOfWeek**.

2. In the view controller's **viewDidLoad** method, initialize the new **daysOfWeek** array. To do this, create an **NSArray** object using the **initWithObjects:** method, and then store the result in the **daysOfWeek** instance variable.

3. Change the last line of code in the **viewDidLoad** method to retrieve an object from the new **daysOfWeek** array, rather than from the **names** array.

4. In the **pickerView:numberOfRowsInComponent:** method, change the code to return the **count** property of the **daysOfWeek** array instead of from the **names** array.

5. Change the **pickerView:titleForRow:forComponent:** method to return an object from the **daysOfWeek** array instead of from the **names** array.

6. Change the **pickerView:didSelectRow:inComponent:** method to retrieve an object from the **daysOfWeek** array rather than from the **names** array.

7. Run the App in the Simulator to make sure that you can see a list of days of the week. Select different days of the week from the picker view and make sure that the day of week is displayed in the label at the top of the view.

Solution Movie 11.1

To see a video providing the solution for this exercise, go to the following link in your web browser.

http://www.iOSAppsForNonProgrammers.com/B2M111.html

Chapter 12: Looping Statements

At times, you need to loop through all of the items in a collection. Objective-C has a few looping statements that let you do just that. In fact, the looping statements can be used to repeatedly execute a set of code for a wide variety of purposes.

Sections in This Chapter

Objective-C Looping Statements

The primary looping statements in Objective-C are:

- **for** statement

- **for in** statement

- **while** statement

- **do** statement

for Statement

You can use two different versions of the **for** statement to repeat a set of code.

The first type of **for** statement has the following syntax:

```
for ( initialization; condition; increment)
{
        statements
}
```

Typically, this type of **for** statement is used to loop a specified number of times.

- The *initialization* expression executes before the first iteration of the **for** loop is run. Normally, it is used to initialize an index variable that specifies the current item number.

- The loop ***condition*** is tested at the top of the **for** loop before each iteration to determine if another iteration should be executed.

- The *statements* between curly braces are executed.

- The loop *increment* is executed at the bottom of the **for** loop after each iteration. It's normally used to increment the index variable created in the initialization expression. Although less common, you can also decrement the index to go backward through a loop, or even loop through every other item by setting the increment statement to **i += 2**.

To see the for loop in action, you are going to edit the **CollectionsDemo** project in these steps:

1. Open the **CollectionsDemo** project.

2. Add the following code at the bottom of the **viewDidLoad** method in **ViewController.m**:

```
for (int i=0; i < names.count; i++) {

        NSLog(@"For name = %@",
            [names objectAtIndex:i]);
    }
}
```

3. Let's look at this code in the order in which it runs with the help of the following image.

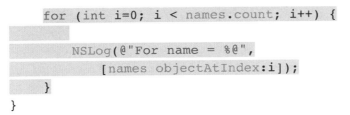

Here's a description of each step:

1. The *initialization* expression executes just once right before the first iteration of the loop. In this example, it creates an integer variable named **i** and sets its value to zero.

2. The loop *condition* check runs next. In this example, it checks to see if the index variable **i** is less than the number of items in the **names** array. If it's less, the statements between the curly braces are executed. Otherwise, the loop is exited, and the next line of code after the loop is executed.

3. The code between the **for** statement's curly braces runs next. In this example, the **NSLog** statement uses the index variable **i** to retrieve an object from the **names** array. The first time through, the variable **i** is set to zero; the next time through, it's set to **one**, and so on.

4. The loop *expression* increments the index variable **i** at the end of the loop, and now control goes back to step 2, where the loop condition is checked again.

Now let's run the App to see how the **for** loop works at run time.

1. Press the **Run** button in Xcode to see the output from this loop. After the Simulator displays the App, you can see the output of the **NSLog** statements in the Console window by selecting **View > Debug Area > Activate Console**. The Console window should look as shown in Figure 12.1.

```
All Output ÷                                        Clear  ☐ ▥ ☐
2012-07-26 21:31:44.845 CollectionsDemo[15470:f803] For name = Jordan
2012-07-26 21:31:44.845 CollectionsDemo[15470:f803] For name = Timothy
2012-07-26 21:31:44.845 CollectionsDemo[15470:f803] For name = Alexander
2012-07-26 21:31:44.846 CollectionsDemo[15470:f803] For name = Mia
2012-07-26 21:31:44.846 CollectionsDemo[15470:f803] For name = Luca
```

*Figure 12.1 The **NSLog** output of the **for** loop*

2. Press Xcode's **Stop** button to stop the App from running in the Simulator.

for Loop Code Completion

Xcode's Code Completion is a great help when you are first getting used to the syntax of the **for** loop. If you type the keyword **for** in a code window, the Code Completion popup shown in Figure 12.2 displays.

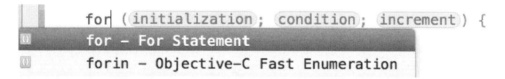

*Figure 12.2 Xcode's popup helps with **for** loop syntax.*

If you press **Enter** with the first option selected, Xcode adds the code template shown in Figure 12.3.

```
for (initialization; condition; increment) {
    statements
}
```

*Figure 12.3 The **for** loop code template*

As you enter each portion of the **for** statement, this template guides you, making sure that you get the syntax right! You move between each gray placeholder by pressing **Tab** to go forward and **Shift+Tab** to go backward.

for in Statement

You may have noticed in Figure 12.2 that the second option in the Code Completion list is **for in**. This is a different type of **for** loop especially designed for looping through collections. It's also known as *fast enumeration*.

Here is the syntax of the for in statement:

```
for (type *object in collection) {

        statements
}
```

The **for in** statement doesn't require that you keep track of either the number of items in the collection or the current index number. The loop is automatically executed once for each item in a collection. Nice and easy.

Here is an explanation of the different parts of the **for in** loop:

- *type* specifies the type of objects in the collection.

- *object* specifies the name of the variable used to reference the current object in the collection.

- *collection* specifies the collection containing the objects that you want to loop through.

- *statements* represents the statements enclosed in curly braces executed for each iteration of the loop.

To see the **for in** loop in action, follow these steps:

1. If it's not already open, in Xcode, open the **CollectionsDemo** project.

2. In the Project Navigator, select the **ViewController.m** implementation file and add the following code at the bottom of the **viewDidLoad** method:

```
for (NSString *name in names) {

    NSLog(@"For In Name = %@", name);
}
```

This code is much simpler than the previous **for** loop! In each iteration of the **for in** loop, the next item is automatically retrieved from the **names** array and stored in the **name** variable for you, and then the code between the curly braces executes. This continues until the statements have been executed for all items in the collection.

3. Press the **Run** button in Xcode, and you can see the output of the **NSLog** statements in the Console (Figure 12.4).

```
All Output ⬦                                                    Clear  ⬜ ⬛ ⬜

2012-07-26 22:13:59.816 CollectionsDemo[15594:f803] For In Name = Jordan
2012-07-26 22:13:59.816 CollectionsDemo[15594:f803] For In Name = Timothy
2012-07-26 22:13:59.816 CollectionsDemo[15594:f803] For In Name = Alexander
2012-07-26 22:13:59.816 CollectionsDemo[15594:f803] For In Name = Mia
2012-07-26 22:13:59.816 CollectionsDemo[15594:f803] For In Name = Luca
```

*Figure 12.4 The **NSLog** output of the **for in** loop*

4. Press the **Stop** button in Xcode to stop the App from running in the Simulator.

When using the **for in** loop, you should never change the collection over which you are iterating by adding or removing items. If you change the collection, you will get an error at run time!

while Statement

The **while** statement provides another way to loop through a set of statements. Here is the syntax of the **while** statement:

```
while (expression) {
        statements
}
```

The *expression* is evaluated at the top of the loop for every iteration. If it evaluates to true, the *statements* are executed; otherwise, the loop exits and passes control to the next statement after the closing curly brace.

To see the while statement in action, follow these steps:

1. If it's not already open, in Xcode, open the **CollectionsDemo** project.

2. In the Project Navigator, select the **ViewController.m** implementation file and add the following code to the bottom of the **viewDidLoad** method:

```
int index = 0;
while (index < names.count) {

    NSLog(@"While Name = %@",
        [names objectAtIndex:index]);
    index++;
}
```

The first line of code creates an integer variable named **index** and initializes it to zero before the **while** loop begins. At the start of each iteration of the loop, the condition checks to see if the index is less than the number of items in the **names** array. If it is, the **NSLog** statement executes. Otherwise, the **while** loop is exited.

3. Run the project, and you should see the "While Name" items displayed in the Console.

4. Press the **Stop** button in Xcode to stop the App from running in the Simulator.

If you are thinking that you could have used a **for** loop in this situation, you are right! Ultimately, you can use a **for** loop in place of a **while** loop and vice versa.

do Statement

The Objective-C **do** statement provides another looping option with a twist— the condition that determines if the associated statements should be executed is checked at the *bottom* rather than the *top* of the loop. This means that the statements always run at least once.

Here is the syntax of the do statement:

```
do {
      statements
} while ( expression );
```

When the **do** statement is first executed, the statements within curly braces are executed unconditionally. At the bottom of the loop, the expression is evaluated. If it evaluates to **true**, the loop is executed again. If it evaluates to **false**, execution passes to the statement immediately after the **do** statement.

To see how the **do** statement works, follow these steps:

1. Open the **CollectionsDemo** project.

2. In the Project Navigator, select the **ViewController.m** implementation file and add the following code to the bottom of the **viewDidLoad** method:

```
int doIndex = 0;
do {
    NSLog(@"Do Name = %@",
        [names objectAtIndex:doIndex]);
    doIndex++;
} while (doIndex < names.count);
```

3. Run the project again and you can see the "Do Name" items displayed in the Console.

4. Press Xcode's **Stop** button to stop the App from running in the Simulator.

Avoiding Infinite Loops

An infinite loop is a looping statement that continues forever. You can inadvertently create an infinite loop if the condition checked at the beginning or end of the loop never evaluates to **false**. For example, the following code produces an infinite loop:

```
int index = 0;
while (index < names.count) {

    NSLog(@"While Name = %@",
        [names objectAtIndex:index]);
}
```

It's an infinite loop because **index** is always set to zero—it's never incremented in the **while** loop, so it is always less than the value of **names.count**. To fix the problem, just add the following statement:

```
int index = 0;
while (index < names.count) {

    NSLog(@"While Name = %@",
        [names objectAtIndex:index]);
    index++;
}
```

This new statement increments the **index** value so that the loop is eventually exited when the **index** value is no longer less than the value of **names.count**.

Summary

Here are the main points to remember regarding Objective-C looping statements:

for Statement

* The **for** statement is typically used to loop a specified number of times.

* Here is an example of a **for** statement:

```
for (int i=0; i < names.count; i++) {

    NSLog(@"For name = %@",
        names objectAtIndex:i]);
}
```

* The *initialization* expression (**int i = 0**) executes before the first iteration of the **for** loop is run. Normally it is used to initialize an index variable that specifies the current item number.

* The loop *condition* (**i < names.count**) is tested at the top of the **for** loop before each iteration to determine if another iteration should be executed.

* The *statements* between curly braces are executed if the condition is met.

* The loop *increment* (**i++**) is executed at the bottom of the **for** loop after each iteration. It's normally used to increment the index variable created in the initialization expression.

for in Statement

The **for in** statement (also known as *fast enumeration*), doesn't require you to keep track of either the number of items in the collection or the current index number. The loop is automatically executed once for each item in a collection.

* Here is an example of a **for in** statement:

```
for (NSString *name in names) {

    NSLog(@"For In Name = %@", name);

}
```

- In each iteration of the **for in** loop, the next item is automatically retrieved from the array and stored in the variable for you (the **name** variable in this example). Afterwards, the code between the curly braces executes. This continues until the statements have been executed for all items in the collection.

while Statement

- The **while** statement provides another way to loop through a set of statements.

- Here is an example of a **while** statement:

```
while (index < names.count) {

    NSLog(@"While Name = %@",
        [names objectAtIndex:index]);
    index++;
}
```

- At the start of each iteration of the loop, the condition is checked. If the condition is **true**, the statements between curly braces are executed. If the condition is **false**, the while loop is exited.

do Statement

- The Objective-C **do** statement provides another way to loop through a set of statements.

- Here is an example of a **do** statement:

```
do {
    NSLog(@"Do Name = %@",
        [names objectAtIndex:doIndex]);
    doIndex++;
} while (doIndex < names.count);
```

- The condition that determines if the associated statements should be executed is checked at the bottom rather than the top of the loop. This means that the statements always run at least once.

Infinite Loops

- To avoid infinite loops, make sure that the condition in your loop eventually evaluates to **false**. This usually means making sure that the index value gets incremented.

Exercise 12.1

In this exercise, you change the **CollectionsDemo** project to use a **for** loop to display items in the **daysOfWeek** array that you created in **Exercise 11.1**.

1. At the bottom of the view controller's **viewDidLoad** method, add a **for** loop that uses **NSLog** to output a list of the **daysOfWeek** array to the Console.

2. Add to the bottom of the **viewDidLoad** method a **for in** loop that uses **NSLog** to output a list of the **daysOfWeek** array to the Console.

3. Run the App and make sure that you have two lists of days of the week in the Console window.

Solution Movie 12.1

To see a video providing the solution for this exercise, go to the following link in your web browser.

http://www.iOSAppsForNonProgrammers.com/B2M121.html

Chapter 13: Conditional Statements

Conditional statements in your App allow you to make choices that execute one set of code under one condition and one or more other sets of code under other conditions. They are a very core programming concept that you need to master before writing any real-world Apps. This chapter provides real-world examples of conditional statements that will help you grasp the concepts.

Sections in This Chapter

8. *Conditional Operator*

9. *Summary*

The Sample Code

Let's take the no-nonsense approach and dive right into the sample code project for this chapter since looking at conditional statements in the context of an App is the best way to learn about them.

1. If you have another project open, close it by selecting **File > Close Project** from the Xcode menu

2. Open the **ConditionalStatements** project by selecting **File > Open...** from the Xcode menu. In the **Open** dialog, navigate to the folder where you have stored this book's sample code. Drill down into the **ConditionalStatements** folder, select the **ConditionalStatements.xcodeproj** file, and then click **Open** as shown in Figure 13.1.

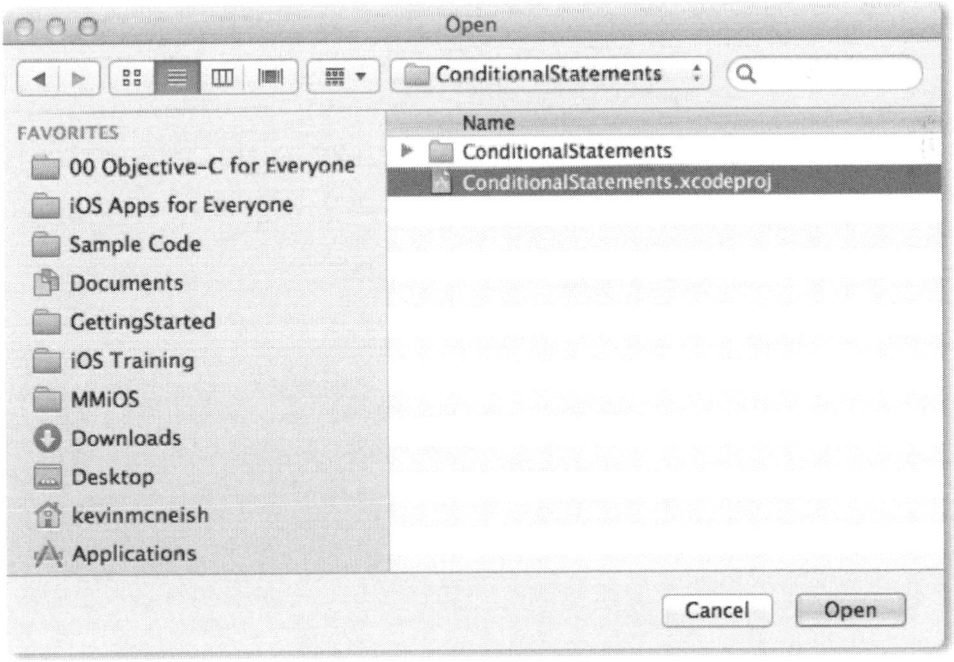

*Figure 13.1 Opening the **ConditionalStatements** project*

3. In the Project Navigator, click the white triangle to the left of the **ConditionalStatementsDemo** node to expand it, and then click the

gray arrow to the left of the **ConditionalStatements** sub node to expand it, and finally select the **MainStoryboard.storyboard** file. You will see the view displayed in Figure 13.2. This is a very simple view that contains a label, a picker view, and a switch control with another label.

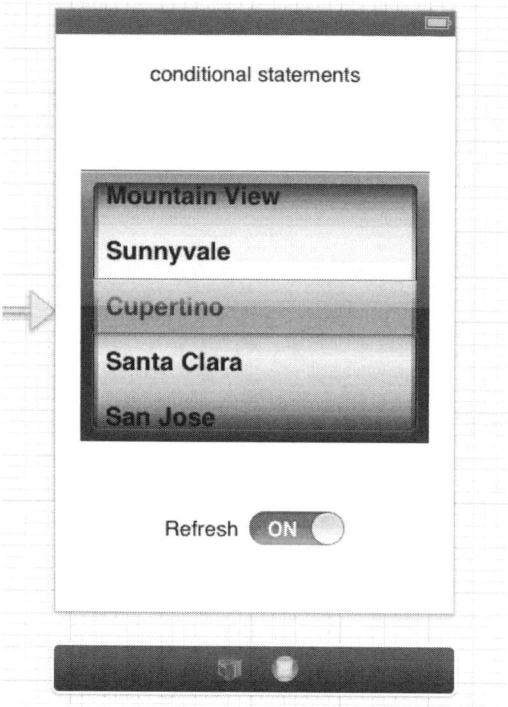

Figure 13.2 The picker view

4. Click Xcode's **Run** button to see this simple App run in the iOS Simulator. Notice that it looks a little different when you run it. Rather than list California cities in the picker view, it lists two options—**Upper Case** and **Lower Case** (Figure 13.3).

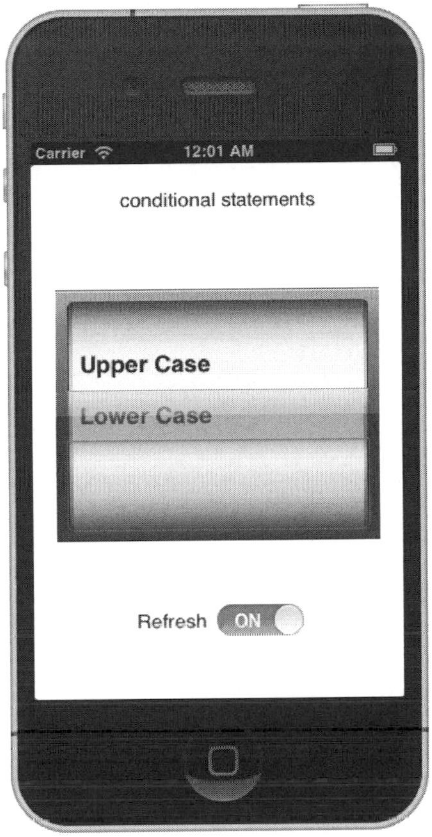

Figure 13.3 The picker view at run time

For now, note that selecting any option in the picker view or changing the setting of the **Refresh** switch has no effect.

5. Go back to Xcode and click the **Stop** button. In the Project Navigator, select the **ViewController.m** file. Notice the **@synthesize** statements at the top of the code window. The **lblDemo** property references the label at the top of the view; **pckOptions** references the picker view; and **swtRefresh** references the switch control. There is also a declaration for an **NSArray** variable named **choices**.

```
@implementation ViewController
{
    NSArray *choices;
}
@synthesize lblDemo;
@synthesize pckOptions;
@synthesize swtRefresh;
@synthesize scrollView;
```

6. Scroll down to see the **viewDidLoad** method:

```
- (void)viewDidLoad
{
    [super viewDidLoad];

    choices = [[NSArray alloc]
            initWithObjects:
            @"Upper Case",
            @"Lower Case",
            nil];

    [self.pckOptions selectRow:1
                inComponent:0
                animated:NO];
}
```

The code in this method initializes the **choices** array with the two options that you saw at run time: "Upper Case" and "Lower Case."

Afterwards, it sets the default selection to the second item in the **choices** array (remember, collections are zero-based, so the number 1 indicates the second item in the collection) by using the picker view's **selectRow:inComponent:animated:** method.

Three other methods of interest are associated with the picker view:

1. The **pickerView:numberOfRowsInComponent:** method is called automatically by the picker view when it first loads items into its list. This method just returns the **count** of items in the **choices** array.

2. The **pickerView:titleForRow:forComponent:** method is used at run time to get the title, or text to be displayed for each item. It is automatically called once for each row in the **choices** array.

3. The **pickerView:didSelectRow:inComponent:** method is called automatically when the user selects an item from the list. The second parameter, **row**, specifies the row selected by the user.

This third method is the main method of interest because it is the one you use to add code that reacts to the user's selection.

if Statements

The **if** statement in Objective-C allows you to run one or more lines of code if a particular condition is **true**. The **if** statement has the following syntax:

```
if ( condition ) {

    // statements to be executed
}
```

When creating an **if** statement, you first type **if**, and then enter an expression to be evaluated between parentheses, and follow it with the code to be executed (if the evaluated expression is true) within curly braces. If there is only one line of code to be executed, you *can* leave out the curly braces, but it's considered good form to leave them in. Let's give it a try.

1. If it's not already open, in Xcode, open the **ConditionalStatements** project.

2. Go to the **pickerView:didSelectRow:InComponent:** method, and enter the **if** statement on an empty line. Notice that Xcode's Code Completion pops up the options shown in Figure 13.4.

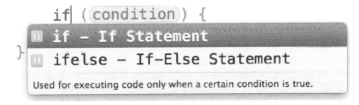

*Figure 13.4 Code Completion for the **if** statement*

3. You want the first item in the list, a simple **if** statement, so press **Tab** and focus is placed on the **condition** placeholder (Figure 13.5).

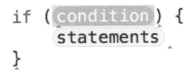

*Figure 13.5 Focus is on the **condition** placeholder*

4. Next, type **row == 0** as shown in Figure 13.6. In Objective-C, the **==** operator is used for comparison, so this code is comparing the row that was selected by the user to see if it's zero.

```
if (row == 0) {
    statements
}
```

Figure 13.6 Set the condition.

5. Press **Tab** again and focus is placed on the **statements** placeholder (Figure 13.7).

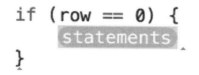

*Figure 13.7 Focus is on the **statements** placeholder.*

6. Enter the following code between the curly braces:

```
- (void)pickerView:(UIPickerView *)
        pickerView
        didSelectRow:(NSInteger)row
        inComponent:(NSInteger)component {

    if (row == 0) {
        self.lblDemo.text =
        [self.lblDemo.text uppercaseString];
    }
}
```

The code in this method does the following:

• It uses an **if** statement to see if the currently selected row is zero.

• If the row is zero, it sends an **uppercaseString** message to the label's **text** object, which converts the text string to uppercase.

• It stores the uppercased return value back into the label's **text** property.

7. Add a breakpoint on the **if** statement by clicking to the left of it in the gutter (Figure 13.8).

```
if (row == 0) {
    self.lblDemo.text =
        [self.lblDemo.text uppercaseString];
}
```

*Figure 13.8 Set a breakpoint on the **if** statement.*

8. Next, press the **Run** button to run this App in the Simulator. Select **Upper Case** in the picker view and you will hit the breakpoint (Figure 13.9).

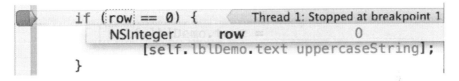

```
if (row == 0) {          Thread 1: Stopped at breakpoint
    self.lblDemo.text =
        [self.lblDemo.text uppercaseString];
}
```

*Figure 13.9 The **if** statement breakpoint is hit.*

9. If you hover your mouse pointer over the **row** variable, you can see that it's set to zero which is the row number that you selected in the picker view (Figure 13.10).

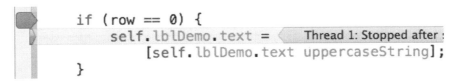

```
if (row == 0) {          Thread 1: Stopped at breakpoint 1
    NSInteger     row                    0
        [self.lblDemo.text uppercaseString];
}
```

*Figure 13.10 The **row** number is zero.*

10. Click the **Step Over** button. Since the condition is **true** (**row == 0**), the code between the curly braces executes (Figure 13.11).

```
if (row == 0) {
    self.lblDemo.text =     Thread 1: Stopped after :
        [self.lblDemo.text uppercaseString];
}
```

*Figure 13.11 The **if** statement is executed.*

11. Press **Continue**. You should see the label text uppercased in the Simulator (Figure 13.12).

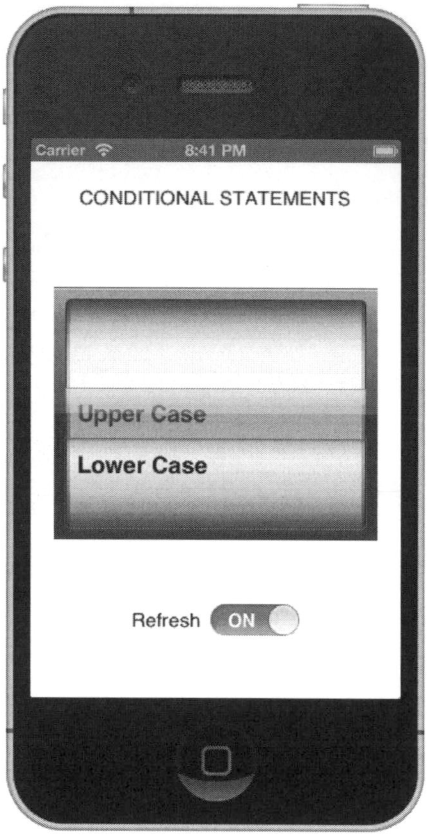

Figure 13.12 The label is uppercased.

If you click the **Lower Case** option in the picker view, notice that the item gets selected, but the label text doesn't change. That requires a code change that you will make in this section.

12. Go back to Xcode and press the **Stop** button to stop the App running in the Simulator.

if else Statements

When you want to perform an alternate set of code in an **if** statement, you add an **else** statement. Here is the syntax of the **if else** statement:

```
if ( condition ) {
      statements
}
else {
      alternate statements
}
```

If the condition in the **if** statement evaluates to **true**, the first set of code is executed; if it evaluates to **false**, the **else** alternate statements are executed. To see the **if else** statement in action, follow these steps:

1. If it's not already open, in Xcode, open the **ConditionalStatements** project.

2. Add the following **else** statement to the **if** statement:

```
if (row == 0) {
    self.lblDemo.text =
    [self.lblDemo.text uppercaseString];
}
else {
    self.lblDemo.text =
    [self.lblDemo.text lowercaseString];
}
```

3. Disable the first breakpoint by clicking on it, and then add a second breakpoint to the **else** statement (Figure 13.13).

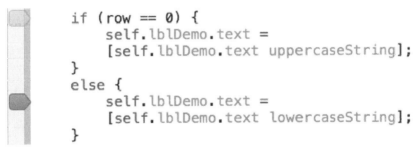

```
if (row == 0) {
    self.lblDemo.text =
    [self.lblDemo.text uppercaseString];
}
else {
    self.lblDemo.text =
    [self.lblDemo.text lowercaseString];
}
```

Figure 13.13 Add a second breakpoint.

4. Next, click the **Run** button to run the App in the Simulator. After the App is displayed, select the **Upper Case** option from the list in order to see the label text displayed in upper case. Next, by selecting the **Lower Case** option from the picker view, you will hit the breakpoint (Figure 13.14).

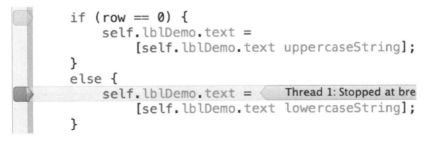

```
if (row == 0) {
    self.lblDemo.text =
        [self.lblDemo.text uppercaseString];
}
else {
    self.lblDemo.text =        Thread 1: Stopped at bre
        [self.lblDemo.text lowercaseString];
}
```

*Figure 13.14 The **else** breakpoint is hit.*

5. If you hover your mouse pointer over the **row** variable, you can see that it is set to **1** (Figure 13.15).

```
        if (row == 0) {
NSInteger    self.lblDemo.text =    1
            [self.lblDemo.text uppercaseString];
        }
        else {
            self.lblDemo.text =    Thread 1: Stopped at bre
                [self.lblDemo.text lowercaseString];
        }
```

*Figure 13.15 The **row** value is 1.*

Since the row is **1**, the condition (**row == 0**) evaluates to **false**, and the **else** statement is executed as evidenced by the fact that your breakpoint was hit.

6. Press the **Continue** button and see that the label text is now lowercased (Figure 13.16).

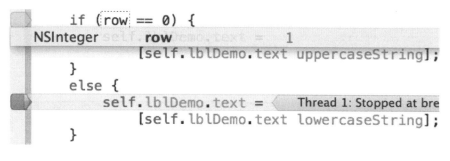

Figure 13.16 The label is lowercased.

7. Go back to Xcode and press the **Stop** button to stop the App running in the Simulator.

Now let's see how to handle three picker view options.

else if Statements

In Objective-C (and other programming languages for that matter), it's common to check two different conditions and provide three alternate sets of code to be executed based on these conditions.

This is where the **else if** statement comes in handy. Here is the syntax of the **else if** statement:

```
if ( condition 1 ) {

        statements executed on first condition
}
else if (condition 2 ) {

        statements executed on second condition
}
else {
        statements executed otherwise
}
```

If the first condition is **true**, then the first set of statements is executed. If the second condition is **true**, the second set of statements is executed. If neither condition is **true**, the third set of statements is executed.

1. If it's not already open, in Xcode, open the **ConditionalStatements** project.

2. Next, go to the **viewDidLoad** method and add a third option, **Capitalized**, to the list of choices:

```
choices = [[NSArray alloc]
        initWithObjects:
            @"Upper Case",
            @"Lower Case",
            @"Capitalized",
            nil];
```

3. Go to the **pickerView:didSelectRow:inComponent:** method and change the code to the following:

```
- (void)pickerView:(UIPickerView *)
        pickerView
        didSelectRow:(NSInteger)row
     inComponent:(NSInteger)component {

    if (row == 0) {
        self.lblDemo.text =
        [self.lblDemo.text uppercaseString];
    }
    else if (row == 1) {
        self.lblDemo.text =
        [self.lblDemo.text lowercaseString];
    }
    else {
      self.lblDemo.text =
        [self.lblDemo.text capitalizedString];
    }
}
```

Note the addition of **if (row == 1)** as well as the new **else** statement at the end.

4. Before running this code, delete the old breakpoints (just right-click and select **Delete breakpoint** from the shortcut menu) and add the breakpoints shown in Figure 13.17.

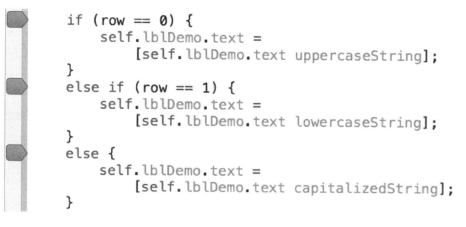

```
if (row == 0) {
    self.lblDemo.text =
        [self.lblDemo.text uppercaseString];
}
else if (row == 1) {
    self.lblDemo.text =
        [self.lblDemo.text lowercaseString];
}
else {
    self.lblDemo.text =
        [self.lblDemo.text capitalizedString];
}
```

*Figure 13.17 Add breakpoints to the **if else** statement.*

5. Click the **Run** button in Xcode and see the new **Capitalized** option in the picker view (Figure 13.18).

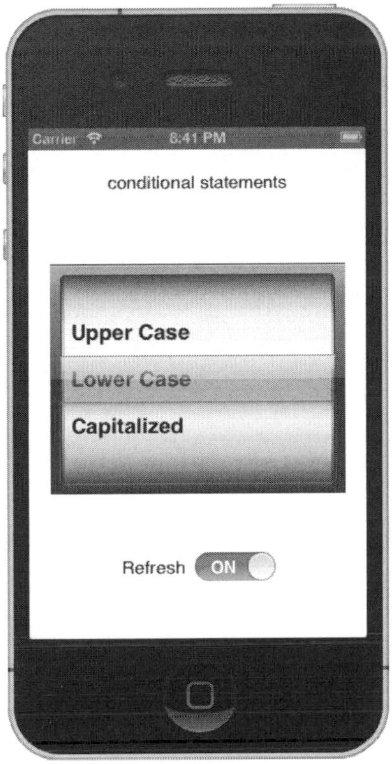

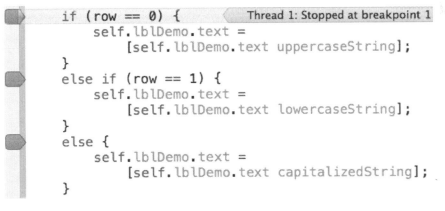

*Figure 13.18 The **Capitalized** option appears in the picker.*

6. Select **Capitalized**, and you will hit your new breakpoint (Figure 13.19).

```
if (row == 0) {                    Thread 1: Stopped at breakpoint 1
    self.lblDemo.text =
        [self.lblDemo.text uppercaseString];
}
else if (row == 1) {
    self.lblDemo.text =
        [self.lblDemo.text lowercaseString];
}
else {
    self.lblDemo.text =
        [self.lblDemo.text capitalizedString];
}
```

*Figure 13.19 The **if** is evaluated.*

7. If you hover your mouse pointer over the **row** variable, you can see that it is set to **2**. This means that the first and second conditions, which check for **row == 0** and **row == 1**, will evaluate to **false** and their associated code will not be executed. Only the code in the final **else** statement will be executed.

8. Click the **Step over** button. This causes execution to jump to the second condition to be evaluated (Figure 13.20).

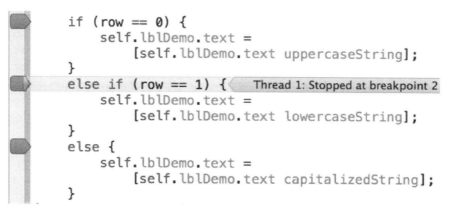

*Figure 13.20 The **else if** is evaluated.*

9. Again, since this condition also evaluates to **false**, click **Step over** again and execution jumps to the statements bracketed within the final **else** statement (Figure 13.21).

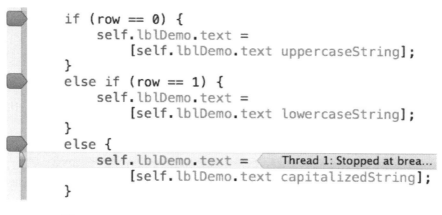

*Figure 13.21 The final **else** statement is executed.*

10. Click the **Continue** button, and you can see in the Simulator that the label text has changed. The first letter of each word is capitalized and all other characters are lowercased (Figure 13.22).

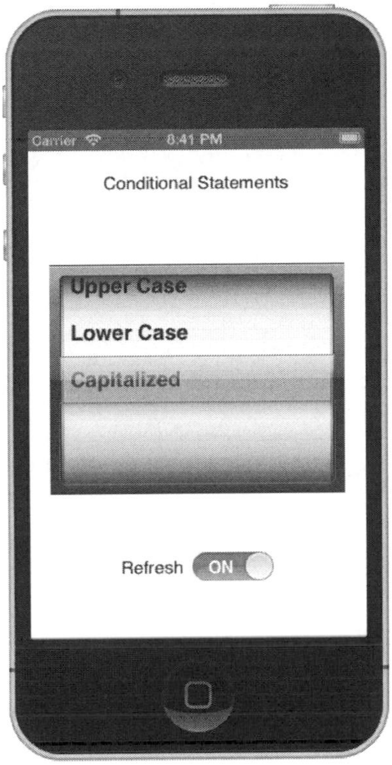

Figure 13.22 The label text s capitalized.

11. Press the **Stop** button to stop the App running in the Simulator.

Nested if statements

So far, we have ignored the **Refresh** switch at the bottom of the view. When the **Refresh** switch is **On**, the label text should be refreshed whenever the user makes a new selection. If the switch is **Off**, the label text should not change when the user makes a new selection.

In the next section, you will learn how to handle this situation with nested **if** statements.

Although it's a little more complex, it's very common to nest one set of **if** statements inside another.

```
if ( condition 1 ) {

        statements to be executed

        if (condition 2) {
```

```
        statements to be executed
    }
}
```

This is exactly what you need in order to handle the situation of deciding whether to refresh the label.

1. Open the **ConditionalStatements** project.

2. Go back to the **if** statements that you just entered and, right before the first **if**, add the new partially complete **if** statement shown in Figure 13.23 (ignore any errors for now).

```
if ([self.swtRefresh isOn]) {
    statements
}

if (row == 0) {
    self.lblDemo.text =
        [self.lblDemo.text uppercaseString];
}
else if (row == 1) {
    self.lblDemo.text =
        [self.lblDemo.text lowercaseString];
}
else {
    self.lblDemo.text =
        [self.lblDemo.text capitalizedString];
}
```

Figure 13.23 Add a new if statement.

Within the condition of this new **if** statement, an **isOn** message is passed to the switch. The method returns **true** if it's on, and **false** if it's off.

3. Since you only want the label to be refreshed when the switch is on, select all of the old **if** statements by clicking, holding the mouse button down, and then dragging your mouse as shown in Figure 13.24.

```
if (row == 0) {
    self.lblDemo.text =
        [self.lblDemo.text uppercaseString];
}
else if (row == 1) {
    self.lblDemo.text =
        [self.lblDemo.text lowercaseString];
}
else {
    self.lblDemo.text =
        [self.lblDemo.text capitalizedString];
}
```

*Figure 13.24 Select the old **if** statements.*

4. Next, type **Command+X** to cut these lines of code from the source code
    file, and then click on the **statements** placeholder (Figure 13.25).

```
if ([self.swtRefresh isOn]) {
    statements
}
```

*Figure 13.25 Click on the **statements** placeholder.*

5. Now type **Command+V** to paste these lines inside the new **if** statement.
    Afterwards, add a breakpoint at the top of the new code (Figure 13.26).

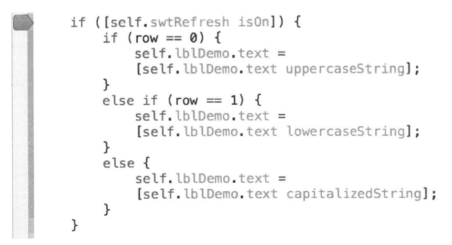

```
if ([self.swtRefresh isOn]) {
    if (row == 0) {
        self.lblDemo.text =
        [self.lblDemo.text uppercaseString];
    }
    else if (row == 1) {
        self.lblDemo.text =
        [self.lblDemo.text lowercaseString];
    }
    else {
        self.lblDemo.text =
        [self.lblDemo.text capitalizedString];
    }
}
```

*Figure 13.26 Paste the **if** statements and add a breakpoint.*

6. Click **Run** to run the new code in the Simulator. Leave the **Refresh**
    switch **On**, and then select **Upper Case** from the picker view. You will hit
    your breakpoint on the outer **if** statement (Figure 13.27).

```
if ([self.swtRefresh isOn]) {
    if (row == 0) {          Thread 1: Stopped at breakpoin
        self.lblDemo.text =
        [self.lblDemo.text uppercaseString];
    }
    else if (row == 1) {
        self.lblDemo.text =
        [self.lblDemo.text lowercaseString];
    }
    else {
        self.lblDemo.text =
        [self.lblDemo.text capitalizedString
    }
}
```

*Figure 13.27 The breakpoint is hit on the outer **if** statement.*

7. The outer **if** statement condition is evaluated first. Since the switch is on, the **isOn** method returns **true** and the nested code executes. To see this, click the **Step Over** button, and execution should move to the nested **if** statement. Click **Continue** and see that the label text is uppercased.

8. Next, click on the **Refresh** switch to turn it off, and then select another option in the picker view. Again, you should hit the outer **if** statement, which checks to see if the switch is on. Click **Step Over**, and you will see execution jump over the nested **if** statements and go to the bottom of the method (Figure 13.28). This is exactly as it should be.

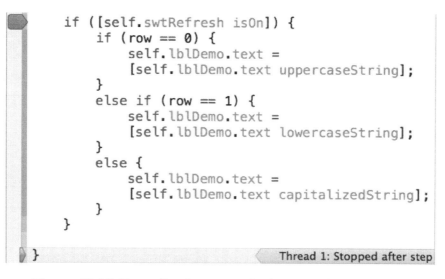

```
if ([self.swtRefresh isOn]) {
    if (row == 0) {
        self.lblDemo.text =
        [self.lblDemo.text uppercaseString];
    }
    else if (row == 1) {
        self.lblDemo.text =
        [self.lblDemo.text lowercaseString];
    }
    else {
        self.lblDemo.text =
        [self.lblDemo.text capitalizedString];
    }
}
}                              Thread 1: Stopped after step
```

Figure 13.28 Execution jumps to the bottom of the method.

9. Press **Continue** in the Debug area, and you will see that the text in the

label is unchanged. Now click the **Refresh** switch to turn it back on. Select an option in the picker view, and you will hit the outer **if** statement again. Click the **Continue** button, you will see that the label text is now updating again.

10. Press Xcode's **Stop** button to stop the App running in the Simulator.

Compound Comparisons

Before moving on from **if** statements, you need to learn about ***compound comparisons***. A compound comparison allows you to perform multiple tests in a single condition.

For example, if you want to check the value of an IQ (intelligence quotient) to see if it falls within the gifted range (130-139), you can create a compound comparison something like this:

```
if (iq >= 130 && iq <= 139) {

        // statements to be executed

}
```

This compound comparison checks two conditions. First, it checks to see if the value of **iq** is greater than or equal to 130, and then it checks to see if the value of **iq** is less than or equal to 139.

You are most likely familiar with the greater than or equal to (>=) and the less than or equal to (<=) operators, but you may not be familiar with the Objective-C **AND** operator (**&&**). When used in a compound condition, the condition is only **true** if both comparisons are **true**. So, if the value of **iq** is 140, the first check in the condition is **true**; but because the second check in the condition is **false**, the entire condition is **false**.

Here is another example of a compound comparison that uses the Objective-C OR operator (||):

```
if (iq < 20 || iq > 140) {

        // statements to be executed

}
```

In this code sample, the value of the **iq** variable is checked to see if it is extreme on either scale—less than 20 *or* greater than 140.

When using the **OR** operator in a compound condition, the condition is **true** if either comparison is **true**. So, if the value of **iq** is 19 and the first check is **true**, the entire compound condition is **true**. If the value of **iq** is 141, the first check is **false**, but the second check is **true**, then the entire compound condition is **true**. If the value of **iq** is anything between 20 and 140, both checks evaluate to **false** and, therefore, the entire condition is **false**.

Note that you can combine multiple comparisons in a single condition. For example:

```
if (iq < 20 || (iq >= 130 && iq <= 139) ||
    iq > 140) {
    // statements to be executed
}
```

In the previous code, there are two **OR** conditions and one **AND** condition. For the sake of clarity, parentheses have been added to the middle condition. You can create endless combinations of these conditional checks.

switch Statements

In the course of writing an App, there are many times when you need to check to see if a value is one of several different values—just as you did with the **iq** variable in the previous section.

Rather than using the **if** statement, which can become difficult to read when comparing several values, you can use the **switch** statement. The **switch** statement has the following syntax:

```
switch ( expression )
{
    case value1:
        // statements to be executed
        break;
    case value2:
        // statements to be executed
        break;
    case value3:
        // statements to be executed
        break;
    default:
```

```
        // statements to be executed
        break;
}
```

When a **switch** statement executes at run time, the value of the *expression* at the top of the **switch** is evaluated. The value of the expression is then compared against each **case** value until a match is found. If no match is found, the statements in the **default** case are executed. The **break** statement in each **case** causes execution to exit, or break out of, the **switch** statement.

Here are the **switch** statement ground rules:

- The **switch** statement's expression can be either an integral value or an expression that returns an integral value. In Objective-C, integer values include the **long**, **BOOL**, and **char** data types (this means that you can't **switch** on an **NSString** value—a common request). The specified value in each **case** must be a simple constant or constant expression. No two **case** values can be the same.

- If you forget to put a **break** statement in a **case**, execution automatically continues to the next **case** *even if it doesn't have a matching value*!

- If you *do* want the same statements executed for different values, you can list multiple **cases** before the statements to be executed. In the following **switch**, a **currentValue** of 0 or 1 executes the statements listed after **case 1**:

```
switch ( currentValue )
{
    case 0:
    case 1:
        // statements to be executed
        break;
    case 2:
        // statements to be executed
        break;
    default:
        // statements to be executed
        break;
}
```

To see a live example of how the **switch** statement works:

1. If it's not already open, in Xcode, open the **ConditionalStatements** project.

2. Let's comment out the **if** statements that you have created so far. Select all of the code inside the **pickerView:didSelectRow:inComponent:** method; then press the **Command+/** (forward slash) (Figure 13.29).

```objc
- (void)pickerView:(UIPickerView *)pickerView
        didSelectRow:(NSInteger)row
        inComponent:(NSInteger)component {

//   if ([self.swtRefresh isOn]) {
//       if (row == 0) {
//           self.lblDemo.text =
//           [self.lblDemo.text uppercaseString];
//       }
//       else if (row == 1) {
//           self.lblDemo.text =
//           [self.lblDemo.text lowercaseString];
//       }
//       else {
//           self.lblDemo.text =
//           [self.lblDemo.text capitalizedString];
//       }
//   }
}
```

*Figure 13.29 Comment out all of the **if** statements.*

3. In the **pickerView:didSelectRow:inComponent:** method, below the commented **if** statements, add the following code:

```objc
switch (row) {
    case 0:
        lblDemo.text =
        [lblDemo.text uppercaseString];
        break;
    case 1:
        lblDemo.text =
        [lblDemo.text lowercaseString];
        break;
    case 2:
        lblDemo.text =
        [lblDemo.text capitalizedString];
        break;
    default:
        break;
```

```
    }
```

Let's look at this code in the order in which it runs with the help of the following image:

```
          ①
switch (row) {
    case 0:
        lblDemo.text = [lblDemo.text uppercaseString];
        break;
 ②  case 1:
        lblDemo.text = [lblDemo.text lowercaseString];
      ③ break;
    case 2:
        lblDemo.text = [lblDemo.text capitalizedString];
        break;
    default:
        break;
}
 ④
```

Here's a description of each step:

1. The value of the **row** variable is evaluated.

2. The value is compared against each **case** value until a match is found, and then the statements associated with that **case** are executed.

3. The **break** statement causes execution to break out of the **case** statement.

4. Execution continues with the next line of code after the ending curly brace of the **case** statement.

Now let's see how the case statement works at run time:

1. Click the **Run** button in Xcode to see whether this works the same as the **if** statements that it replaced. The real point is that the **switch** statement is much easier to write and to understand. As an App developer, you should take pride in writing code that is easily understood. Six months after you have written code, you don't want to be scratching your head trying to figure out what on earth it does.

2. Press the **Stop** button to stop the App running in the Simulator.

switch Statements and Curly Braces

One little oddity about the switch statement is that you need to use curly braces within a particular case if the first statement is a declaration (such as a variable declaration). For example, check out the **switch** statement in Figure 13.30. Notice Xcode displays the error "Expected expression".

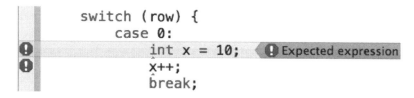

```
switch (row) {
    case 0:
        int x = 10;     Expected expression
        x++;
        break;
```

Figure 13.30 Add curly braces to avoid this error.

To fix this error, simply put the code in the **case** between curly braces:

```
switch (row) {
    case 0:
    {
    int x = 10;
    x++;
    break;
    }
}
```

Conditional Operator

One other conditional statement to discuss, oddly enough, is called the *conditional operator*.

It's a bit of an odd duck because it takes three operators. Here is its basic syntax:

```
condition ? expression1 : expression2
```

When this line of code executes, the *condition* is evaluated first. If the condition evaluates to **true**, *expression1* is evaluated and its result becomes the result of the entire operation. If the condition evaluates to **false**, *expression 2* is evaluated and its result becomes the result of the entire operation.

If that seems confusing, the following example should help clear it up:

```
BOOL goodGrade = ( grade > 85 ) ? YES : NO;
```

In this code sample, the condition **(grade > 85)** is evaluated first. If it's **true**, the value **YES** is stored in the **goodGrade** variable. If it's **false**, the value **NO** is stored in the **goodGrade** variable.

Summary

Here is an overview of conditional statements in Objective-C:

if Statements

- The **if** statement in Objective-C allows you to run one or more lines of code if a condition is true.

- Here is an example of an if statement:

```
if (row == 0) {
    self.lblDemo.text =
        [self.lblDemo.text uppercaseString];
}
```

In this example, if the condition **(row == 0)** is **true**, then the statement between the curly braces is executed. If the condition is **false**, the statement is not executed.

if else Statements

- An **if else** statement allows you to run one of two different set of statements.

- Here is an example of an **if else** statement:

```
if (row == 0) {
    self.lblDemo.text =
        [self.lblDemo.text uppercaseString];
}
else {
    self.lblDemo.text =
        [self.lblDemo.text lowercaseString];
}
```

In this example, if the condition in the **if** statement **(row == 0)** evaluates to **true**, the code between the first set of curly braces is executed. If it evaluates to **false**, the **else** alternate statement is executed.

else if Statements

- An **else if** statement allows you to check two different conditions and to provide three alternate sets of code to be executed based on these conditions.

- Here is an example of an **else if** statement:

```
if (row == 0) {
    self.lblDemo.text =
      [self.lblDemo.text uppercaseString];
}
else if (row == 1) {
    self.lblDemo.text =
      [self.lblDemo.text lowercaseString];
}
else {
    self.lblDemo.text =
      [self.lblDemo.text capitalizedString];
}
```

In this example, if the first condition **(row == 0)** is **true**, the code between the first set of curly braces is executed. If the second condition **(row == 1)** is **true**, the code between the second set of curly braces is executed. If neither condition is **true**, code between the third set of curly braces is executed.

Nested if Statements

- In Objective-C, you can nest one set of **if** statements inside another.

- Here is an example of a nested **if** statement:

```
if ([self.swtRefresh isOn]) {
    if (row == 0) {
        self.lblDemo.text =
        [self.lblDemo.text uppercaseString];
    }
    else if (row == 1) {
        self.lblDemo.text =
```

```
        [self.lblDemo.text lowercaseString];
    }
    else {
     self.lblDemo.text =
     [self.lblDemo.text capitalizedString];
    }

}
```

In this example, the outer **if** statement condition (**[self.swtRefresh isOn]**) is evaluated first. If it's **true**, the nested **if** statement is executed. If it's **false**, the nested **if** statement is NOT executed.

Compound Comparisons

- A compound comparison allows you to perform multiple tests in a single condition.

- Here is an example of a compound comparison:

```
if (iq >=  130 && iq <= 139) {

    // statements to be executed

}
```

In this example, the compound comparison checks two conditions. First, it checks to see if the value of **iq** is greater than or equal to **130**, *and* then it checks to see if the value of **iq** is less than or equal to **139**.

- When the Objective-C **AND** operator (**&&**) is used in a compound condition, the condition is only **true** if both comparisons are **true**.

- When using the **OR** operator in a compound condition, the condition is **true** if either comparison is **true**.

- You can combine multiple comparisons in a single condition. For the sake of clarity, you can add parentheses to conditions:

```
if (iq < 20 || (iq >= 130 && iq <= 139) ||  iq > 140) {

    // statements to be executed

}
```

switch Statements

- Rather than using the **if** statement, which can become difficult to read when comparing several values, you can use the **switch** statement, which makes your code much clearer.

- Here is an example of a **switch** statement:

```
switch (row) {
    case 0:
        lblDemo.text =
          [lblDemo.text uppercaseString];
        break;
    case 1:
        lblDemo.text =
          [lblDemo.text lowercaseString];
        break;
    case 2:
        lblDemo.text =
          [lblDemo.text capitalizedString];
        break;
    default:
        break;
    }
```

- When a **switch** statement executes at run time, the value of the expression at the top of the **switch** is evaluated. The value of the expression is then compared against each **case** value until a match is found. If no match is found, the statements in the **default** case are executed. The **break** statement in each **case** causes execution to exit, or break out of, the **switch** statement.

- The **switch** statement's expression can be either an integral value or an expression that returns an integral value.

- The specified value in each **case** must be a simple constant or constant expression.

- No two **case** values can be the same.

- If you forget to put a **break** statement in a **case**, execution automatically continues to the next **case** even if it doesn't have a matching value.

- If you *do* want the same statements executed for different values, you can list multiple **cases** before the statements to be executed.

Conditional Operator

- The conditional operator allows you to check a condition and to perform one of two expressions based on the result.

- Here is an example of the conditional operator:

```
BOOL goodGrade = ( grade > 85 ) ? YES : NO;
```

In this code sample, the condition **(grade > 85)** is evaluated first. If it's **true**, the value **YES** is stored in the **goodGrade** variable. If it's **false**, the value **NO** is stored in the **goodGrade** variable.

Chapter 14: Working With Strings

In the process of creating Apps, you work with a lot of character strings—so often that it deserves its own topic. You have already learned much of the basics about strings, but this chapter goes a bit deeper and even teaches you how to make the strings in your App multi-lingual.

Sections in This Chapter

1. *Converting Values to NSString With Format Specifiers*

2. *Converting NSString to Numeric Values*

3. *Removing Characters From a String*

4. *Appending Strings*

5. *Dividing Strings*

6. *Comparing and Identifying Characters in a String*

7. *The unichar Data Type*

8. *Multi-Lingual Support*

9. *Summary*

10. *Exercise 14.1*

11. *Solution Movie 14.1*

Converting Values to NSString With Format Specifiers

Often, you need to convert numeric values to a string value for display or other purposes. The **NSString** class has a **stringWithFormat:** method that allows you to do this and more.

The **NSString** Class Reference says of **stringWithFormat:**

> *Returns a string created by using a given format string as a template into which the remaining argument values are substituted.*

In Objective-C, you can use a special format string as a placeholder for another value to be inserted into the string. You can then use the **stringWithFormat:** method to substitute the value into the placeholder.

For example, the following string contains a **%u** placeholder for a number of attendees, followed by a variable that holds the attendee count:

```
@"There are %u attendees", count;
```

In this example, you don't want to hard-code the number of attendees in the string because the number of attendees may change. It's much better to get the number of attendees from a variable. The **%** character in this string indicates a placeholder. The character that follows is a *format specifier*, which indicates the kind of value to be inserted. In this case, **u** indicates an unsigned integer stored in the **count** variable (for a list of other commonly used format specifiers, see Appendix D – String Format Specifiers).

You can use the **stringWithFormat:** method of the **NSString** class to substitute the **count** value into the string. Check out the *signature* (method name and parameters) of the **stringWithFormat:** method:

```
+ (id)stringWithFormat:(NSString *)format,...
```

The plus sign indicates that it is a class method, so you need to call the method directly on the **NSString** class. For example:

```
NSString *myString =
        [NSString stringWithFormat:
        @"There are %u attendees", count];
```

This code passes a **stringWithFormat:** message to the **NSString** class. It passes a string argument containing the **%u** placeholder and a second integer variable named **count** which is converted to a string and inserted into the placeholder by the **stringWithFormat:** method. The return value of the message is stored in a local **NSString** variable named **myString**.

To see another example of **stringWithFormat:**, let's check out the **StringsDemo** sample project:

1. To open the project, select **File > Open...** from the Xcode menu. In the **Open** dialog, navigate to the folder where you have copied this book's sample code. Drill down into the **StringsDemo** folder, select the **StringsDemo.xcodeproj** file, and click the **Open** button.

2. In the Project Navigator, drill into the **StringsDemo** node and select the **MainStoryboard.storyboard** file. You should see the view displayed in Figure 14.1.

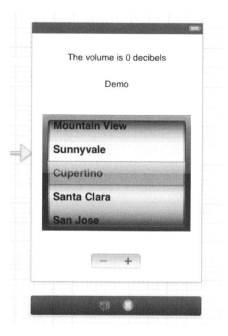

Figure 14.1 The stepper control changes the volume.

This view contains two labels, a picker view and a control that you haven't seen yet—a stepper. The stepper has plus and minus buttons, often used to change a numeric value in another control.

3. You are going to add code so that the user's pressing the minus/plus buttons on the stepper changes the volume level displayed in the label (the **Demo** label and the picker view are used to demonstrate other string functions later in this section).

   In the Project Navigator select the **ViewController.m** file. Near the top of the code file, you should see the **stepValueChanged:** method:

   ```
   - (IBAction)stepValueChanged:(id)sender {
   }
   ```

4. This method is automatically called when the user touches the minus or plus buttons on the stepper control. Add the following code to this method:

   ```
   - (IBAction)stepValueChanged:(id)sender {

       NSUInteger decibels = self.stpDemo.value;

       self.lblDemo.text =
       [NSString stringWithFormat:
        @"The volume is %u decibels", decibels];
       self.lblDemo2.text = @"";
   }
   ```

The first line of code gets the current **value** from the stepper control and stores it into an **NSUInteger** variable. This is necessary because the **value** property of the stepper control is of type **double** and, if you remember, a **double** contains a decimal point with several zeroes to the right of it—not what you want in this case. Storing the **double** value into the **NSUInteger decibels** variable converts the value to an unsigned integer, which is exactly what you want (for more information on converting data types, check out Chapter 16: Advanced Objective-C under the section Converting Objective-C Data Types).

The second line of code is the main point of this example. The **stringWithFormat:** method of the **NSString** class substitutes the

decibels value for the **%u** placeholder in the string, and the string is then assigned to the **text** property of the **lblDemo** label. The third line of code clears the **Demo** label text.

5. Press the **Run** button to see this code at work in the Simulator (Figure 14.2).

Figure 14.2 The stepper control at run time

Converting NSString to Numeric Values

The **NSString** class has a number of instance methods that allow you to convert a string to a numeric data type. All of these methods ignore any white space at the beginning of the string:

```
// Convert to a double value
double d = [@"1.1" doubleValue];

// Convert to a float value
float f = [@"2.2" floatValue];
```

```
// Convert to an integer value
int i = [@"10" intValue];
```

If these methods do not encounter a valid numeric string of the specified type, they return a 0.0 (**doubleValue** and **floatValue**) and 0 (**intValue**).

Boolean (true/false) values are also considered numeric since they evaluate to a one (**true**) or zero (**false**). You can convert a string to a Boolean value as follows:

```
bool b = [@"T" boolValue];
```

The **boolValue** method returns **true** if the first character is **Y, y, T, t**, or a number 1-9. Otherwise, it returns **false**.

Removing Characters From a String

At times, you need to remove characters from a string. This section provides examples showing how to do this.

Removing Characters From the End of a String

For example, if there is a single unwanted character at the end of a string, you can remove the final character by using this code:

```
NSString *myString = @"Steve Jobs.";
myString = [myString
       substringToIndex:myString.length - 1];
```

The **substringToIndex:** instance method of the **NSString** class returns a portion of the string starting with the first character up to the index, or character position, that you specify. As you might imagine, the index is zero-based, so to remove the last character, you specify the length of the string minus one. This changes the value in **myString** to **Steve Jobs** (without the period at the end).

Removing Characters From the Beginning of a String

To remove characters from the beginning of a string, you can do the following:

```
NSString *myURL = @"http://www.apple.com";
myURL = [myURL substringFromIndex:7];
```

The **substringFromIndex:** instance method of the **NSString** class returns a portion of a string starting at the specified index position. In this example, the first seven characters are removed (0 through 6). This changes the value in **myURL** to **www.apple.com**.

Removing Characters From the Middle of a String

You can also pull characters out of the middle of a string. For example:

```
myString = @"iPod Touch, iPhone, iPad";
NSRange myRange = {12, 6};
myString = [myString
  substringWithRange:myRange];
```

The **substringWithRange:** instance method of the **NSString** class returns a portion of a string. In this example, the **NSRange** variable created in the second line of code specifies a starting index of 12, with a range of 6 characters. Passing the **subStringWithRange:** message to the **myString** object with this range returns the string "iPhone".

Removing All Occurrences of a Character From a String

Sometimes you need to remove all occurrences of a specific character (or sequence of characters) from a string. The **stringByReplacingOccurrencesOfString:** method is just right for this job. For example:

```
myString = [myString
  stringByReplacingOccurrencesOfString:@","
  withString:@""];
```

This code removes all commas from the string.

Trimming White Space From a String

Another common task is removing spaces from the beginning and end of a string. To do this, you can use the **stringByTrimmingCharactersInSet:** method:

```
myString = [myString
```

```
stringByTrimmingCharactersInSet:
[NSCharacterSet whitespaceCharacterSet]];
```

If you also want to remove "new line" characters from the string (the **\n** character combination in a string creates a new line, so that subsequent characters are displayed on the next line), you can use the following character set:

```
myString = [myString
  stringByTrimmingCharactersInSet:
  [NSCharacterSet
    whitespaceAndNewlineCharacterSet]];
```

> **Note:** You can see some of these methods at work in the **StringsDemo** project. To see the demo code, select the **ViewController.m** file in the Project Navigator and look in the **pickerView:didSelectRow:InComponent** method. To see these methods do their magic at run time, run the project in the Simulator and select different items from the picker view.

Appending Strings

Earlier in this chapter, you learned about appending strings with the **stringByAppendingString:** method. I'll mention it again briefly in this section so that it will be here when you come looking for it!

In the following code sample:

```
NSString *myString = [@"iPhone "
  stringByAppendingString:@"5"];
```

This statement takes the strings "iPhone " and "5", appends them and stores the resulting "iPhone 5" value into the **myString** variable.

You can also use format specifiers to append numeric values to strings. For example:

```
NSString *myString = [@"iPhone "
  stringByAppendingFormat:@"@u", 5];
```

In this example, the iPhone version number is an integer, so you use the format specifier **@u** to convert the number to a string. The result "iPhone 5" is stored into the **myString** variable.

Dividing Strings

The **componentsSeparatedByString:** method is one of the most common methods used to divide a string. For example:

```
NSString *devices =
  @"iPod Touch, iPhone, iPad";
NSArray *deviceArray =
 [devices componentsSeparatedByString:
   @", "];
```

In this example, the **componentsSeparatedByString:** method searches for the ", " string in the **devices** string and creates an array containing three strings, "iPod Touch," "iPhone," and "iPad".

Comparing and Identifying Characters in a String

Although mentioned earlier in this book, the topic of how to compare two strings bears repeating since this one can really make you chase your tail around.

Comparing Strings

Rather than using the usual == operator to compare strings, you must use the **isEqualToString:** instance method of **NSString** instead. For example:

```
BOOL areStringsEqual =
  [self.lblDemo.text
    isEqualToString:@"Demo"];
```

The **isEqualToString:** method compares the string "Demo" to the text of the **lblDemo** label (which is also "Demo") and finds that they are equal. If you try this:

```
BOOL areStringsEqual =
  (self.lblDemo.text == @"Demo");
```

The == comparison returns **NO**, rather than the expected **YES**, because the == operator is not checking the value of the strings; instead, it's checking to see if they are the exact same object instance (they are not).

Save yourself some frustration and remember to use the **isEqualToString:** method!

Checking for One String at the Beginning or End of Another String

Two other common **NSString** methods are the **hasPrefix:** and **hasSuffix:** methods:

```
NSString *url = @"http://apple.com";
BOOL hasHTTP = [url hasPrefix:@"http://"];
BOOL hasDotCom = [url hasSuffix:@".net"];
```

In this code, the **hasPrefix:** method checks the beginning of the **url** string for an "http://" suffix, finds it, and returns **true**. The **hasSuffix:** method checks the **url** string for a ".com" suffix, finds it, and returns **false**.

Checking if a String Contains Another String

Often, you need to check to see if one string contains another string. This is easy to do by using **NSString's rangeOfString:** method. For example, to check to see if a string contains a period, you can perform this check:

```
if ([value rangeOfString:@"."].location
  != NSNotFound) {
      // It does contain a period
}
```

By default, this search is case-sensitive, meaning that it searches for an exact match for a string with the same upper and lowercase letters. If you want to perform a case-insensitive search, use the **options** argument:

```
if ([value rangeOfString:@"AbC"
   options:NSCaseInsensitiveSearch].location
   == NSNotFound)
{
```

```
    // Doesn't contain any "abc" combination
}
```

Checking for an Empty String

You can easily check if a string is empty by seeing if its **length** is equal to zero:

```
if (value.length == 0)
{
        // The string is empty
}
```

This not only checks to see if the string is empty, but also checks to see if the string is **nil**, since calling **length** on a **nil** string also returns zero.

The unichar Data Type

NSString objects are comprised of **unichar** characters. A **unichar** represents a single character such as a letter of the alphabet. You declare a character literal by surrounding the character with single quotes:

```
unichar letter = 'a';
unichar digit = '1';
```

There are a number of **NSString** methods that accept **unichar** values, so it's good to know about this data type. For example, **characterAtIndex:** returns the **unichar** at the specified index in the string:

```
unichar *myChar = [name characterAtIndex:0];
```

Multi-Lingual Support

In many cases, you can expand your user base by offering your App in multiple languages. The term *localize* is used in iOS and other software platforms to describe the process of translating and adapting your App to different cultures, countries, regions, or groups of people. This section isn't an exhaustive discussion of localization, but simply addresses how to make sure that the strings in your App can be translated to other languages.

Not every string in your App needs to be localized, but any string that is displayed to the user interface should be made localizable. So far, all of the samples in this book have used hard-coded strings. For example:

```
self.lblDemo.text = @"screen";
```

This code always stores the text "screen" to the label's **text** property regardless of the user's language setting on his or her iOS device (specified in the **Settings** App under **General > International > Language**).

Rather than hard-coding strings in your App, you can use the **NSLocalizedString()** function instead. Here is the signature of the **NSLocalizedString()** function:

```
NSString * NSLocalizedString(NSString *key,
  NSString *comment)
```

This function accepts two arguments:

- **key** - The text *string* that you want to display

- **comment** - A description of the text that you want to display

Here is the same line of code used as an example above but modified to use the **NSLocalizedString()** function instead:

```
self.lblDemo.text =
  NSLocalizedString(@"screen",
                @"An iOS display");
```

When this function executes at run time, it checks to see if a translation of the text "screen" has been provided for the user's current language. If it has, the *translated string* is returned from the function. If no translation has been provided, the text "screen" is returned from the function.

This means that you don't have to translate your App strings until you have finished creating your App. At that time, you can decide which languages you want to support and then translate your App to those languages.

In this example, the comment "An iOS display" describes the "screen" text string. In this case, the comment is important because the English word screen has multiple meanings. It could mean the screen on your iPhone or it could mean "to examine something closely," as when you are screened at airport security. Providing a meaningful comment helps translators to produce an accurate localization of your App's strings!

Summary

Here is an review of string manipulation in Objective-C:

Converting to and from Strings

- You can use the **stringWithFormat:** method in conjunction with format specifiers to convert numeric values to a string. For example:

```
NSString *myString =
  [NSString stringWithFormat:
      @"There are %u attendees", count];
```

- The **NSString** class has a number of instance methods that allow you to convert a string to a numeric data type. For example:

```
// Convert to a double value
double d = [@"1.1" doubleValue];

// Convert to a float value
float f = [@"2.2" floatValue];

// Convert to an integer value
int i = [@"10" intValue];
```

Removing Characters from a String

- To remove characters from the end of a string, you can use the **substringToIndex**: method:

```
myString = [myString
    substringToIndex:myString.length - 1];
```

- To remove characters from the beginning of a string, you can use the **substringFromIndex:** method:

```
myURL = [myURL substringFromIndex:7];
```

- To remove characters from the middle of a string, you can use the **substringWithRange:** method:

```
myString = [myString
  substringWithRange:myRange];
```

- The **stringByReplacingOccurencesOfString**: can be used to remove all occurrences of one or more characters from a string:

```
myString = [myString
  stringByReplacingOccurencesOfString:@","
  withString:@""];
```

- To trim white space from the beginning and end of a string, use the **stringByTrimmingCharactersInSet**: method:

```
myString = [myString
  stringByTrimmingCharactersInSet:
  [NSCharacterSet whitespaceCharacterSet]];
```

Appending Strings

- You can append strings together by using the **stringByAppendingString**: method:

```
NSString *myString = [@"iPhone "
    stringByAppendingString:@"5"];
```

- You can also use format specifiers to append numeric values to strings. For example:

```
NSString *myString = [@"iPhone "
    stringByAppendingFormat:@"%u", 5];
```

Dividing Strings

- You can divide a string by using the **componentsSeparatedByString**: method:

```
NSArray *deviceArray = [devices
    componentsSeparatedByString:@", "];
```

Comparing and Identifying String Characters

- You can test if strings contain the same characters by using the **isEqualToString**: method:

```
BOOL areStringsEqual = [self.lblDemo.text
    isEqualToString:@"Demo"];
```

- You can test if a string begins with a specific set of characters by using the **hasPrefix:** method:

```
BOOL hasHTTP = [url hasPrefix:@"http://"];
```

- You can test if a string ends with a specific set of characters by using the **hasSuffix:** method:

```
BOOL hasDotCom = [url hasSuffix:@".net"];
```

- You can test if one string contains another string by using **rangeOfString:**

```
if ([value rangeOfString:@"."].location
   != NSNotFound) {
      // It does contain a period
}
```

Checking for an Empty String

- You can check for an empty string by checking to see if the string's **length** is equal to zero:

```
if (myString.length == 0)
```

The unichar Data Type

- **NSString** objects are comprised of **unichar** characters. A **unichar** represents a single character such as a letter of the alphabet. You declare a character literal by surrounding the character with single quotes:

```
unichar letter = 'a';
```

Multi-Lingual Support

- You should use the **NSLocalizedString** function to make the strings in your App localizable:

```
self.lblDemo.text =
    NSLocalizedString(@"screen",
```

```
@"An iOS display");
```

Exercise 14.1

In this exercise, you add an option to the **StringsDemo** project that trims white space from a string.

1. In the **ViewController.m** implementation file, go to the **pickerView:didSelectRow:inComponent:** method and add a new **NSString** local variable at the top of the method called **paddedString**.

2. Further down in the same method, add a **case 5** to the **switch** statement that:

    *   Stores the string " One Infinite Loop" (with three leading spaces) to the **paddedString** variable

    *   Stores the **paddedString** variable to the **lblDemo** label's **text** property

    *   Uses the **stringByTrimmingCharactersInSet:** method to trim leading spaces from the **paddedString** variable, and stores the result back into the **lblDemo2** label's **text** property

3. In the **viewDidLoad** method, add a new "Trimming" item at the end of the **tests** array.

4. Run the App and select the new **Trimming** option to make sure that the label displays the *untrimmed string in the upper label* and the *trimmed string in the lower label*. If you have succeeded, the labels should look like Figure 14.3.

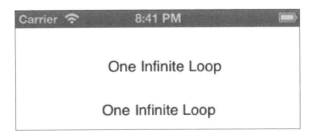

Figure 14.3 The untrimmed and trimmed strings

Solution Movie 14.1

To see a video providing the solution for this exercise, go to the following link in your web browser.

http://www.iOSAppsForNonProgrammers.com/B2M141.html

Chapter 15: Comments, Constants & Enumerations

In this chapter, you will learn more about adding quality comments to your code—something you will thank yourself for many times over. You will also learn why and how you should declare your own constants and enumerations. You will even learn how to extend Objective-C enumerations to make them more powerful for your iOS Apps.

Sections in This Chapter

1. *Commenting Your Code*

2. *Creating Constants*

3. *Declaring Constants*

4. *Creating Your Own Enumerations*

5. *Extending Objective-C Enumerations*

6. *Summary*

7. *Exercise 15.1*

8. *Solution Movie 15.1*

Commenting Your Code

Commenting your code is important. It allows others to quickly look at your code and understand what it does. It also helps when you come back to your code several months later to try to figure out what's going on without spending precious time staring at the code. A well-written comment can save you time and speed you along to the fun part—writing code.

Some of the most important comments that you create are in your class header file. Here you can provide a succinct comment on what each method does in a way that is more efficient than looking at the return value and method signature to figure it out.

Comments in Objective-C come in two forms. The single line comment, as you have already seen, looks like this:

```
// This is a single line comment
```

When the compiler sees the two forward slashes indicating a comment, it ignores all other characters on that line. You can also create a comment on the same line as an Objective-C statement. For example:

```
return YES; // We are on an iPad
```

You can also create multi-line comments by placing "/*" at the beginning of the comment line and "*/" after the last comment line. For example:

```
/*      Here is a multi-line comment
        Here is the second line
        And the third line */
```

You can use a multi-line comment to comment out a block of code containing single line comments, but a multi-line comment cannot contain another multi-line comment.

Good Comments and Bad Comments

There are good comments and bad comments. Here's an example of a bad comment:

```
count++;   // increment the count
```

This comment is unnecessary because it's painfully obvious what it does. It probably takes longer to read the comment than to read the code!

Here's an example of a good comment:

```
// iPhone should not be flipped upside down.
// iPad can have any orientation
if ([[UIDevice currentDevice]
        userInterfaceIdiom]
        == UIUserInterfaceIdiomPhone)
{
    return (interfaceOrientation !=
     UIInterfaceOrientationPortraitUpsideDown);
    } else {
        return YES;
}
```

If you are not familiar with this code that checks the orientation of the device, it takes a few minutes to look at the code to figure out what the code does. In contrast, the comment can be read and understood in just a few seconds.

Create comments when you need them; do *not* create comments when you don't need them.

Creating Constants

You learned how to use constants earlier in this book. Now it's time to learn how to create your own constants.

To review, *constants* are similar to variables in that they provide a place in memory where a value can be stored. The difference is that a constant's value cannot be changed once it is assigned—that's what makes it a constant.

Why You Should Use Constants

Constants are useful in situations where you use a specific value repeatedly throughout your App. Rather than hard-coding, or manually entering the same value each time, you can declare a constant with that same value using the constant instead. Doing this makes changing the value much easier if needed in the future.

Constants also make your code more readable. For example, in the following line of code, you readily understand the code is checking if the value is less than or equal to the maximum allowed digits:

```
if (value <= MaxDigits)
```

In the following line of code, what the number **10** represents is not as clear:

```
if (value <= 10)
```

Using constants makes your code more readable and, therefore, cuts down on maintenance time when you revisit the code at a later date. It's a best practice not to have any hard-coded "magic numbers" in your code other than the commonplace numbers one (1) and zero (0). For all other numbers, you should use constants!

Declaring Constants

Here is the simplest way to declare a constant:

```
const int MaxDigits = 10;
```

This statement declares an integer constant named **MaxDigits** whose value is 10. Declaring a constant is similar to declaring an instance variable, except that you add the **const** keyword. In addition, you specify the value of the constant when you declare it.

There are a variety of common naming conventions for constants. Apple recommends using a one- or two-character, uppercase prefix, followed by the name of the constant in Pascal case. For example:

```
const float NSLightGray;
```

Another common naming convention is to use the lowercase letter "k" as a prefix. For example:

```
const float kLightGray;
```

Constant Scope

If you only need a constant in a single class, you can declare the constant in the class implementation file. Typically, constants are declared near the top of the code file where you declare your instance variables.

If you have constants that you want to use throughout your project, you can declare them in a class header (.h) file and implement them in a class implementation (.m) file. For example:

```
// MyClass.h
extern const int MaxDigits;
extern const NSString *FileExtension;

@interface MyClass
```

Notice the use of the **extern** keyword. This tells the compiler that the constant is *declared* in the header file, but *defined* elsewhere (in this case, the implementation file). You can implement these constants in an implementation file like this:

```
// MyClass.m
const int MaxDigits - 10;
const NSString *FileExtension = @".xml";
```

To use these constants from another class, just include the **MyClass.h** header file in that class.

Creating Your Own Enumerations

As you learned earlier in this book, an *enumeration*, or enum, is a group of related constants. Although you have used enumerations, you haven't created your own. In this section you are going to do just that.

Currently, the **Calculator** class that you created in this book performs five operations—add, subtract, multiply, divide, and clear. It's a good idea to create an enumeration that represents all of the available operations. An enumeration helps document the available operations to anyone who uses the **Calculator** class. And, as you will see, it also allows you to create methods that accept an argument specifying the current operation. This **Calculator** class has also been defined for you in a sample code project for use in the next few chapters named **AdvancedObjectiveCDemo**.

Enumeration names are *Pascal cased* (the first character of the word is capitalized, as is the first letter of every word in a compound word). The members of an enumeration are also Pascal cased and typically begin with a prefix that describes what type that they are. For example, earlier in this book you worked with the **UITextBorderStyle** enumeration.

Each member of the enumeration begins with the prefix "UITextBorderStyle":

- UITextBorderStyleBezel

- UITextBorderStyleLine

- UITextBorderStyleNone

- UITextBorderStyleRoundedRect

Including the parent enumeration name in the member names allows each member of the enumeration to be self-documenting.

Follow these steps to declare an enumeration that defines the various operations available in the **Calculator** class:

1. If you have another project open, close it by selecting **File > Close Project** from the Xcode menu.

2. Open the **AdvancedObjectiveCDemo** project by selecting **File > Open...** from the Xcode menu. In the **Open** dialog, navigate to the folder where you have saved this book's sample code. Drill into the **AdvancedObjectiveC** folder by double-clicking it and select the **AdvancedObjectiveC.xcodeproj** file and then click **Open**.

3. Expand the **AdvancedObjectiveCDemo** node in the Project Navigator and then expand the **AdvancedObjectiveCDemo** subnode.

4. In the Project Navigator select the **Calculator.h** header file and add the following enumeration declaration above the **@interface** declaration:

```
#import <Foundation/Foundation.h>

typedef enum {
    OperationAdd,
    OperationSubtract,
    OperationMultiply,
    OperationDivide,
    OperationClear
} Operation;

@interface Calculator : NSObject {
```

This code declares an enumeration named Operation, containing five items: OperationAdd, OperationSubtract, OperationMultiply, OperationDivide, and OperationClear.

If you don't specify otherwise, the underlying value of the first item in an enumeration is 0, the second item is 1, the third is 2, and so on. Usually, the actual value of an enumeration item is not important. Throughout your App, you refer to a member of the enumeration without worrying about its behind-the-scenes value.

Notice the use of the keyword typedef. For a thorough explanation of this keyword, check out the topic Declaring a Structure Using typedef in *Chapter 11: Arrays and Other Collections.*

When you use an enumeration in code, you only reference a single member of the enumeration, not the enumeration itself. So, for example, the following code stores the OperationAdd enumeration member in a local variable:

```
Operation currentOperation = OperationAdd;
```

It's obvious by the name of the enum member that it belongs to the Operation enumeration.

That's it! It's pretty easy to create your own enumerations. You will use this enumeration in *Chapter 16: Advanced Objective-C* under the section Creating "Private" Methods With Class Extensions.

Extending Objective-C Enumerations

Often, the out-of-the-box functionality of Objective-C enumerations is all you need in your Apps. However, there may be times where you want to:

1. Get the string value associated with an enumeration member

2. Get the enumeration member based on a string value

3. Get the number of items in an enumeration

Typically, you need this functionality if you are displaying enumeration values in the user interface. Unfortunately, it's not easy to get this information from a standard Objective-C enumeration. Fortunately, it's not too difficult to roll your own enumeration *wrapper class* that wraps or encapsulates the functionality of an Objective-C enumeration and adds the desired features.

To see an example of such a wrapper class:

1. If it's not already open, in Xcode, open the **AdvancedObjectiveCDemo** project.

2. **DeviceFamilyEnum** is the enumeration wrapper class. Select the **DeviceFamilyEnum.h** header file in the Project Navigator. This class wraps the enum that lists Apple device families found at the top of the header file:

```
typedef enum {
    DeviceFamilyiPhone,
    DeviceFamilyiPod,
    DeviceFamilyiPad,
    DeviceFamilyAppleTV
} DeviceFamily;
```

This is a standard Objective-C enumeration.

3. Directly below the enumeration is the definition of the strings associated with each enumeration member:

```
#define DeviceFamilyStrings \
NSLocalizedString(@"iPhone", @""),  \
NSLocalizedString(@"iPod", @""), \
NSLocalizedString(@"iPad", @""), \
NSLocalizedString(@"AppleTV", @""), nil
```

I prefer to put the string definitions directly below the enumeration declaration so that if I need to add an enumeration member at a later date, I'll have a visual reminder to add an associated string.

4. Next in the header file is the declaration of the **DeviceFamilyEnum** wrapper class:

```
@interface DeviceFamilyEnum : NSObject

// Returns the string for the specified enum member
+(NSString *) enumToString:(DeviceFamily)enumVal;

// Returns an enum member for the specified string
+(DeviceFamily) stringToEnum:(NSString *)strVal;
```

```
// Returns the number of members in the enumeration
+(NSUInteger) count;

@end
```

This interface declares three class methods (indicated by the plus (+) sign). As shown in the comments, these methods allow you to:

- Get the string for an enum member

- Get the enum member for a specified string

- Get the number of members in the enumeration

5. Now let's take a look at the method implementations. Go to the Project Navigator and select the **DeviceFamilyEnum.m** implementation file. You will see the **initialize** and **count** methods:

```
@implementation DeviceFamilyEnum

NSArray *enumArray;

+ (void)initialize
{
    enumArray = [[NSArray alloc]
       initWithObjects:DeviceFamilyStrings];
}

+ (NSUInteger)count {
    return enumArray.count;
}
```

In the **initialize** class method, the **enumArray** instance variable is initialized with the **DeviceFamilyStrings** declared in the header file. The **count** method simply returns the number of items in the **enumArray**.

Further down, the **enumToString:** method simply returns the string from the **enumArray** that matches the index of the specified enum member:

```
+ (NSString *) enumToString:
    (DeviceFamily)enumValue
{
    return [enumArray objectAtIndex:enumValue];
```

```
}
```

Finally, the **stringToEnum:** method returns the enum member that matches the specified string. If there is no matching string in the **enumArray**, an exception is raised indicating an "Unexpected DeviceFamily string was specified:

```
+ (DeviceFamily) stringToEnum:(NSString *)stringValue
{
    NSUInteger index =
      [enumArray indexOfObject:stringValue];
    if (index == NSNotFound) {
       [NSException raise:NSGenericException
        format:
        @"Unexpected DeviceFamily string"];
    }
    return (DeviceFamily)index;
}
```

As you come across situations where you need additional functionality from your enums, you can use this class as a model to create your own enum wrapper classes.

Summary

Here are the key points in this chapter.

Comments

- You can create single-line comments by using two forward slashes:

```
// This is a single line comment
```

- You can create multi-line comments by placing "/*" at the beginning of the comment line and "*/" after the last comment line. For example:

```
/*  Here is a multi-line comment
    Here is the second line
    And the third line */
```

Constants

- Constants are similar to variables in that they provide a place in memory where a value can be stored. The difference is that a constant's value cannot be changed once it is assigned.

- Here is a simple constant declaration. It begins with the keyword **const**, and then declares the type and name of the constant as well as a value:

```
const int MaxDigits = 10;
```

- Constants are useful in situations where you use a specific value repeatedly throughout your App. Rather than hard-coding, or manually entering the same value each time, you can declare a constant with that same value and use the constant instead.

- If a constant is used in just one class, you can declare it at the top of the class implementation file.

- If you need to use a constant in multiple classes, you can declare it in a class header file:

```
// MyClass.h
extern const int MaxDigits;
```

and then implement the constant in an implementation file:

```
// MyClass.m
const int MaxDigits = 10;
```

Enumerations

- An *enumeration*, or enum, is a group of related constants.

- Here is an example of an enumeration definition:

```
typedef enum {
    OperationAdd,
    OperationSubtract,
    OperationMultiply,
    OperationDivide,
    OperationClear
```

```
} Operation;
```

The enumeration is named **Operation** and has five members.

- Enumeration names and members are Pascal cased.

Exercise 15.1

In this exercise, you will create a custom enumeration in the
AdvancedObjectiveCDemo project.

1. In the **ScientificCalculator** class, create a new **ScientificOperation**
   enum that lists all the scientific operations the **ScientificCalculator**
   class performs.

Solution Movie 15.1

To see a video providing the solution for this exercise, go to the following link
in your web browser.

http://www.iOSAppsForNonProgrammers.com/B2M151.html

Chapter 16: Advanced Objective-C

This chapter contains a number of topics that help you understand some of the more advanced features of Objective-C by showing them to you in the context of real-world iOS App development. Understanding these topics is critical in taking full advantage of the Objective-C language and producing world-class iOS Apps.

Sections in This Chapter

9. *Understanding Protocols and Delegates*

10. *Declaring Your Own Protocols*

11. *Understanding Inheritance*

12. *Extending Classes With Categories*

13. *Creating "Private" Methods with Class Extensions*

14. *Key-Value Coding*

15. *Creating Initializers for Your Custom Classes*

16. *Polymorphism*

17. *Converting Objective-C Data Types*

18. *Summary*

Understanding Protocols and Delegates

Objective-C has an advanced feature known as ***protocols***. Because it is used in many places throughout the Cocoa Touch Framework, it's important for you to get a good grasp of the subject (for those of you with programming experience, protocols are equivalent to interfaces in languages such as Java and C#).

Outside the realm of software, the word protocol is defined as:

> *The established code of behavior in any group, organization, or situation.*

This definition isn't far off the mark when it comes to protocols in Objective-C. As you will see, they also define a standard set of behavior.

One of the first uses of protocols that you encounter in Cocoa Touch Framework documentation is in conjunction with user-interface controls. In fact, you have already used a few protocols without knowing it. The **CollectionsDemo**, **ConditionalStatements**, and **StringsDemo** projects all used a picker view control, which requires the use of protocols. All the picker views that you have seen so far contained just one component, or column. However, as you dive a little deeper into using picker views, you should know that they can have multiple components, as shown in Figure 16.1.

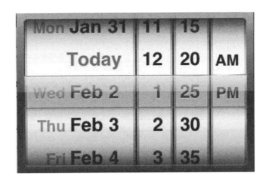

Figure 16.1 A multi-component picker view

The **UIPickerView** control works in conjunction with a *data source* and a *delegate* object to fill its rows and respond to user selection. In fact, the **UIPickerView** class has both a **dataSource** and a **delegate** property that you can use to specify these objects (Figure 16.2).

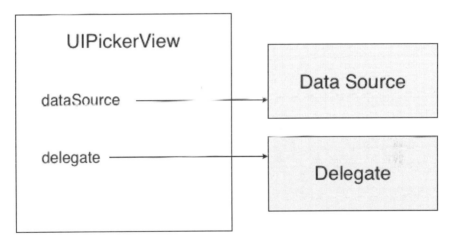

*Figure 16.2 **UIPickerView** uses a data source and delegate.*

The *data source* object tells the picker view how many components, or columns, are in the picker and how many rows are in each component.

The *delegate* provides help constructing each row in the picker view and can also respond to the user's selecting an item. In object-oriented programming, a delegate is an object that performs a task for another object—which is definitely true in this case.

The beauty of the design in Figure 16.2 is that any object can act as the data source or the delegate. You just store a reference to the objects that you want to use in the picker view's **dataSource** and **delegate** properties, and at different points in time, the picker view calls specific methods on the data source and delegate objects. You can even have the same object act as both the data source and the delegate (this is actually a common practice, as you shall see in just a bit).

So, what methods does the picker view call on each of these objects? How can you guarantee that the objects specified in the **dataSource** and **delegate** properties have the methods that the picker view needs? The answer is *protocols*.

The **UIPickerViewDataSource** protocol declares methods required by an object that wants to act as a data source for the picker view. In turn, the **UIPickerViewDelegate** protocol declares methods required by an object that wants to act as a delegate for the picker view. Let's take a closer look at each of these protocols.

UIPickerViewDataSource Protocol

The **UIPickerViewDataSource** protocol declares these methods:

Method	Description
numberOfComponentsInPickerView:	Called by the picker view when it needs the number of components
pickerView:numberOfRowsInComponent	Called by the picker view when it needs the number of rows for a specific component

Both methods in this protocol are required. So, any object that wants to act as a data source for a picker view *must* implement these two methods.

UIPickerViewDelegate Protocol

The **UIPickerViewDelegate** protocol declares these methods:

Method	Description
pickerView:didSelectRow:InComponent:	Called by the picker view when the user selects a row in a component
pickerView:titleForRow:forComponent:	Called by the picker view when it needs the title (the text displayed in the picker) for a given row in a given component
pickerView:viewForRow:forComponent:reusingView:	Called by the picker view when it needs to know which view to use for a given row in a given component
pickerView:rowHeightForComponent:	Called by the picker view

	when it needs the row height to use for drawing row content
	Called by the picker view when it needs the row width to use for drawing row content
pickerView:widthForComponent:	

None of the methods in the **UIPickerViewDelegate** protocol are marked "required," but your picker view won't work very well without implementing the two most commonly used methods:

- pickerView:titleForRow:forComponent: and

- pickerView:didSelectRow:inComponent:.

The **pickerView:titleForRow:forComponent:**, returns a title for the specified row and component. The second method, **pickerView:didSelectRow:inComponent:**, provides a place where you can put code to respond to a user selecting an item from the picker view.

Adopting Protocols

A class *adopts* a protocol to indicate that it implements all of the required methods and often some of the optional methods too. Rather than have a separate object act as the data source and delegate, Figure 16.3 shows a common iOS convention whereby a view controller adopts both protocols for the picker view.

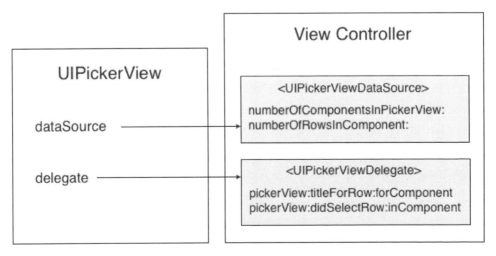

Figure 16.3 A view controller often implements UI control protocols.

A class declares that it adopts specific protocols in its header file. For example, in the following code, the **ViewController** class adopts the **UIPickerViewDataSource** and **UIPickerViewDelegate** protocols:

```
@interface ViewController : UIViewController
 <UIPickerViewDataSource, UIPickerViewDelegate>
```

The protocols adopted by a class are listed after the superclass declaration between angled brackets and are separated by commas.

Protocols Step by Step

To help you fully understand the use of protocols in this context, you are going to write code from scratch that fills a picker view and responds to a selection of an item in the picker view.

1. Open the **ProtocolDemo** project by selecting **File > Open...** from the Xcode menu. In the Open dialog, navigate to the folder where you have stored this book's sample code. Drill into the **ProtocolDemo** folder, select the **ProtocolDemo.xcodeproj** file and then click **Open**.

2. In the Project Navigator, drill into the **ProtocolDemo** node and select the **MainStoryboard.storyboard** file. You should see the view displayed in Figure 16.4.

*Figure 16.4 The **ProtocolDemo** main storyboard*

Currently, there is no code in the **ViewController** class associated with the picker view although there are properties that you can use to reference the picker view and label. There is also a **fifaWinners** array containing the last four FIFA World Cup winners, which you will use to fill the picker view.

3. Your next step is to create a data source and delegate for the picker view. As mentioned previously, it's common to make the associated view controller both the data source and delegate. This means that it needs to adopt both the **UIPickerViewDataSource** and **UIPickerViewDelegate** protocols.

   To do this, select the **ViewController.h** header file in the Project Navigator and change the interface declaration to the following:

   ```
   @interface ViewController : UIViewController
   <UIPickerViewDataSource,UIPickerViewDelegate>
   ```

4. Now you need to implement the methods of the protocols. To do this, select the **ViewController.m** file in the Project Navigator. Notice the warning icon next to the **@implementation ViewController**

declaration. If you click on the warning symbol it tells you "Method in protocol not implemented (Figure 16.5) (depending on the version of the compiler you are using, the warnings will be slightly different).

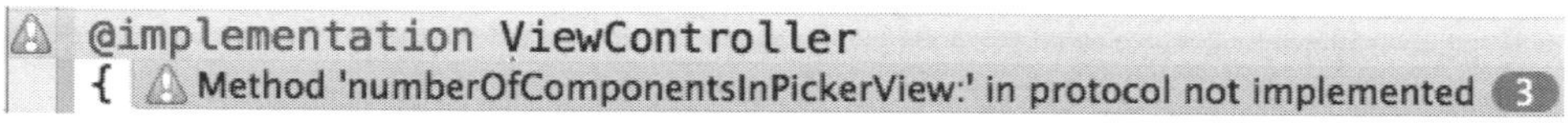

Figure 16.5 "Protocol not implemented" warning

The number **3** on the far right indicates that there are three warnings. If you click the **3**, it shows the warnings listed in (Figure 16.6).

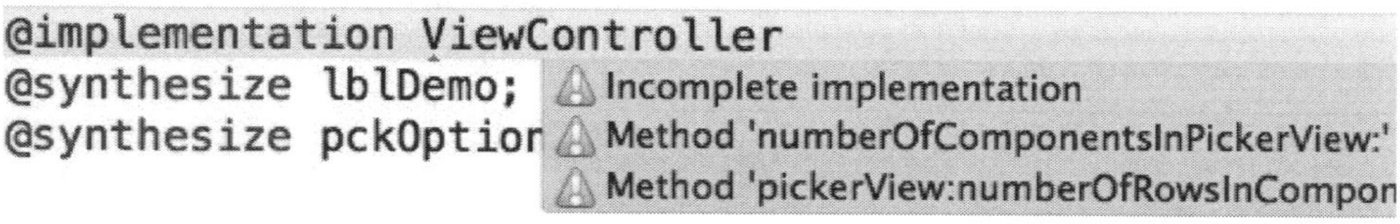

Figure 16.6 Incomplete implementation warning detail

This is exactly right. You have declared in the class header file that the **ViewController** class implements the picker view protocols, but you have not added the method implementations yet. Newer versions of the compiler show the names of methods that need to be implemented as in Figure 16.6.

5. Let's get rid of these warnings by implementing the methods of the **UIPickerViewDataSource** protocol first. At the top of the **ViewController.m** implementation file, directly below the declaration of the **fifaWinners** array, add the following methods:

```
NSArray *fifaWinners;
```

```
-(NSInteger)numberOfComponentsInPickerView:
    (UIPickerView *)pickerView
{
    return 1;
}
```

```
- (NSInteger)pickerView:
    (UIPickerView *)pickerView
    numberOfRowsInComponent:
    (NSInteger)component
{
    return fifaWinners.count;
}
```

As soon as you do this, the warnings automatically go away.

If you look at the code that you just entered, the **numberOfComponentsInPickerView:pickerView:** method returns **1** because you only want one column, or component, in the picker view.

The **pickerView:numberOfRowsInComponent:** method returns the count of items in the **fifaWinners** array. Since there is only one component in the picker view, the component parameter is ignored.

6. Now let's implement the **UIPickerViewDelegate** protocol. In **ViewController.m**, directly below the methods that you just added, add these two new methods:

```
- (NSString *)pickerView:
    (UIPickerView *)pickerView
    titleForRow:(NSInteger)row
    forComponent:(NSInteger)component
{
    return [fifaWinners objectAtIndex:row];
}

- (void)pickerView:
    (UIPickerView *)pickerView
    didSelectRow:(NSInteger)row
    inComponent:(NSInteger)component
{
    self.lblDemo.text =
    [fifaWinners objectAtIndex:row];
}
```

The **pickerView:titleForRow:forComponent:** method returns the item from the **fifaWinners** array for the currently selected picker view row.

The **pickerView:didSelectRow:inComponent:** method automatically executes when a user selects an item from the picker view. It gets the text of the currently selected picker view row from the **fifaWinners** array and stores it into the **text** property of the label at the top of the view.

Now that you have implemented methods for both protocols, press the **Run** button to run the App in the Simulator. Oddly enough, the picker view is not visible (Figure 16.7)!

Figure 16.7 The picker view is not visible!

What's going on? Although you have implemented the protocols on the view controller, you haven't told the picker view which objects to use as data source and delegate. To do this, you have to set the picker view's **dataSource** and **delegate** properties.

I intentionally had you "forget" to set these properties because you will often forget to do this in your day-to-day App development. Now you can see what a picker view looks like at run time when its **dataSource** and **delegate** properties are not set—it doesn't appear at all!

7. First, let's look at the **dataSource** and **delegate** properties in Xcode. To do this, go back to Xcode and click the **Stop** button. Next, select the **MainStoryboard.storyboard** file in the Project Navigator to open it up in the design surface. Then, select the picker view by clicking on it.

   You can view the **dataSource** and **delegate** properties in Xcode's Connections Inspector, located in the Utilities panel on the right side of the Xcode window. If Xcode's Utilities panel is not visible, click the far-right button in the **View** button group at the top of the Xcode window (the Utilities panel is visible if this button is depressed as shown in Figure

16.8).

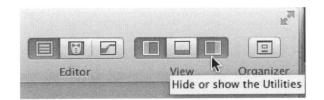

Figure 16.8 You can hide or show the Utilities panel.

In the Utilities panel, view the Connections Inspector by selecting the button on the far right (Figure 16.9).

Figure 16.9 Displaying the Connections Inspector

The picker view's **dataSource** and **delegate** properties are at the top of the Inspector (Figure 16.10).

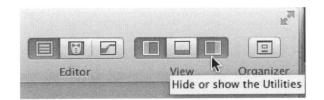

*Figure 16.10 The **dataSource** and **delegate** properties*

Notice the circles to the right of the properties. These are called *connection wells*. When they are empty, it indicates that the properties are not connected to anything. Let's change that.

8. Go to the storyboard file, hold the **Control** key down, and click the picker view. While still holding the **Control** key, drag down to the **View Controller** icon in the scene dock (Figure 16.11).

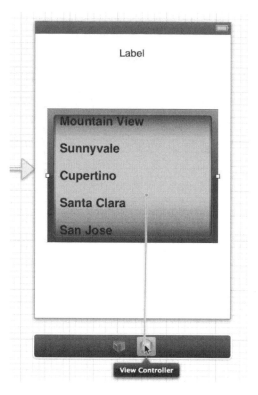

*Figure 16.11 **Control+Drag** to the view controller icon.*

When you see the View Controller popup appear, let go of the mouse button and **Control** key and you will see the **Outlets** popup shown in Figure 16.12.

*Figure 16.12 The **Outlets** popup*

Notice the **dataSource** and **delegate** outlets. First, select the **dataSource** outlet by clicking on it (you will see the small View Controller icon flash, indicating the connection has been made).

9. Next, **Control+Drag** again between the picker view and the **View Controller** icon. Notice the small white dot to the left of the **dataSource** outlet, indicating that it has already been selected. This time, select the **delegate** outlet (Figure 16.13).

*Figure 16.13 Select the **delegate** outlet.*

Now look at the Connections Inspector and you can see both the **dataSource** and **delegate** outlets are shown as connected to the View Controller, and the connection wells are no longer empty (Figure 16.14).

Figure 16.14 The outlets are connected.

10. Click Xcode's **Run** button. When the App appears in the Simulator, you can see that the picker view contains a list of winning FIFA teams (Figure 16.15).

Figure 16.15 The picker view is populated!

11. Select an item from the list. When you do, the

263

pickerView:didSelectRow:inComponent: method is automatically called and the selected item is displayed in the label's **text** property (Figure 16.16).

Figure 16.16 The selected item is displayed in the label.

The pattern of using protocols in conjunction with the picker view is a common approach that you will use many times with different user-interface controls in iOS.

Declaring Your Own Protocols

At times you may need to declare your own protocols that you want other classes to implement. It's very easy to do. Here is the syntax for declaring a protocol:

```
@protocol ProtocolName
     // Method declarations
@end
```

For example, you could declare a protocol for retrieving and setting App settings:

```
@protocol AppSetting

-(NSString *)getSettingForKey:(NSString *)key;
-(void)setSetting:(NSString *) forKey:
      (NSString *)key;

@end
```

Multiple classes can implement this protocol, but provide completely different implementations for the methods. For example, one class that implements the protocol could read and write settings to a local file on the iOS device, and another class could read and write settings to a database on the device.

By default, methods declared in a protocol are required—meaning any class adopting the protocol must implement that method. You can indicate that a particular method is optional by using the **@optional** keyword. If you want to be explicit, there is also a **@required** keyword you can use to indicate specific methods are required. For example:

```
@protocol AppSetting

@required
-(NSString *)getSettingForKey:(NSString *)kcy;
-(void)setSetting:(NSString *) forKey:(NSString *)key;

@optional
-(void)deleteSettingForKey:(NSString *)key;

@end
```

In this code sample, the **getSettingForKey:** and **setSetting:ForKey:** methods are required, and the **deleteSettingForKey:** method is optional.

You can either declare a protocol in its own class header file, or you can declare a protocol in the header file of a class that uses the protocol to define functionality for a delegate. For example, the **UIPickerView** class has an associated **UIPickerViewDelegate** protocol it uses to define the methods it needs implemented. In this case, it makes sense to declare the protocol in the header file of the **UIPickerView** class.

Understanding Inheritance

You learned the basics of Objective-C *inheritance* earlier in this book, but now you are going to dive in a bit deeper, and see live examples of inheritance at work.

As a refresher, inheritance allows you to create new classes that are based on other classes. For example, Figure 16.17 shows a **ScientificCalculator** class subclassed from a **Calculator** class.

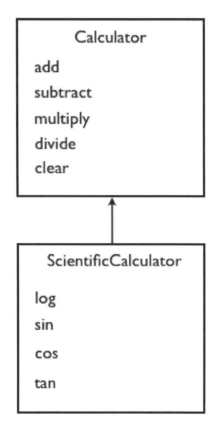

Figure 16.17 ***ScientificCalculator*** *is a subclass of the* ***Calculator*** *class.*

The beauty of inheritance is that you don't have to create every class from scratch. You can create a subclass from an existing class, inherit all of its properties, methods and protected instance variables, and extend it to suit your needs. In this example, the **ScientificCalculator** inherits all the functionality of its **Calculator** superclass, including **add**, **subtract**, **multiply**, **divide**, and **clear** methods. You don't have to rewrite these methods for the **ScientificCalculator** class. They are simply inherited. You can then add methods in the **ScientificCalculator** class—such as **log**, **sin**,

cos, and **tan**—that extend its functionality and specialize it.

Overriding Methods

At times, you may need to ***override*** a method inherited from a superclass. As you learned when working with the **dealloc** method earlier (*Chapter 10: Object Lifetime and Memory Management* under the section Overriding the dealloc Method), you can override a method inherited from a superclass by creating a method with the same signature in the subclass. Overriding a method allows you to:

- *Extend* the superclass method by doing something additional in the subclass and

- *Override* the superclass method by doing something completely different in the subclass.

To see an example of how overriding works, you are going to look at the **AdvancedObjectiveCDemo** project where the **ScientificCalculator** class is subclassed from the **Calculator** class.

1. Open the **AdvancedObjectiveCDemo** project.

2. In the Project Navigator, drill down into the **AdvancedObjectiveCDemo** node to see the Calculator and **ScientificCalculator** classes (Figure 16.18).

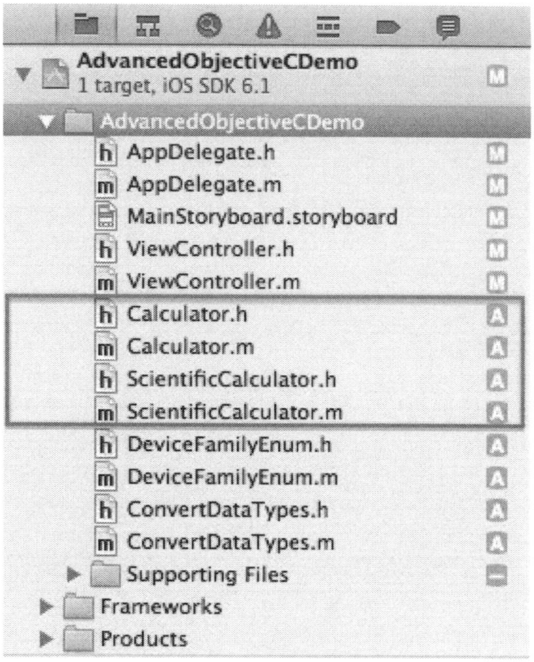

Figure 16.18 **Calculator** *and* **ScientificCalculator** *classes*

3. Select the **Calculator.m** implementation file in the Project Navigator and check out the **clear** method:

```
- (void) clear
{
    self.total = 0.00;
}
```

4. Select the **ScientificCalculator.h** header file in order to see that it is a subclass of the **Calculator** class:

```
@interface ScientificCalculator : Calculator
```

5. Select the **ScientificCalculator.m** file in the Project Navigator. Notice that there is also a **clear** method which is inherited from the **Calculator** class:

```
- (void)clear
{
    [super clear];
    self.memory = 0.00;
}
```

This method *overrides* the **clear** method in the **Calculator** superclass.

Remember, you override an inherited method by adding a method with the same signature in the subclass, as you see here.

In the first line of code is a call to **[super clear]**, which calls the **clear** method in the **Calculator** superclass. This is very common. When overriding a method, you often make a call to the superclass method in addition to the custom code that you have added. Doing this allows you to extend the existing functionality of the method—extending it because you are still running the method in the superclass, and you are doing something extra in the subclass.

When the method is executed in the subclass:

- First, a call is made to the **Calculator** *superclass* **clear** method which clears the **total** property, and then

- Execution continues in the **ScientificCalculator** subclass **clear** method and the **memory** property is cleared.

To see this at run time:

1. Select the **ViewController.m** implementation file in the Project Navigator, and then add the following **import** statement at the top of the file:

```
#import "ViewController.h"
#import "ConvertDataTypes.h"
#import "ScientificCalculator.h"
```

2. Next, add the following code to the bottom of the **viewDidLoad** method:

```
- (void)viewDidLoad
{
    [super viewDidLoad];

    ScientificCalculator *sc =
        [[ScientificCalculator alloc] init];
    [sc clear];
}
```

An instance of the **ScientificCalculator** class is created and passed a **clear** message in this code.

3. Next, set a breakpoint on the second line of code by clicking in the gutter to the left (Figure 16.19).

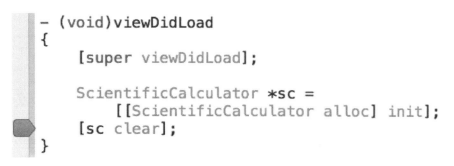

*Figure 16.19 Set a breakpoint on the **clear** message call.*

4. Click the **Run** button to run the App in the Simulator and you will hit the breakpoint (Figure 16.20).

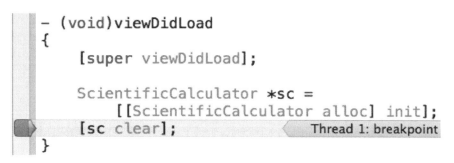

Figure 16.20 The breakpoint is hit.

5. Click the **Step into** button in the Debug area to execute this line of code. This takes you into the **ScientificCalculator clear** method (Figure 16.21).

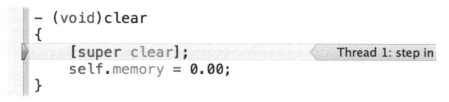

*Figure 16.21 Inside the **clear** method*

6. Click the **Step into** button again to run the code that makes a call to **[super clear]**. Notice that doing so takes you to the **clear** method of the **Calculator** superclass (Figure 16.22).

```objc
- (void) clear
{
    self.total = 0.00;          Thread 1: step in
}
```

*Figure 16.22 You are in the **Calculator clear** method.*

So, the call to **superclass** works as advertised!

7. Click the **Step out** button in the Debug area to get out of the superclass method. Notice that doing so takes you back to the **clear** method of the **ScientificCalculator** subclass (Figure 16.23).

```
- (void)clear
{
    [super clear];
    self.memory = 0.00;              Thread 1: step out
}
```

*Figure 16.23 Back to **ScientificCalculator**'s **clear** method*

8. At this point you can click the **Step out** button, which takes you back to the code in the **ViewController** (Figure 16.24).

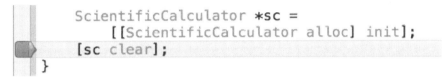
```
    ScientificCalculator *sc =
        [[ScientificCalculator alloc] init];
    [sc clear];
}
```

Figure 16.24 Back to the View Controller

9. Click **Stop** in Xcode to end execution of the App.

A few additional notes on overriding—when you override a method, you can choose to add custom code *before* the call to **super**, or *after* the call to **super** (or both). For example:

```
- (void) clear
{
    // Custom subclass code
    [super clear];
    // More custom subclass code
}
```

Also, if you eliminate the call to the superclass method, you *completely* override the code in the superclass because that code never executes. It's more common to *extend* a method by including the call to **super**.

Extending Classes With Categories

Objective-C provides another powerful tool for extending classes—*categories*. A **category** allows you to extend a class without creating a subclass. You can even extend the Cocoa Touch Framework classes!

It's better to create a category to extend a Cocoa Touch Framework class than to create a subclass. For example, if you add functionality directly to the **NSString** class by using a category, you can still use **NSString** throughout your App. You don't have to remember to use a custom subclass in some places and **NSString** in others.

Creating a Custom Category Step by Step

To see how this works, let's add a new method to the **NSString** class. By default, **NSString** does *not* have a method that tells you the number of times a specific string occurs in another string. For example, you may want to know how many commas are in a string.

Since **NSString** doesn't have this method, you can add it by using a category. Let's create a category called **Occurs**, which has one method named **occurrencesOfString**:

1. Open the **AdvancedObjectiveCDemo** project.

2. In the Project Navigator, right-click the **AdvancedObjectiveCDemo** subfolder and select **New File...** from the shortcut menu

3. In the New File dialog, make sure **Cocoa Touch** is selected in the left panel, select the **Objective-C category** template, and then click the **Next** button (Figure 16.25).

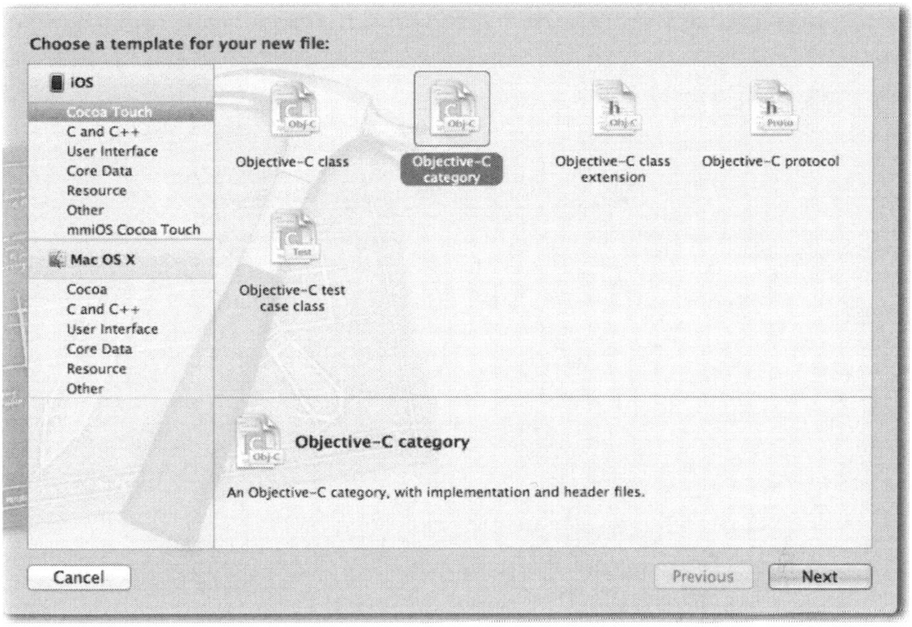

Figure 16.25 Creating a new category

4. In the next step of the New File dialog, enter **Occurs** in the **Category** box and enter **NSString** in the **Category On** box (Figure 16.26). This specifies the name of the category and the class that you are extending. Afterwards, click the **Next** button.

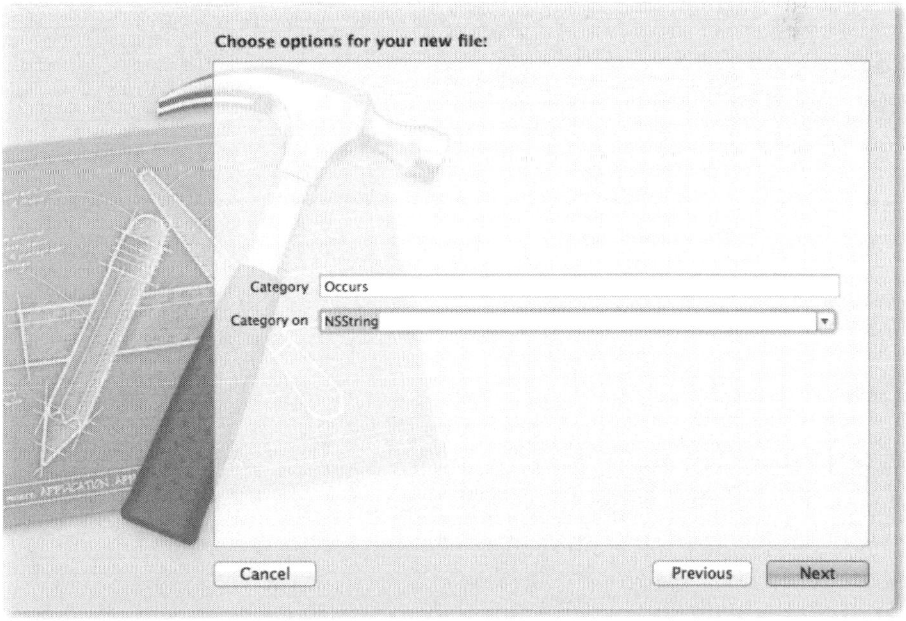

Figure 16.26 Name the category and the class that you are extending.

5. In the File Save dialog, click the **Create** button to save the new category in the root folder of the project. You should see two new files in the Project Navigator (Figure 16.27).

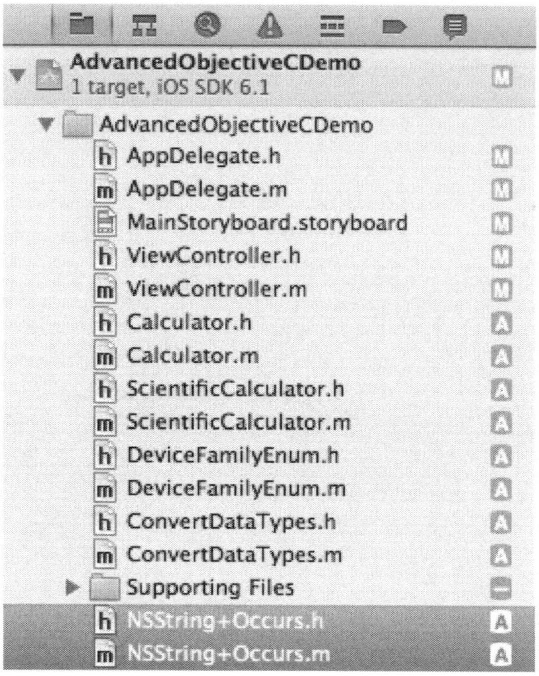

Figure 16.27 Two new category files

Notice the name of the files that Xcode generated. It took the name of the class that you are extending (**NSString**), inserted a plus sign (+), and then added the name of the category (**Occurs**). This is a standard naming convention for Objective-C categories.

6. In the Project Navigator, select the **NSString+Occurs.h** header file and check out the category interface declaration:

```
@interface NSString (Occurs)


@end
```

As you can see, this looks a lot like a regular class interface declaration except the name of the category is listed in parentheses after the class name and there is no superclass listed.

7. Add the following method declaration to the **NSStrings+Occurs.h** header file. This is the new method that you are adding to the **NSString**

class. As you can see, it returns an unsigned integer, its name is **occurrencesOfString**, and it accepts a string argument (the string that you are searching for):

```
@interface NSString (Occurs)

// Returns the number of occurrences
// of a string within the receiver
- (NSUInteger) occurrencesOfString:
      (NSString *)aString;

@end
```

8. Now select the **NSStrings+Occurs.m** implementation file in the Project Navigator. Notice that it looks very much like a regular class implementation file, except the category name (**Occurs**) is listed after the name of the class that you are extending (**NSString**):

```
@implementation NSString (Occurs)

@end
```

9. If you don't want to type a lot of code, just add the following code to implement the new method. This hard-codes the value to **3**, but it saves some typing:

```
@implementation NSString (Occurs)

- (NSUInteger) occurrencesOfString:
    (NSString *)aString
{
    return 3;
}

@end
```

If you don't mind typing and want to see the method work for real, add the following code to implement the new **occurrencesOfString** method:

```
@implementation NSString (Occurs)

- (NSUInteger) occurrencesOfString:
      (NSString *)aString
{
    NSUInteger occurrences = 0;
```

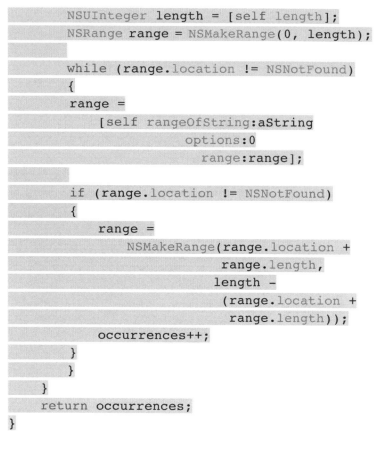

```
        if (aString != nil) {

            NSUInteger length = [self length];
            NSRange range = NSMakeRange(0, length);

            while (range.location != NSNotFound)
            {
            range =
                [self rangeOfString:aString
                            options:0
                              range:range];

            if (range.location != NSNotFound)
            {
                range =
                    NSMakeRange(range.location +
                                range.length,
                                length -
                                (range.location +
                                range.length));
                occurrences++;
            }
            }
        }
        return occurrences;
}
```

@end

This method contains a **while** loop that cycles through the string searching for occurrences of the specified string. Notice the references to **self**. Because you are adding this method to the **NSString** class, you reference the string object by means of the **self** keyword. Notice that there is also a check for a null string at the top of the method. It's best to bulletproof your code and check to make sure a value was actually passed to your method!

Using Your Custom Category

Now that you have created a custom category, let's see how it works by using it in a project.

1. In the Project Navigator, select the **ViewController.m** file. At the bottom of the **viewDidLoad** method, add the following line of code:

```
NSString *myString = @"iPod, iPhone, iPad";
```

This creates a new string that you are going to check for occurrences of the letter **i**.

2. Directly below this line of code, add the following partial line of code:

```
NSUInteger occurrences = [myString o
```

Notice that, as soon as you type the letter "o", the Code Completion pops up, but the new **occurrencesOfString:** method is not in the list. Why not? Because you need to import the header file for the new category in order to use it.

3. Delete this partial line of code before continuing.

4. Although you *could* just import the header file at the top of the **ViewController.m** implementation file, there is a better approach.

In *Chapter 7: Referencing Classes*, you learned that prefix header files can be used to add import statements to all source code files in your project. This is a great choice for categories because you only have to import the category once in your project, rather than adding an import statement to each source code file individually.

So, in the Project Navigator, expand the **Supporting Files** folder, select the **AdvancedObjectiveCDcmo -Prefix.pch** file, and add the following import statement:

```
#ifdef __OBJC__
    #import <UIKit/UIKit.h>
    #import <Foundation/Foundation.h>
    #import "NSString+Occurs.h"
#endif
```

5. Before continuing, build your project by pressing **Command+B**. This makes Xcode aware of the change that you just made in the prefix header file.

6. Now go back to the **ViewController.m** file and enter the following lines of code at the bottom of the **viewDidLoad** method. As you type, notice that Xcode's Code Completion is now aware of the new method that you added to **NSString**:

```
NSString *myString = @"iPod, iPhone, iPad";
```

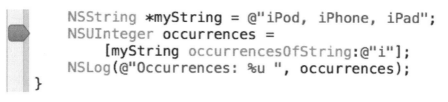

Testing Your Custom Category

Now it's time to test your custom category at run time.

1. Clear the first breakpoint that you created in the previous section by clicking on it once, and then add a new breakpoint on the line of code that calls the new **occurrencesOfString:** method (Figure 16.28).

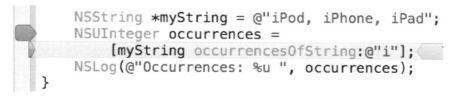

Figure 16.28 Add a new breakpoint.

2. Press the **Run** button, and you should hit your breakpoint (Figure 16.29).

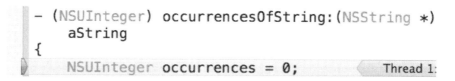

Figure 16.29 The breakpoint is hit at run time.

3. Press the **Step into** button in the Debug area, and you can see the new method that you added to the **NSString** class being run (Figure 16.30).

```
- (NSUInteger) occurrencesOfString:(NSString *)
    aString
{
    NSUInteger occurrences = 0;                    Thread 1:
```

Figure 16.30 Step into the category method.

4. Press the **Step out** button to return to the **viewDidLoad** method, and then press **Step over** twice to run the statement that logs the return value to the Console.

    If the Console is not visible, select **View > Debug > Activate Console** from the Xcode menu. You should see that three occurrences of the letter **i** were found (Figure 16.31).

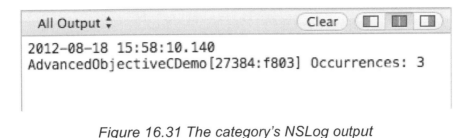

Figure 16.31 The category's NSLog output

That's it—you have officially felt the power that comes from extending one of the Cocoa Touch Framework classes!

Just a few more things to note about categories:

- You can add more than one method to a class in a single category.

- It's a best practice to add related methods to a single category.

- There is no limit to the number of categories that you can add to a class.

- You can't add new instance variables to a class, but a category can access all instance variables declared in the class that it is extending.

- Methods that you add to a class by using a category are inherited by subclasses—making categories an extremely powerful feature!

Creating "Private" Methods With Class Extensions

So far, all the methods that you have created have been public. This means that anyone who creates an instance of a class can access these methods. In many cases, that's what you want.

However, it's a best practice to only expose methods publicly that are useful to someone using your class. Rather than cluttering the public interface of a class with methods that are for internal use, these methods should be hidden from the public interface.

Fortunately, in Objective-C there is a way to hide the method by using a ***class extension***. Class extensions are similar to categories except:

- They are usually found in the implementation (.m) file *of the class that they are extending*.

- There is no name listed between the parentheses.

- They allow you to declare *required* methods.

Ultimately, methods declared in this way are not truly private—they are simply hidden (thus the quotation marks around the word "private" in this section's title). If someone knows a hidden method exists, they can still make a message call to that method, but for all practical purposes, it's private.

A picture is worth a thousand words, so you are going to create a class extension in the **Calculator** class that adds a private method named **setCurrentOperation:** which lets you set the current calculator operation.

1. Open the **AdvancedObjectiveCDemo** project if it's not already open.

2. Select the **Calculator.h** header file in the Project Navigator. If the following enumeration declaration is not at the top of this file, add it (it won't be there if you didn't follow the step-by-step instructions in the *Chapter 15: Constants, Comments and Enumerations* under the section Creating Your Own Enumerations):

```
typedef enum {
    OperationAdd,
    OperationSubtract,
    OperationMultiply,
    OperationDivide,
    OperationClear
} Operation;
@interface Calculator : NSObject {
```

3. Select the **Calculator.m** implementation file in the Project Navigator, and add the following code. Make sure that you place these two sections of code *exactly* where they are shown here:

```
#import "Calculator.h"

// Class extension
@interface Calculator()

// Sets the current operation
-(void)setCurrentOperation:(Operation)operation;

@end
```

```
@implementation Calculator

@synthesize total = _total;

Operation currentOperation;

-(void)setCurrentOperation:(Operation)operation
{
    currentOperation = operation;
}
```

The first block of highlighted code at the top of the file is a class extension. It looks a lot like a category, except there is no name between the parentheses. This class extension declares a private method named **setCurrentOperation:** that returns **void** and accepts a single **Operation** argument. Normally, an **@interface** declaration is found in the *public* header (.h) file, but in this case, because you are declaring a private method, you put it in the *private* implementation (.m) file.

The second set of highlighted code declares a **currentOperation** instance variable to store the current operator. It also implements the **setCurrentOperation:** method.

You may have noticed that, when you added the class extension, the warning in Figure 16.32 appeared.

```
@interface Calculator()

// Sets the current operation
-(void)setCurrentOperation:(Operation)operation;

@end

⚠ @implementation Calculator   ⚠ Incomplete implementation
```

Figure 16.32 The "Incomplete Implementation" warning

This happened because, unlike categories, methods declared in a class extension are *required*. Since you had not added the method to the implementation section yet, you received this warning!

4. Now change the other methods in the **Calculator** class to use the new private method. Each method calls the new, private **setCurrentOperation:** method, passing the current operation:

```
- (void) clear
```

```
{
    self.total = 0.00;
    [self setCurrentOperation:OperationClear];
}


- (double) addToTotal:(double)value
{
    self.total += value;
    [self setCurrentOperation:OperationAdd];
    return self.total;
}


- (double) subtractFromTotal:(double)value
{
    self.total -= value;
    [self setCurrentOperation:OperationSubtract];
    return self.total;
}


- (double) multiplyTimesTotal:(double)value
{
    self.total *= value;
    [self setCurrentOperation:OperationMultiply];
    return self.total;
}


- (double) divideIntoTotal:(double)value
{
    self.total /= value;
    [self setCurrentOperation:OperationDivide];
    return self.total;
}
```

5. Now, to prove the new private **setCurrentOperation:** method cannot be accessed outside the class, select the **ViewController.m** implementation file in the Project Navigator, and add the following code to the bottom of the **viewDidLoad** method. This code instantiates the **Calculator** class and tries to call the new, private **setCurrentOperation:** method:

```
Calculator *calc =
    [[Calculator alloc] init];
[calc setCurrentOperation:OperationAdd];
```

6. You should immediately get an error. If you click the error icon, you will see the error description in Figure 16.33.

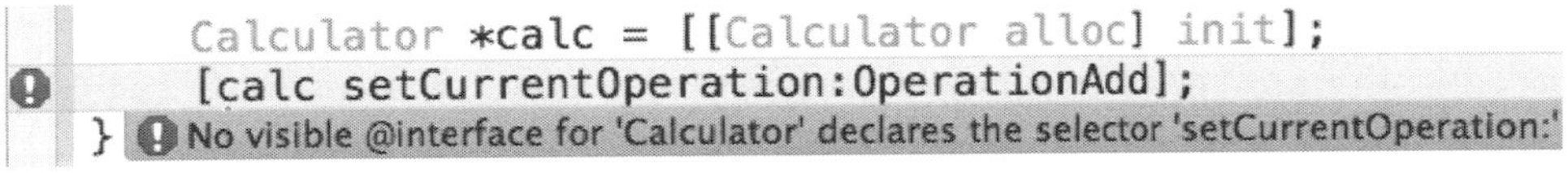

```
Calculator *calc = [[Calculator alloc] init];
[calc setCurrentOperation:OperationAdd];
} ❶ No visible @interface for 'Calculator' declares the selector 'setCurrentOperation:'
```

Figure 16.33 You can't access the private method!

Fortunately, this error is very descriptive. The **setCurrentOperation:** method can't be found in a *visible*, or *public*, **@interface** declaration (although it is in a private **@interface** declaration). This means that the private method declaration worked—you can access **setCurrentOperation:** inside the **Calculator** class, but it's not accessible outside the class by the usual means!

7. Delete the two lines of code you just added so that the project can be built without error.

That's it! So, a public method is declared in the public header (.h) file and a private method is declared in the private implementation (.m) file by using a class extension.

Just a few things more to note about class extensions:

- You can add more than one method to a class in a single class extension.

- You can also declare properties and instance variables in a class extension.

- Methods that you add to a class by using a category are private and are therefore not inherited by subclasses.

- You can use class extensions to redeclare a public, read-only property as **readwrite** (meaning, you can read and write to it).

> **Note:** There is a way to declare a private method without using a class extension. You can simply declare the method in the **@implementation** block of the implementation file without declaring it in the **@interface** of the class. Although you can do this, it's better to be explicit with your coding and declare private methods in a class extension.

Key-Value Coding

Key-value coding (KVC) is an advanced feature of Objective-C that allows you to access an object's properties indirectly by using the string value of the property name rather than directly by using the standard getter and setter methods.

Key-value coding is used by the Cocoa Touch Framework's Core Data to set and retrieve values on the properties of your entity objects. Key-value coding functionality is part of **NSObject**, so all your classes and all Cocoa Touch Framework classes automatically inherit this magic.

Key-value coding is also useful when writing framework-level code—high-level, generic code you can use in multiple Apps. I've spent much of my programming career writing framework-level code—it helps eliminate redundant code and makes your life as an App developer far easier.

Getting a Property Value

Normally, you get a property value either by using dot notation, or by means of the property's getter, like this:

```
// dot notation
firstName = customer.firstName;

// property getter
firstName = [customer firstName];
```

Using key-value coding, you get the property by using the **valueForKey:** method. The *key* is the property name passed as a string:

```
firstName = [customer
      valueForKey:@"firstName"];
```

Setting a Property Value

You usually set a property's value either by using dot notation or by means of the property's setter:

```
// dot notation
customer.firstName = @"Steve";

// property setter
[customer setFirstName:@"Steve"];
```

Using key-value coding, you set the property by using the **setValue:forKey:** method. You pass the value that you want to store in the property and, again, the *key* is the property name passed as a string:

```
[customer setValue:@"Steve"
      forKey:@"firstName"];
```

Working With Scalar Values

Not only does key-value coding work with properties that reference objects, you can also use it with properties that hold **scalar** values—primitive data types that contain only a single value such as Boolean, integer, and double. However, you need to take one extra step when dealing with scalar values.

If you try to set a scalar value by using **setValue:forKey:** like this:

```
[customer setValue:123 forKey:@"customerID"];
```

then you are going to get a compiler error such as:

Implicit conversion of 'int' to 'id' is disallowed with ARC.

To set a scalar value, you need to convert the scalar type to an object. If you are using Xcode 4.4 or later, you can just add an @ sign in front of the value and it will be converted to an object:

```
[customer setValue:@123 forKey:@"customerID"];
```

If you are using an earlier version of Xcode, you can use the **NSNumber** class to make the conversion:

```
[customer setValue:[NSNumber numberWithInt:123]
      forKey:@"customerID"];
```

If you try to *get* a scalar value by using **valueForKey:** like this:

```
int customerID = [customer valueForKey:@"customerID"];
```

then you are going to get a compiler warning such as:

Incompatible pointer to integer conversion initializing 'int' with an expression of type 'id'

because **valueForKey:** returns an **NSNumber** value for scalar properties.

To get a scalar value, you need to store the return value in an **NSNumber** variable like this:

```
NSNumber *customerID =    [customer valueForKey:@"customerID"];
```

For more information on converting scalar types to objects and vice versa, see the Boxing Scalar Data Types topic later in this chapter.

Avoiding Run-Time Errors

When using key-value coding, if you specify a property name that doesn't exist, you do not get a warning or error at compile time when you build your project. That's because the property name is a string that is evaluated at run time. However, at run time, you will get an **NSUnknownKeyException** such as:

> 'NSUnknownKeyException', reason: '[<Customer 0x6c156e0> valueForUndefinedKey:]: this class is not key value coding-compliant for the key firstname.'

So, be careful with the spelling and the case of your strings to make sure that they exactly match the property name!

Creating Initializers for Your Custom Classes

When you create your own custom classes in Objective-C, one of your tasks includes creating an ***initializer***, or **init** method. When a new object is instantiated from your custom class, all its instance variables are initialized to zero (or **nil** if it's a pointer). The only exception is the **isa** variable (all Objective-C classes have an **isa** variable, which is a special pointer that points back to the class that created it).

There are times when a zero or **nil** value may not be a good default value for some variables. It's expected that when the **init** method of your class is called, it initializes, or sets the value of any instance variables that need to have some other default:

```
// Initialize ivars in the init!
Calendar *calendar =
        [[Calendar alloc] init];
```

Also, you can create multiple initializer methods for a custom class that allow consumers of your class to initialize objects in a variety of ways.

When creating a custom initializer method for your class, here are some ground rules to remember. I will list the ground rules first, and then explain them afterwards:

- The name of the initializer method starts with **init**.

- The return type of an initializer method should be **id**.

- You must invoke the superclass's ***designated initializer*** (more on that in a moment).

- You should assign the value returned by the superclass initializer to **self**.

- If the superclass initializer does *not* return **nil**, then perform initialization of your instance variables.

- When setting the value of instance variables, do so directly rather than by using property accessor methods in order to avoid unwanted side effects.

- At the end of the initializer, return **self**; if the initialization fails, then you should return **nil**.

Let's walk through the process of creating a class with multiple initializers to help you understand this laundry list a little better. In these steps you are going to create a new **Calendar** class and create multiple initialization methods for it. Typically, a Calendar object has today's date automatically set, so this is a good example of initializing a variable in the **init** method.

1. Open the **AdvancedObjectiveCDemo** project in Xcode. Right-click the **AdvancedObjectiveCDemo** sub folder and select **New File...** from the shortcut menu.

2. In the left panel of the New File window under **iOS**, select **Cocoa Touch**. In the right panel of the dialog, select **Objective-C class**, and then click the **Next** button.

3. In the next step of the New File window, in the **Class** box enter **Calendar**, and then in the **Subclass of** box select **NSObject**. Afterwards, click the **Next** button.

4. In the final step of the New File window, click the **Create** button to save the new class in the root folder of the project. You should now have two new files, **Calendar.h** and **Calendar.m**, displayed in the Project

Navigator (Figure 16.34).

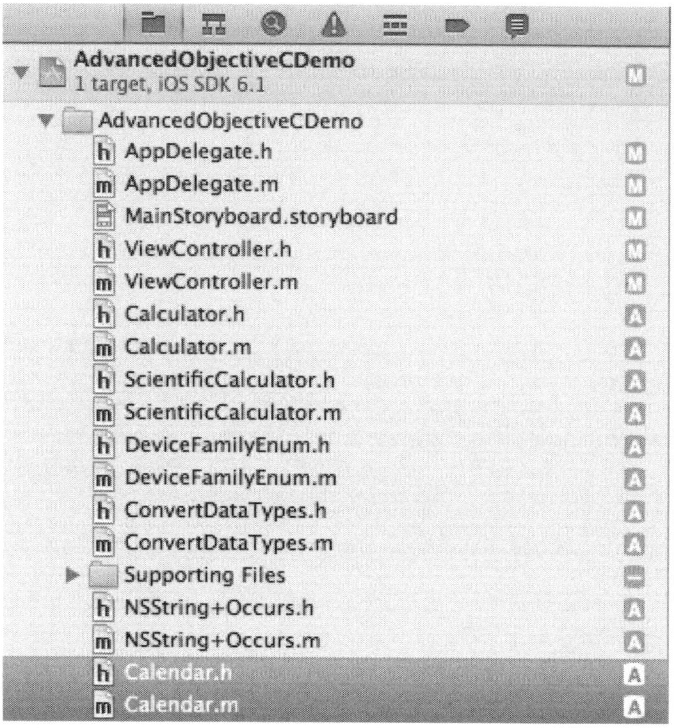

*Figure 16.34 The new **Calendar** class files*

5. In the Project Navigator, select the **Calendar.h** header file. Add the following property and method declaration:

```
@interface Calendar : NSObject

@property (strong, nonatomic) NSDate *today;

// Returns an initialized object
- (id)init;

@end
```

6. Select the **Calendar.m** implementation file in the Project Navigator.

   If you are using Xcode 4.4 or later, you can skip this step. Otherwise, add the following **@synthesize** statement:

```
@implementation Calendar

@synthesize today = _today;
```

7. Now you're ready to create the **init** method. To automate this process, you can use Xcode's **init** code snippet. First create a new empty line above the **@end** declaration. Next, type **init** and in the Code Completion popup, select **init – Objective-C init Method** and press **Enter** (Figure 16.35).

Figure 16.35 Select the **init** code snippet.

This adds the code shown in Figure 16.36 to the **Calculator.m** file.

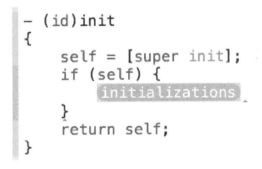

Figure 16.36 The **init** code snippet template

Change the **initializations** placeholder to the following code that initializes the **_today** instance variable:

```
- (id)init
{
    if (self = [super init])
    {
        _today = [NSDate date];
    }
    return self;
}
```

If you look closely at this **init** method, you can see that it follows the ground rules listed earlier. Let's look at these in more detail.

*   **Initializer Naming**

    As required, this method starts with the keyword **init**:

    ```
    (id)init
    ```

If you look back, you can see every Cocoa Touch class initialization method you have used so far starts with "init"—such as **initWithCoder:**, **initWithFrame:** and **initWithObjects:** methods.

- **Initializer Return Type**
  The return type of the initializer is **id**:

  ```
  (id)init
  ```

  The **init** method always returns an initialized instance of the new object, and **id** indicates the method returns an object.

- **Calling the Designated Initializer**
  The call to **[super init]** fills the need to call the superclass's *designated initializer*:

  ```
  - (id)init
  {
      if (self = [super init])
      {
          _today = [NSDate date];
      }
      return self;
  }
  ```

It's important to call the superclass **init** method first to make sure the instance variables further up the inheritance chain are initialized properly. Since a class can have more than one initializer method, you need to make sure that you call the designated initializer. The designated initializer for a class is the initializer method that guarantees all instance variables are initialized. How do you know which method this is?

It's a convention in the Cocoa Touch Framework documentation that the designated initializer is the one with the most arguments (or said another way, the method that allows the most freedom to determine the character of the new instance).

Ultimately, the only way to determine the true designated initializer is to read the documentation for the class. In this case, there is only one **init** method in the superclass, so that makes it easy.

- **Assigning self**

  Notice that the value returned from the superclass's designated initializer is assigned to **self**:

```
- (id)init
{
    if (self = [super init])
    {
        _today = [NSDate date];
    }
    return self;
}
```

  Remember, the **init** method always returns an initialized version of the newly created object, so you assign that initialized object to **self** before performing your own initialization.

- **Checking for nil**

  The return value from the superclass **init** method is checked to see if it's **nil**:

```
- (id)init
{
    if (self = [super init])
    {
        _today = [NSDate date];
    }
    return self;
}
```

  Within the condition for this **if** statement, there are three things going on, in this order:

  1. A call is made to the superclass **init** method.

  2. The return value from the **init** method is assigned to **self**, using the assignment operator.

  3. **self** is checked to see if it's **nil.**

  In Objective-C, you can check for **nil** explicitly:

```
if (self == nil)
```

or implicitly:

```
if (!self)
```

which is effectively what is happening in the **init** method code. In this case, if the superclass **init** method returns **nil**, the code that initializes the **_today** variable doesn't execute.

- **Initializing Instance Variables**
  This is the main reason for creating the **init** method—initializing the **_today** instance variable to today's date as shown here:

```
- (id)init
{
    if (self = [super init])
    {
        _today = [NSDate date];
    }
    return self;
}
```

Notice that the initialization code accesses the instance variable directly, rather than by using the **today** property. Usually, it's a bad idea to access instance variables directly when accessor methods are available, but inside an initializer method, you should bypass accessor methods in order to avoid unwanted side effects. You don't know what code is in a particular accessor method and what side effects it might cause, so in this case it's best to store the value in the instance variable directly.

By default, instance variables are initialized to zero (or **nil**), so you don't need to manually initialize all instance variables unless the value needs to be non-zero for the object to function properly.

- **Returning self**
  At the end of the initializer method, **self** is returned:

```
- (id)init
{
    if (self = [super init])
    {
        _today = [NSDate date];
    }
```

```
    return self;
}
```

Developers using your class expect you to return an initialized instance of the class, so this is a good thing! At this point, **self** may be **nil** if a **nil** was returned from the superclass **init** method. If something fails in your initialization (in this example, there's nothing to go wrong), you should return **nil**.

Initializers With Parameters

Now let's ratchet things up a notch and create a second initializer for the **Calendar** class that accepts a parameter. Typically **Calendar** objects track both today's date and the currently selected date, so let's add an initializer that allows you to specify the current date.

1. Select the **Calendar.h** file in the Project Navigator and add the following **currentDate** property and **initWithCurrentDate:** method declaration:

```
@interface Calendar : NSObject

@property (strong, nonatomic) NSDate *today;
@property (strong, nonatomic) NSDate
    *currentDate;

// Returns an initialized object
- (id)init;

// Returns an object initialized with the
// currently selected date
// (Designated initializer)
- (id)initWithCurrentDate:(NSDate *)aDate;

@end
```

As per our guidelines, the method begins with the word **init** and returns a value of type **id**. It accepts a single argument of type **NSDate**. In the comments, it's documented as the designated initializer.

2. Select the **Calendar.m** implementation file in the Project Navigator.

If you are using Xcode 4.4 or later, you can skip this step. Otherwise, add the following code that synthesizes the **currentDate** property:

```
@implementation Calendar

@synthesize today = _today;
@synthesize currentDate = _currentDate;
```

3. Next, add the following code that implements the **initWithCurrentDate:** method directly above the **init** method:

```
- (id)initWithCurrentDate:(NSDate *)aDate
{
    if (self = [super init])
    {
        _currentDate = aDate;
        _today = [NSDate date];
    }
    return self;
}
```

4. Remove all of the existing code in the original **init** method and replace it with this code:

```
- (id)init
{
    return [self initWithCurrentDate:nil];
}
```

Notice that the code initializing the **_today** instance variable has been moved from the **init** method to the **initWithCurrentDate:** method. Also, the original **init** method has been changed to call the new **initWithCurrentDate:** method, passing **nil** as the default value for the current date.

This is a best practices pattern. The initialization methods that have fewer parameters should call the initialization methods with more parameters, passing default values along the way. This provides a single method (**initWithCurrentDate:**) whereby all instance variables are initialized. It allows someone to create a subclass of your class and have one method that they can call to initialize all variables.

Testing the Initializers

Now let's see how the initializers work at run time.

1. First, you need to add some code that instantiates the **Calendar** class.

Select the **ViewController.m** file in the Project Navigator and add the
following **import** statement at the top of the code file:

```
#import "ViewController.h"
#import "ConvertDataTypes.h"
#import "ScientificCalculator.h"
#import "Calendar.h"
```

2. Now add the following code to the bottom of the **viewDidLoad** method:

```
Calendar *calendar = [[Calendar alloc] init];
NSLog(@"Today is: %@", calendar.today);
```

This code calls the **init** method of the **Calendar** class.

Did you notice that the **init** and **initWithCurrentDate:** methods were
listed in the Code Completion popup? Nice! Also, notice that the **today**
property is of type **NSDate**, and the format specifier in the **NSLog**
command is a **%@**. This means that the date is taken from the
description method of the **NSDate** class.

3. Set a breakpoint on the first line of code (Figure 16.37).

*Figure 16.37 Set a breakpoint on **Calendar** creation.*

4. Click the **Run** button to run the App in the Simulator, and you will hit the
breakpoint (Figure 16.38).

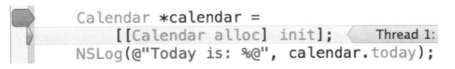

*Figure 16.38 The **Calendar** creation breakpoint is hit.*

5. Click the **Step into** button in the Debug area, and control will jump to the
init method (Figure 16.39).

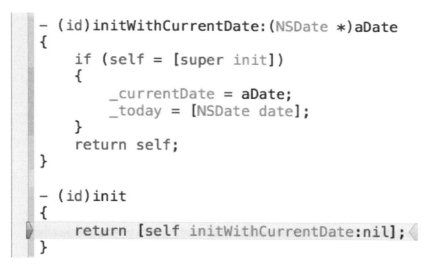

```
- (id)initWithCurrentDate:(NSDate *)aDate
{
    if (self = [super init])
    {
        _currentDate = aDate;
        _today = [NSDate date];
    }
    return self;
}

- (id)init
{
    return [self initWithCurrentDate:nil];
}
```

*Figure 16.39 Step into the **init** method.*

6. Click the **Step into** button, and control will jump to the **initWithCurrentDate:** method (Figure 16.40).

```
- (id)initWithCurrentDate:(NSDate *)aDate
{
    if (self = [super init])
    {
        _currentDate = aDate;
        _today = [NSDate date];
    }
    return self;
}

- (id)init
{
    return [self initWithCurrentDate:nil];
}
```

*Figure 16.40 Step into the **initWithCurrentDate:** method.*

The **nil** value passed to this method gets stored in the **_currentDate** instance variable and today's date gets stored in the **_today** instance variable. You can step through this code and check out the instance variable values by hovering your mouse pointer over them if you like.

7. When you're ready, press the **Continue** button. You should now be able to see today's date displayed in the Console as shown in Figure 16.41 (if the Console isn't visible, select **View > Debug Area > Activate Console** from the Xcode menu).

```
All Output ▲▼                                    Clear  ▢  ▥  ▢
2012-07-31 19:03:47.194 AdvancedObjectiveCDemo[7318:f803]
Today is: 2012-08-01 05:03:47 +0000
```

Figure 16.41 Today's date is displayed in the Console.

Following these basic guidelines will help you to create custom initializers that work well under all circumstances.

Polymorphism

Polymorphism is one of the core principles of object-oriented programming, and you really need to understand it well to write the most effective code.

So far, whenever you have declared a variable of a particular type, you have always stored an object of that exact same type into the variable. For example, the following code declares a variable of type **UITextField**, and then creates an instance of **UITextField** and stores it in the **textField** variable:

```
UITextField *textField =
        [[UITextField alloc] init];
```

No surprises here. However, in Objective-C, when you declare a variable of a particular type, it can also hold a reference to any *subclass* of that type. Take for example the class hierarchy shown in Figure 16.42, which shows **UITextField**, **UIButton**, and **UISlider** which are just a few of the subclass of the **UIControl** class.

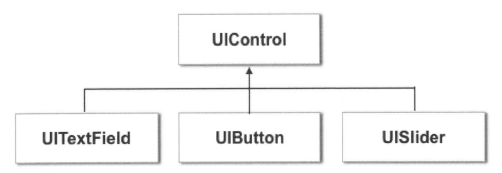

Figure 16.42 When you declare a variable of a particular type, it can hold a reference to any subclass of that type.

The word "polymorphism" literally means "many forms," and in this example you can see the **UIControl** class can take many different forms—a text field, a button, or a switch.

Given this hierarchy, you can declare a variable of type **UIControl** and then store a reference to the **UITextField**, **UIButton** or **UISwitch** object in this variable. For example:

```
UIControl* control;
control = [[UITextField alloc] init];
control = [[UIButton alloc] init];
control = [[UISwitch alloc] init];
```

Polymorphism allows you to write more generic code that works with families of objects, rather than writing code for a specific class. In this example, regardless of which class you instantiate, you can access all the properties and methods declared in the **UIControl** class that are inherited by all the subclasses.

For example, the **UIControl** class has an **enabled** property, so you can write the following line of code:

```
control.enabled = true;
```

The **UIControl** class also declares an **isMultiTouchEnabled** method, so you can pass the following message to the control object:

```
bool multiTouch =
          [control isMultipleTouchEnabled];
```

As you continue to write more iOS Apps over time, you will find great uses for polymorphism as you build generic code and class libraries that can be reused in many different Apps.

Converting Objective-C Data Types

In *Chapter 14: Working With Strings*, you learned how to convert values to a string and convert strings to numeric values. However, this isn't the only situation where you need to convert from one data type to another.

There are two main kinds of conversions—*implicit* and *explicit*. **Implicit conversions** occur automatically, and **explicit conversions** require you to specifically write code that performs the conversion.

As you read about the different types of conversions in the next sections, you can refer to the **ConvertDataTypes** class in the **AdvancedObjectiveCDemo** project from which the code samples were taken.

Implicit Conversions

The Objective-C compiler automatically, or implicitly, performs any data conversions for you that it considers "safe." For example, check out the following code:

```
NSInteger i = 10;
double d = i;
```

The first line of code declares an integer variable named **i** and stores the number **10** in the variable. The next line of code stores the integer value into a variable named **d** whose data type is **double**. When this second line of code executes, the **integer** value is converted to **double** before getting stored in the **d** variable. Note that the value in the **i** variable remains of type **integer**.

The compiler performs this conversion implicitly because it's safe. The **integer** data type holds a smaller maximum value than the **double** data type, so there's no danger in losing data when converting from **integer** to **double**.

Suppressed Compiler Warnings

What happens if we reverse the conversion—convert a double value to an integer value?

```
double d = 1.567f;
NSInteger i = d;
```

In this example, the **f** at the end of **1.567** is used in Objective-C to indicate a floating point number. When the second line of code executes, the **double** value is converted to an **integer** before it is stored in the **i** variable, and data is definitely lost. Since integers are always whole numbers, the numbers to the right of the decimal pointed are truncated—that's right—the value is rounded. The numbers to the right of the decimal point are "dropped".

Normally, you would expect the compiler to warn you about this situation, but by default it doesn't. If you would like to turn these warnings on for your project:

1. In the Project Navigator, select the very first node to display the Project Editor.

2. On the left side of the Project Editor, select your project under the **Project** section. Next, select the **Build Settings** tab, and then scroll down to the Apple **LLVM compiler 4.2 – Warnings** section. Change the **Suspicious Implicit Conversions** setting to **Yes** as shown in Figure 16.43.

Setting	AdvancedObjectiveCDemo
▼Apple LLVM compiler 4.2 – Warnings – All languages	
Check Switch Statements	Yes ⬍
Deprecated Functions	Yes ⬍
Empty Loop Bodies	No ⬍
Four Character Literals	No ⬍
Hidden Local Variables	No ⬍
Implicit Constant Conversions	Yes – $
Implicit Conversion to 32 Bit Type	No ⬍
Implicit Enum Conversions	Yes – $
Implicit Integer to Pointer Conversions	Yes – $
Implicit Signedness Conversions	No ⬍
Initializer Not Fully Bracketed	No ⬍
Mismatched Return Type	**Yes ⬍**
Missing Braces and Parentheses	Yes ⬍
Missing Fields in Structure Initializers	No ⬍
Missing Function Prototypes	No ⬍
Missing Newline At End Of File	No ⬍
Other Warning Flags	
Pointer Sign Comparison	Yes ⬍
Sign Comparison	No ⬍
▶ Suspicious Implicit Conversions	**Yes ⬍**

Figure 16.43 Turn on compiler warnings for suspicious implicit conversions.

3. Now when you build your project, you will get a compiler warning when you are performing a "suspicious" implicit conversion (Figure 16.44).

```
double d = 1.567f;
NSInteger i = d;
```
⚠ Implicit conversion turns floating-point number into integer: 'double' to 'NSInteger.

Figure 16.44 The compiler warns of a suspicious implicit conversion.

To get rid of this compiler warning, you need to perform an explicit conversion, which is discussed in the upcoming Explicit Conversions section.

Implicit Conversion of Complex Data Types

Not only does the compiler perform explicit conversions of basic data types such as integer, float, and double, it can also implicitly convert complex data types.

For example, in the **AdvancedObjectiveCDemo** project, the **ScientificCalculator** is a subclass of the **Calculator** class. Since the **ScientificCalculator** class inherits all of the public and protected properties and methods of the **Calculator** class, it's safe for the compiler to perform the following implicit conversion for you:

```
Calculator *calc =
        [[ScientificCalculator alloc] init];
```

At run time, the **ScientificCalculator** object is implicitly converted to an object of type **Calculator** before it's stored in the **calc** variable. Ultimately, the compiler can always implicitly convert a class to a class higher in the inheritance chain.

Explicit Conversions

Let's go back to the code that converts a **double** to an **integer** value:

```
double d = 1.567f;
NSInteger i = d;
```

If you have turned on the "Suspicious implicit conversion" compiler warning, you can get rid of the warning by performing an explicit conversion, also known as a *cast*. For example, notice the highlighted code:

```
double d = 1.567f;
NSInteger i = (NSInteger)d;
```

To perform an explicit conversion or cast, you simply place the data type you want to convert to in parentheses directly before the value to be converted. This explicitly tells the compiler to convert the value stored in the **d** variable to an **NSInteger** before storing it in the **i** variable.

When you declare an explicit conversion, the compiler "looks the other way" and doesn't try to make sense of the conversion. It assumes you know what you're doing. However, if you explicitly tell the compiler to make a conversion that is invalid, you will get an error at run time. For example, check out the following explicit conversion:

```
ScientificCalculator *calc =
  (ScientificCalculator *)[[Calculator alloc]init];
[calc log:10];
```

The first line of code explicitly converts a **Calculator** object to a **ScientificCalculator** object. This is an invalid cast because **Calculator** is the superclass of **ScientificCalculator**. It is not a **ScientificCalculator**, so when the second line of code executes at run time and the **log** message is sent to the object, you will get an "unrecognized selector sent to instance" error, and your App will grind to a halt! So, when you perform an explicit cast, you definitely want to make sure you know what you're doing.

Dynamic Typing With id

As you have already learned, the Objective-C **id** data type represents any object, which allows you to substitute any object at run time. You can cast any object to type **id** and cast **id** to any other type implicitly. For example:

```
id obj = [[Calculator alloc] init];
obj = @"Test";
```

This first line of code declares a variable named **obj** of type **id**, and then stores a reference to a new **Calculator** object in the variable. The second line of code then stores a string object into the same variable. In both cases, there is no explicit conversion necessary.

You can go the other way and convert an object of type **id** to any other type without performing an explicit cast. For example:

```
id obj = [[Calculator alloc] init];
Calculator *calc = obj;
```

In this code, the object in the **obj** variable, which is of type **id**, is stored into the **calc** variable, which is of type **Calculator**, with no explicit conversion required. As you might imagine, if the object stored in the **obj** variable is not of type **Calculator**, you will get the "unrecognized selector sent to instance" exception at run time.

Determining the Type of an Object

There are a few ways you can determine the type of an object in Objective-C. Ultimately, in dynamically typed languages such as Objective-C, you shouldn't normally care about the specific type of an object—you are more interested in whether an object conforms to a particular protocol or if it responds to a particular message or selector.

Duck Typing

You can determine if an object responds to a particular message by passing it a **respondsToSelector:** message. Checking an object's abilities in this way (rather than checking for a particular class or protocol) is known as "duck typing"—if a bird walks like a duck and swims like a duck and quacks like a duck, I call that bird a duck. For example, take a look at the following method:

```
- (void)duckTyping:(id)obj
{
    if ([obj respondsToSelector:
        @selector(addToTotal:)])
    {
        [obj addToTotal:123];
    }
}
```

This method accepts a parameter of type **id**, which says nothing about the object's heritage, or the protocols it implements. The **if** statement checks if it responds to the selector **addToTotal:**, and if it does, it passes that message to the object.

Checking If an Object Conforms to a Protocol

Another common check that you can perform in your code is testing if an object conforms to a particular protocol. To do this, you pass an object the **conformsToProtocol:** message. For example:

```
- (BOOL)checkConformsToProtocol:(id)obj
{
 return [obj conformsToProtocol:
         @protocol(UIPickerViewDataSource)];
}
```

This method passes a **conformsToProtocol:** message, passing the
UIPickerViewDataSource protocol. If the object conforms to that
protocol, the method returns **YES**, otherwise it returns **NO**.

Checking an Object's Type

If you find yourself in a situation where you really need to know the specific
type of an object, you can pass the object an **isMemberOfClass:** or
isKindOfClass: message.

The **isMemberOfClass:** method checks if the object's class is exactly the
same as the specified class. For example, check out the following method:

```
- (BOOL)checkIsMemberOfClass:(id)obj
{
        return [obj isMemberOfClass:
            [Calculator class]];
}
```

This method accepts an **obj** parameter of type **id**, and passes the
isMemberOfClass: message to the object. A **class** message is passed to the
Calculator class. This method returns a class object, which is passed to the
object in the **isMemberOfClass:** message call. If the object is of the
specified type, it returns **YES**, otherwise, it returns **NO**. This means that the
method only returns **YES** if a **Calculator** object is passed to it.

The **isKindOfClass:** method works a little differently. Rather than checking
for an exact match on the class, it checks if the object is an instance of the
specified class, or any subclass of that class. For example, check out the
following method:

```
- (BOOL)checkIsKindOfClass:(id)obj
{
        return [obj isKindOfClass:
            [Calculator class]];
}
```

If a **Calculator** object is passed to this method, it returns true. If a **ScientificCalculator** object is passed to this method, it also returns true—because **ScientificCalculator** is a subclass of **Calculator**.

Boxing Scalar Data Types

As I mentioned earlier in this book, scalar data types such as **integer**, **double**, and **BOOL** are not objects. Often, you need to convert these scalar values to number objects for things like key-value coding or storing literal values into an array. When you convert a scalar data type to an object, it's known as *boxing*.

You can use the **NSNumber** class to box, or convert a scalar data type to an **NSNumber** object. For example:

```
NSUInteger myInt = 123;
double myDouble = 123.45;
float myFloat = 123.45f;
BOOL myBool = YES;
char myChar = 'A';

NSNumber *number;
number = [NSNumber numberWithInt:myInt];
number = [NSNumber numberWithDouble:myDoublc];
number = [NSNumber numberWithFloat:myFloat];
number = [NSNumber numberWithBool:myBool];
number = [NSNumber numberWithChar:myChar];
```

In this example, I first stored literal values into variables, and then passed the variables as arguments to the various **NSNumber** methods. I did this because the value you need to convert is often a variable.

However, if you are converting a hard-coded literal value, and you are using Xcode 4.4 or later, you can convert the value to an **NSNumber** object by simply prefixing it with an @ sign. For example:

```
NSNumber *number;
number = @123;
number = @123.45;
number = @123.45f;
number = @YES;
number = @'A';
```

Summary

Here are the key points in the various sections on Advanced Objective-C features.

Protocols

- Protocols define a standard set of behavior for a class.

- Protocols are equivalent to interfaces in languages such as Java and C#.

- The **UIPickerViewDataSource** protocol declares methods required by an object that wants to act as a data source for the picker view.

- The **UIPickerViewDelegate** protocol declares methods required by an object that wants to act as a delegate for the picker view.

- A class *adopts* a protocol to indicate that it implements all of the required methods and often some of the optional methods too.

- Here is an example of a view controller adopting the **UIPickerViewDataSource** & **UIPickerViewDelegate** protocols:

```
@interface ViewController : UIViewController
<UIPickerViewDataSource, UIPickerViewDelegate>
```

- You can declare your own protocols using the **@protocol** directive. For example:

```
@protocol AppSetting

-(NSString *)getSettingForKey:
    (NSString *)key;
-(void)setSetting:(NSString *) forKey:
    (NSString *)key;

@end
```

- By default, protocol methods are *required*, meaning the class that implements the protocol must implement its methods. You can use the **@optional** keyword to indicate one or more methods are optional. You can also use the **@required** keyword to explicitly declare methods as required. For example:

```
@protocol AppSetting

@required
-(NSString *)getSettingForKey:
    (NSString *)key;
-(void)setSetting:(NSString *)
    forKey:(NSString *)key;

@optional
-(void)deleteSettingForKey:
    (NSString *)key;

@end
```

Inheritance

- Inheritance allows you to create new classes that are based on other classes.

- You can create a subclass from an existing class, inherit all of its properties, methods and protected instance variables, and extend it to suit your needs.

- You can override a method inherited from a superclass by creating a method with the same signature (method name and parameters) in the subclass.

- Overriding a method allows you to:

  1. *Extend* the superclass method by doing something additional in the subclass and

  2. *Override* the superclass method by doing something completely different in the subclass.

Categories

- A category allows you to extend a class without creating a subclass.

- It's better to create a category to extend a Cocoa Touch Framework class rather than creating a subclass, so that you don't have to remember to use a custom subclass in some places and a Cocoa Touch Framework class in others.

- The standard naming convention for categories is to use the name of the class that you are extending as a prefix, append a plus sign (+), and then add the name of the category as a suffix. For example:

  - NSString+Occurs.h

  - NSString+Occurs.m

- A category interface declaration includes the name of the class being extended, followed by the name of the category in parentheses. In the header file you also declare the new method(s) that you are adding to extend the class:

```
@interface NSString (Occurs)
- (NSUInteger) occurrencesOfString:
        (NSString *)aString;
@end
```

- A category implementation declaration also includes the name of the class being extended, followed by the name of the category in parentheses. In the implementation file, you implement the methods that you declare in the category interface file.

```
@implementation NSString (Occurs)

- (NSUInteger) occurrencesOfString:
        (NSString *)aString
{
    // Method code
}


@end
```

- To use a category, you must include its header. Typically, it's best to import the header file in your project's prefix header (.pch) file:

```
#ifdef __OBJC__
    #import <UIKit/UIKit.h>
    #import <Foundation/Foundation.h>
```

```
#import "NSString+Occurs.h"
#endif
```

- You can add more than one method to a class in a single category.

- It's a best practice to add related methods to a single category.

- There is no limit to the number of categories that you can add to a class.

- You can't add new instance variables to a class with a category, but a category can access all instance variables declared in the class that it is extending.

- Methods that you add to a class by using a category are inherited by subclasses.

Class Extensions

- You can declare a private (hidden) method by using a class extension. Class extensions are similar to categories except:

  1. They are usually found in the implementation (.m) file *of the class they are extending*.

  2. There is no name listed between the parentheses.

  3. They allow you to declare *required* methods.

- Here is an example of a class extension:

```
// Class extension
@interface Calculator()

// Sets the current operation
-(void)setCurrentOperation:
    (Operation)operation;

@end
```

- You declare the class extension at the top of the class implementation (.m) file, above the **@implementation** directive, and include any private method declarations.

- In the class extension below the **@implementation** directive, you then implement the methods that you declared.

Key-Value Coding

- Key-value coding (KVC) is an advanced feature of Objective-C that allows you to access an object's properties indirectly by using the string value of the property name rather than directly by using the standard getter and setter methods.

- You get a value with key-value coding by using the **valueForKey:** method:

```
NSString *firstName = [customer  valueForKey:@"firstName"];
```

- You set a value with key-value coding by using the **setValue:forKey:** method:

```
[customer setValue:@"Steve"  forKey:@"firstName"];
```

- To *set* a scalar value, you need to convert the scalar type to an object. If you are using Xcode 4.4 or later, you can just add an @ sign in front of the value and it will be converted to an object:

```
[customer setValue:@123  forKey:@"customerID"];
```

or, if you are using an earlier version of Xcode, you can use the **NSNumber** class to make the conversion:

```
[customer setValue:
    [NSNumber numberWithInt:123]
    forKey:@"customerID"];
```

- To *get* a scalar value, you need to store the return value in an **NSNumber** variable like this:

```
NSNumber *customerID =    [customer
valueForKey:@"customerID"];
```

Initializer Methods

- You need to create an initializer, or **init** method, for your custom classes to initialize variables to values other than zero or **nil**.

- Here is an example of an **init** method:

```
- (id)init
{
        if (self = [super init])
        {
        _today = [NSDate date];
        }
        return self;
}
```

- The name of an initializer starts with **init**.

- The return type of an initializer should be **id**.

- You must invoke the superclass's designated initializer.

- You should assign **self** to the value returned by the superclass initializer.

- If the superclass initializer does not return **nil**, perform initialization of your instance variables.

- When setting the value of instance variables, do so directly rather than by using property accessor methods to avoid unwanted side effects.

- At the end of the initializer, return **self** unless the initialization fails; if it does, you should return **nil**.

- You can create multiple initialization methods that accept a variety of parameters normally used as initialization values.

- The initialization methods that have fewer parameters should call the initialization methods with more parameters, passing default values along the way. This provides a single method whereby all instance variables are initialized.

Polymorphism

- The word "polymorphism" literally means "many forms." This refers to the fact that a class can take many different forms.

- When you declare a variable of a particular type, you can store an instance of that type or any of its subclasses.

- Polymorphism allows you to write more generic code that works with families of objects rather than writing code for a specific class.

Converting Data Types

- The Objective-C compiler implicitly performs any data conversions it considers safe, such as when a smaller data type is converted to a larger data type.

- The compiler can always implicitly convert a class to a class higher in the inheritance chain.

- To perform an explicit conversion, or cast, place the data type you want to convert to in parentheses, directly before the value to be converted. For example:

```
double d = 1.567f;
NSInteger i = (NSInteger)d;
```

- You can convert to and from the **id** data type without casting.

- You can check if an object responds to a message by passing it a **respondsToSelector:** message.

- You can check if an object conforms to a particular protocol by passing it a **conformsToProtocol:** message.

- You can check if an object is an instance of a specific class by passing it an **isMemberOfClass:** message.

- You can check if an object is an instance of a class or any subclass of that class by passing it an **isKindOfClass:** method.

- Converting a scalar data type to an object is known as *boxing*.

- You can use the **NSNumber** class to box, or convert, a scalar data type to an **NSNumber** object. For example:

```
number = [NSNumber numberWithInt:123];
number = [NSNumber numberWithDouble:123.45];
number = [NSNumber numberWithFloat:123.45f];
```

- If you are converting a hard-coded literal value, and you are using Xcode 4.4 or later, you can convert the value to an **NSNumber** object by simply prefixing it with an @ sign. For example:

```
NSNumber *number;
number = @123;
number = @123.45;
number = @123.45f;
number = @YES;
number = @'A';
```

Exercise 16.1

In this exercise, you will use what you learned about categories to extend the **NSNumber** class.

1. In the **AdvancedObjectiveCDemo** project, create a new category named **Math** that extends the **NSNumber** class.

2. Add the following methods to the category:

```
- (float) radiansValue;
- (float) degreesValue;
```

3. Implement the category methods as follows:

```
- (float) radiansValue
{
    return [self floatValue] *
        (float)(M_PI / 180);
}

- (float) degreesValue
{
    return [self floatValue] *
        (float)(180 / M_PI);
}
```

4. Add code to the **ViewController.m** file's **viewDidLoad** method that tests that the category methods have been added to **NSNumber**.

Solution Movie 16.1

To see a video providing the solution for this exercise, go to the following link in your web browser.

http://www.iOSAppsForNonProgrammers.com/B2M161.html

Exercise 16.2

In this exercise you will put to use what you have learned about creating an initializer for a custom class.

1. In the **AdvancedObjectiveCDemo** project, create a new class named **Book** based on **NSObject**.

2. Add a **currentPage** property of type **NSUInteger** to the **Book** class.

3. Add an **initWithCurrentPage:** method to the **Book** class that accepts an **NSUInteger** parameter named **currentPage**.

4. In the **initWithCurrentPage:** method implementation, add code that stores the **currentPage** value into the **currentPage** property's instance variable.

5. Add an **init** method to the **Book** class that accepts no arguments.

6. In the **init** method implementation, call the **initWithCurrentPage:** method, passing **1** as the default page number.

7. Add code to the **ViewController.m** file's **viewDidLoad** method to test both initializer methods.

Solution Movie 16.2

To see a video providing the solution for this exercise, go to the following link in your web browser.

http://www.iOSAppsForNonProgrammers.com/B2M162.html

Chapter 17: Advanced Messaging

One of the identifying features of Objective-C is the concept of sending messages to objects. In this chapter, you will see there is much more to messaging than simply passing a message to a specific object. You will learn advanced messaging techniques that are important for tasks such as responding to UI events, animations, and enumerating collections.

Sections in This Chapter

Invoking Methods With Selectors

As you learned early on in this book, the most common way to execute a method on an object is to pass a message directly to the object, requesting the method be invoked. This is the way you have invoked methods throughout this book so far. You usually invoke methods this way because you know which specific object you want to send the message to, and you want the object to run the method immediately.

At times, you may *not* want a method invoked immediately. For example, you may want a method to be invoked only when the user taps a button. Objective-C provides *selectors* for this very purpose.

In Objective-C, the term *selector* has two meanings:

1. When you pass a message to an object, the name of the method is known as the selector.

2. Selector also refers to a unique identifier that replaces the method name when a project is compiled.

When you compile a project in Xcode, the names of all methods are converted to a unique identifier. All methods with the same name have the same selector. If you had a **Calculator** class with a **save** method, and a **Customer** class with a **save** method, both classes would have the same selector defined for their respective **save** methods as shown in Figure 17.1.

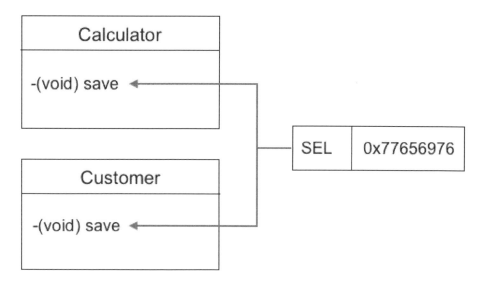

Figure 17.1 All methods with the same name have the same selector.

Getting a Method's Selector

You use the **@selector** directive to get the selector for a particular method. This is the most efficient way to get a selector since the evaluation of the selector occurs at compile time rather than run time. For example, the following code gets the selector for the **done:** method:

```
SEL done = @selector(done:);
```

Just as you see in this code sample, the type of all selectors is **SEL**, which differentiates them from all other data types.

Although it's less efficient, you can also convert a character string to a selector at run time:

```
SEL done = NSSelectorFromString(@"done:");
```

You can also go the other way and get a string containing the method name from a selector. For example:

```
NSString *methodName =
        NSStringFromSelector(done);
```

Invoking a Selector

The **NSObject** protocol has a **performSelector:** method for invoking selectors. This method takes a **SEL** identifier as its first parameter. For example, if you have a **SEL** variable that holds a selector:

```
SEL save = @selector(save);
```

you can send a **performSelector:** message to an object requesting that it invoke the selector stored in the **save** variable:

```
[myObject performSelector:save];
```

This statement is equivalent to:

```
[myObject save];
```

There are two other methods in the **NSObject** protocol that perform selectors:

```
- (id)performSelector:withObject:-
```

```
(id)performSelector:withObject:withObject
```

These methods perform the same task as **performSelector:** but accept either one or two objects that get passed through as arguments to the selector method. For example, if you have a **SEL** variable that holds a selector to a method that accepts a single argument:

```
SEL done = @selector(done:);
```

You can send a **performSelector:withObject:** message to an object, requesting that it invoke the selector stored in the **done** variable and pass the necessary argument:

```
[myObject performSelector:done
        withObject:self];
```

The **NSObject** class has a variety of other methods that perform selectors after a specified delay, in the background, or with other threading options. Check out Apple's *NSObject Class Reference* for details.

All objects that inherit from **NSObject** inherit this family of **performSelector:** methods, so it's widely available in the classes and objects you commonly use in your Apps.

Getting Around the Compiler Warning With PerformSelector

If you have any calls to the **performSelector:** methods in an App that uses ARC (Automatic Reference Counting), you will get the following compiler warning:

PerformSelector may cause a leak because its selector is unknown.

You get this warning because ARC cannot enforce proper memory management. Normally, ARC uses standard Objective-C method naming conventions to add the appropriate **retain** or **release** messages. When you use selectors, the compiler doesn't know the method name, so it gives you this warning.

To get around the warning, you can turn off the −**Warc-performSelector-leaks** flag in each place you use **performSelector:** in your code. For example:

```
#pragma clang diagnostic push
#pragma clang diagnostic ignored "-Warc-performSelector-leaks"
[myObject performSelector:done withObject:self];
#pragma clang diagnostic pop
```

Returning a Value From a Selector

All of the **performSelector:** methods return a value of type **id**. They pass back an object that is the result of the message call. Notice I specifically said an *object*. The **performSelector:** methods cannot return scalar values; they only return objects (if you need to return a scalar value, check out Apple's *NSInvocation Class Reference* documentation).

To return a value from one of the **performSelector:** methods, just store the result into a variable from the **performSelector:** message call. For example:

```
Calculator *result = [self
        performSelector:getCalculator];
```

Messaging With the Target-Action Design Pattern

The place you will most often use selectors is in conjunction with the *Target-Action design pattern*. In this pattern, an object holds two pieces of information for sending a message:

1. A *target*, which is the receiver of the message and

2. An *action*, which is the method to be invoked.

For example, Figure 17.2 shows a **Bar Button Item** (a button found in a navigation bar or toolbar) that has a **target** property and an **action** property. The **target** property points to the **View Controller** object and the **action** property points to the **flipBack:** method. When the user taps the **Bar Button Item**, the **flipBack:** message is sent to the **View Controller**.

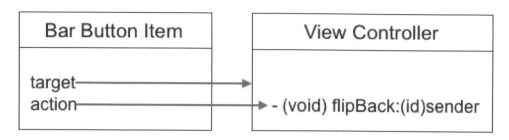

Figure 17.2 A bar button item with target and action properties

For a hands-on example of how this works, let's take a look at the **PickACard** sample project.

1. Open the **PickACard** project by selecting **File > Open...** from the Xcode menu. In the Open dialog, navigate to the folder where you have stored this book's sample code. Expand the **PickACard** folder, select the **PickACard.xcodeproj** file and then click the **Open** button.

2. In the Project Navigator, expand the **PickACard** folder and click on the **MainStoryboard.storyboard** file. Scroll to the right of the storyboard and you will see the two main scenes—**Playing Card Back View** and **Playing Card Front View** (Figure 17.3).

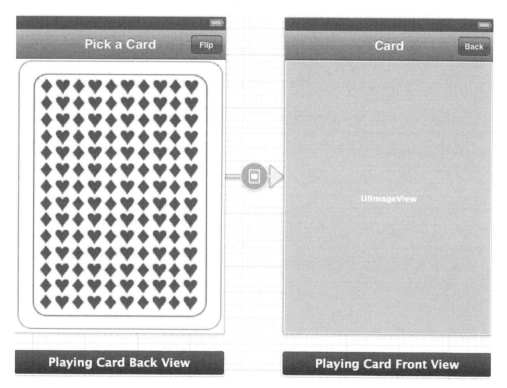

Figure 17.3 The Playing Card Back and Front View

The **Playing Card Back View** shows the back of a playing card. When you tap the **Flip** button on the right side of the navigation bar, the view flips and the **Playing Card Front View** is displayed. There is code in the App that gets a random playing card and displays its image in the **Playing Card Front View**.

3. Let's run the App to see how it works. Just click Xcode's **Run** button and when the App appears in the Simulator, click the **Flip** button. This flips the view horizontally and displays a random card on the flip side of the view as shown in Figure 17.4 (your card will most likely be different!)

Figure 17.4 A random card on the flip side of the view

4. Click the **Back** button, and you can see that nothing happens. You are going to fix this so that clicking the **Back** button flips the view to the back of the card.

5. First, press **Command+Tab** to get back to Xcode then click the **Stop** button.

6. Next, go to the Project Navigator and click on the

PlayingCardFrontViewController.m implementation file to select it. This is the view controller code file associated with the **Playing Card Front View** scene. Scroll to the bottom of the code file and you will see the **flipBack:** method:

```
- (void)flipBack:(id)sender {

    [self dismissViewControllerAnimated:YES
        completion:nil];
}
```

This code sends the view controller (**self**) a **dismissViewControllerAnimated:completion:** message, which flips the view to the back of the card.

7. You need to tell the **Back** button to call this method when it's tapped. To do this, add the following code to the **viewDidLoad** method:

```
- (void)viewDidLoad
{
  [super viewDidLoad];

    self.navBar.topItem.title =
        self.card.cardName;
    self.imgCard.image = [UIImage
    imageNamed:self.card.cardImageName];

    self.btnBack.target = self;
    self.btnBack.action =
        @selector(flipBack:);
}
```

This code sets the **Back** button's **target** property to **self** and its **action** property to **flipBack:**, just as was illustrated in Figure 17.2. Notice you used the **@selector** command to get the selector for the **flipBack:** method.

8. Let's run the App again and see what happens. Click the **Run** button, and when the App appears in the Simulator, click the **Flip** button to display a random card. At this point the **Back** button is "wired up" to a target object and action method. Click the **Back** button, and the view will flip to the back of the card.

At this point you can flip back and forth between the views to display random playing cards.

This is just one example of the target-action design pattern in action. Although you set the target object and action method in code, as you learn more about Xcode, you will see that you can often set the **target** and **action** in the Interface Builder editor by simply dragging from the Connections Inspector to the associated view controller code file.

Enhancing Your Code With Blocks

A **block** is a self-contained chunk of code, usually small in size that can be passed around as an object (in fact, blocks are Objective-C objects). Blocks are a relatively new feature added in iOS 4.0. If you are coming from other programming languages such as Ruby or Python, the concept of blocks should be familiar to you. If you're coming from the Microsoft world, blocks are equivalent to anonymous methods.

Blocks can be executed:

1. As a callback when an operation has finished, or in response to the occurrence of an event

2. Concurrently (simultaneously) on multiple threads of execution

3. Over items in a collection

Apple has implemented the use of blocks in a number of important places in the Cocoa Touch Framework (although not in enough places yet).

One of the best ways to understand how blocks work is to see how code works using older methodologies such as target-selector, and seeing how you can use blocks instead. Let's start by looking at **animations**. An animation is a smooth transition from one user-interface state to another; for example, when the user taps a button and one view slides out and another view slides in its place.

Animation Without Blocks

For a hands-on example of how animation works without blocks, let's take a look at a sample project. In this example, the animation occurs when the App first launches.

1. Open the **PickACard** project.

2. Click Xcode's **Run** button, and notice when the App first appears in the Simulator, a splash image (as shown in Figure 17.5) appears then slowly grows and fades out.

Figure 17.5 The splash image grows and fades out.

3. To see how this animation works, go back to Xcode and press the **Stop** button. Then, go to the Project Navigator and select the **AppDelegate.m** file. The **application:didFinishLaunchingWithOptions:** method is listed first in the code file. It is called automatically when your App has been launched but is not yet active. Towards the bottom of this method, an **animateOldStyle** message call is made.

The **animateOldStyle** method can be found just below this method in the code file. It's called "old style" because its code demonstrates how you used to set up and perform animations prior to iOS 4:

```
- (void)animateOldStyle
{
        // Set up the animation
    [UIView beginAnimations:nil context:nil];
```

```
    [UIView setAnimationDuration:2.0];
    self.splashView.alpha = 0.0;
    self.splashView.frame =
        CGRectMake(-60, -60,
        self.splashView.frame.size.width+120,
        self.splashView.frame.size.height+120);


// Specify the delegate and selector
        [UIView setAnimationDelegate:self];
      [UIView setAnimationDidStopSelector:
        @selector(startupAnimationDone:
        finished:context:)];


// Perform the animation
    [UIView commitAnimations];
}
```

This section of code begins by setting the animation duration to **2.0** seconds, and then specifies the object values to be animated. The image view's **alpha** value will decrease to zero (gradually making it invisible), and the size of the image view will increase in height and width by **120** points simultaneously during the 2-second animation period.

Next, a delegate and selector are set. This specifies the target object (AppDelegate) and selector method to be called when the animation is complete. The selector in this code points to the method located just below it:

```
- (void)startupAnimationDone:
        (NSString *)animationID
        finished:(NSNumber *)finished
        context:(void *)context {

    [self.splashView removeFromSuperview];
}
```

When the animation completes, this code removes the splash view from its parent view, so it's no longer visible.

Figure 17.6 demonstrates the order of events that occur to perform this animation.

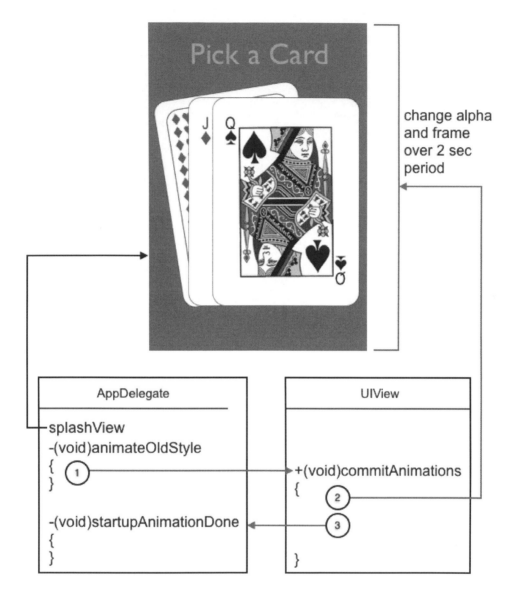

Figure 17.6 Animation message order

Here's the breakdown:

1. After performing the animation setup, the **AppDelegate** calls the **UIView** class method **commitAnimations**.

2. Over a 2-second period, the splash view's **alpha** value is decreased and its **frame** size is increased.

3. After the 2-second animation period, the **UIView** calls the **startupAnimationDone:finished:context:** method, which removes the splash view from its parent view.

Now let's see how animations work when using blocks.

Animation With Blocks

I have included the code that uses blocks for animation in the sample project. Let's take a look at it.

1. Open the **PickACard** project.

2. In the Project Navigator, select the **AppDelegate.m** implementation file and scroll down until you see the **animateWithBlocks** method (Figure 17.7).

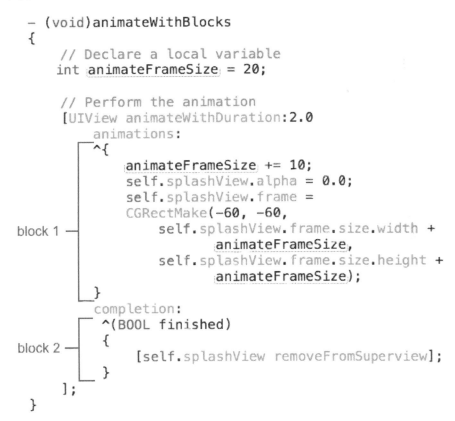

```
- (void)animateWithBlocks
{
    // Declare a local variable
    int animateFrameSize = 20;

    // Perform the animation
    [UIView animateWithDuration:2.0
        animations:
            ^{
                animateFrameSize += 10;
                self.splashView.alpha = 0.0;
                self.splashView.frame =
                CGRectMake(-60, -60,
                    self.splashView.frame.size.width +
                        animateFrameSize,
                    self.splashView.frame.size.height +
                        animateFrameSize);
            }
        completion:
            ^(BOOL finished)
            {
                [self.splashView removeFromSuperview];
            }
    ];
}
```

block 1 — {...}

block 2 — ^(BOOL finished) {...}

*Figure 17.7 Blocks in the **animateWithBlocks** method*

As you can see, this code is far more concise than the animation code that doesn't use blocks.

It takes just a little extra effort to grasp the concepts of blocks, but their use in your Apps will continue to pay dividends as you maintain your Apps over time.

Declaring an Inline Block

The **animationWithDuration:animations:completion:** method of the **UIView** class is called in the code in Figure 17.7. This method has two parameters that accept blocks—**animations** and **completion**.

In this code, the blocks are declared inline and passed directly as arguments. Ultimately, you can pass a block to a method, just as you would pass any other object—this is very powerful!

As you can see, blocks begin with the caret (^) character and the code in the block is enclosed in curly braces. In this example, neither block returns a value. **Block 1** has no parameters, and **block 2** accepts a **BOOL** parameter.

To help grasp the syntax of blocks, let's look at **block 2** and see how it's declared differently than a regular method. Figure 17.8 shows a *method* on top and an equivalent *block* on the bottom.

Method

```
- (void)complete:(BOOL)finished
{
    [self.splashView removeFromSuperview];
}
```

Block

```
^(BOOL finished)
{
    [self.splashView removeFromSuperview];
}
```

Figure 17.8 Comparing a method to a block

Here are a few things to note:

- The method on top specifies a **void** return value.

  The block on the bottom doesn't specify a return value. A block *can* specify the type of its return value, but doesn't *have* to. The compiler can look at the code in the block and infer, or figure out, the type of the value returned from the block. This is known as ***type inference***.

- The name of the method on top is **complete:**.

  Blocks don't have names—they are *anonymous*. In fact, you can think of the tilde (^) character as a placeholder for where you would normally specify a method name.

- The method on top has a single parameter. A colon separates the method name from the parameter. The parameter type (**BOOL**) is enclosed in parentheses, followed by the parameter name (**finished**).

  In a block declaration, there is no colon before the parameter and both the parameter type and name are enclosed in parentheses. Commas are used to separate multiple block parameters.

We'll learn more about block syntax and functionality in just a bit, but let's talk about why they can be more desirable than selectors.

1. They allow you to locate the code to be executed near the code that is invoking it. In the code sample in Figure 17.7, you don't have to create a separate method to be called on completion of the animation. You can pass the code as a block—it's more straightforward, and more obvious what's going on for someone reading your code.

2. Blocks have access to any variables that are in scope at the time the block is declared. This means you don't have to pass arguments to give the block information it needs. It can just access the variables directly.

This second point is discussed further in the next section.

Blocks as Closures

You often hear the term ***closure*** in a discussion of Objective-C blocks. This term describes the ability of a block to close around variables that are in scope at the time the block is declared. If you declare a local variable outside of a block, the block can still access that variable. In Figure 17.9, the **animateFrameSize** variable is declared in the same method as the block, so this variable can be accessed from within the block.

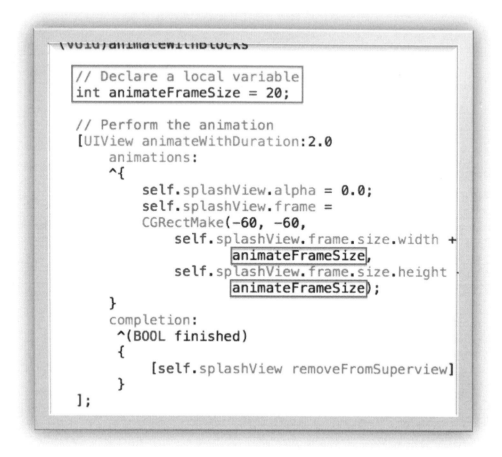

Figure 17.9 Blocks can access local variables.

By default, the block captures the value of the variable at the point in time when the block is declared, and the value of the value of the variable is read-only and can't be changed within the block.

If you *do* need to let a block change the value of a variable, you can use the **___block** modifier (there are two underscores that prefix the block modifier) as shown in Figure 17.10.

```
- (void)animateWithBlocks
{
    // Declare a local variable
    __block int animateFrameSize = 20;

    // Perform the animation
    [UIView animateWithDuration:2.0
        animations:
        ^{
            animateFrameSize += 10;
            self.splashView.alpha = 0.0;
            self.splashView.frame =
            CGRectMake(-60, -60,
                self.splashView.frame.size.width +
                    animateFrameSize,
                self.splashView.frame.size.height +
                    animateFrameSize);
        }
        completion:
        ^(BOOL finished)
        {
            [self.splashView removeFromSuperview];
        }
    ];
}
```

Figure 17.10 Use __block to change variable values.

Declaring Block Variables

In the previous section you learned how to declare a block "inline" with the call to a method. This is the most common way to use blocks. You can also declare a block variable that holds a reference to a block, and then use that variable to pass the block around like an object.

The syntax of declaring a block variable is somewhat unusual, so let's use our familiar block example to break it down. Figure 17.11 declares a block variable and assigns a block to it.

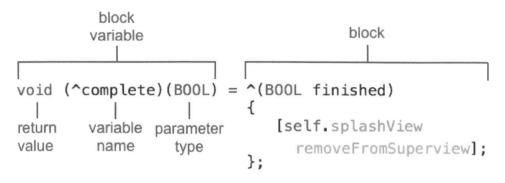

Figure 17.11 Declaring a block variable

The block variable declaration on the left sign of the equal sign has three main parts. Note that all three parts are mandatory:

1. **Return value** – Specifies the type of the block's return value. This block returns nothing (**void**).

2. **Variable name** – The block variable name has a caret (^) prefix and is enclosed in parentheses. This block variable's name is **complete**.

3. **Parameter type(s)** – Parameters types are enclosed in parentheses, and multiple parameters are separated by commas. This block accepts a single parameter of type **BOOL**.

Using Block Variables

After you declare a block variable, you can pass it to a function or method. Figure 17.12 demonstrates the declaration and assignment of a block variable named **complete**. Then, the **complete** block variable is passed to the **animateWithDuration:animations:completion:** method as an argument.

```
// Declare the block variable
// and assign a block to it
void (^complete)(BOOL) = ^(BOOL finished)
{
    [self.splashView
        removeFromSuperview];
};
```

```
// Perform the animation
[UIView animateWithDuration:2.0
    animations:
    ^{
        self.splashView.alpha = 0.0;
        self.splashView.frame =
        CGRectMake(-60, -60,
            self.splashView.frame.size.width +
                animateFrameSize,
            self.splashView.frame.size.height +
                animateFrameSize);
    }
    completion:complete
];
```

Figure 17.12 A block variable passed as an argument

As shown in Figure 17.13, after you declare a block variable, you can call it just as you would a function.

```
// Declare the block variable
// and assign a block to it
void (^complete)(BOOL) = ^(BOOL finished)
{
    [self.splashView
        removeFromSuperview];
};

// Call the block variable as
// you would a function
complete(YES);
```

Figure 17.13 Calling a block variable

Enumerating a Collection Using Blocks

Apple has added support for enumerating the contents of an **NSArray**, **NSDictionary**, and **NSSet** using blocks. For cases where you are doing simple enumeration over the contents of a small collection, it's preferable to use fast enumeration (a **for in** loop) because it's syntax is more straightforward and readable.

However, you may consider enumeration using blocks in these situations:

• If you have a collection with a large number of items, you can get faster performance using blocks because iOS can spread an enumeration over multiple cores (central processing units). Starting with the iPhone 4s and the iPad 2, all newer iOS devices have multiple cores.

• When enumerating the contents of a *dictionary* using blocks, both the object and key are passed to your block. In contrast, with a standard **for in** loop, you enumerate the keys and then make another call to get the associated object, which is slower and clumsier.

• If you need to plug in different algorithms when enumerating a collection, you can create different reusable blocks and choose the one you need at run time.

As a refresher, let's first take a look at using a standard **for in** loop to enumerate a collection.

1. Open the **PickACard** project in Xcode if it's not already open.

2. Go to the Project Navigator and select the **PlayingCardBackViewController.m** implementation file. Add the following code to the bottom of the **viewDidLoad:** method:

```
- (void)viewDidLoad
{
  [super viewDidLoad];

    // Create a dealer, open new deck of cards
    self.dealer = [[Dealer alloc] init];
    [self.dealer openNewDeck];

    // Add the players
    self.players = [[NSDictionary alloc]
      initWithObjectsAndKeys:
      @"Doyle Brunson", @"DB",
      @"John Bonetti", @"JB",
      @"Johnny Chan", @"JC",
      @"Phil Hellmuth", @"PH",
```

```
    nil];

    // Standard for/in loop
    NSLog(@"\n\rStandard for in loop:");

    for (CardEntity *card in self.dealer.deck) {
        NSLog(@"%@", card.cardName);
    }
}
```

At the top of the **viewDidLoad** method, a **Dealer** object is created, and an **openNewDeck** message is sent to it. This creates a new deck of cards with cards ordered in the usual sequence for a new deck:

- Hearts first, Ace to King,

- Clubs second, Ace to King,

- Diamonds third, King to Ace,

- Spades fourth, King to Ace

The code you added is a standard **for in** loop. I had you add this code to remind you what a standard loop looks like. The code within the loop outputs the name of the current card to Xcode's Console.

3. Press Xcode's **Run** button. After the App appears in the Simulator, you will see the list of cards in the Console (Figure 17.14).

```
All Output ⬍    ( Clear )                              [□] [▓] [□]
Standard for in loop:
2012-07-16 13:14:53.561 PickACard[2685:f803] Ace of Hearts
2012-07-16 13:14:53.561 PickACard[2685:f803] 2 of Hearts
2012-07-16 13:14:53.561 PickACard[2685:f803] 3 of Hearts
2012-07-16 13:14:53.562 PickACard[2685:f803] 4 of Hearts
2012-07-16 13:14:53.562 PickACard[2685:f803] 5 of Hearts
2012-07-16 13:14:53.562 PickACard[2685:f803] 6 of Hearts
2012-07-16 13:14:53.563 PickACard[2685:f803] 7 of Hearts
2012-07-16 13:14:53.563 PickACard[2685:f803] 8 of Hearts
2012-07-16 13:14:53.563 PickACard[2685:f803] 9 of Hearts
2012-07-16 13:14:53.564 PickACard[2685:f803] 10 of Hearts
2012-07-16 13:14:53.564 PickACard[2685:f803] Jack of Hearts
2012-07-16 13:14:53.565 PickACard[2685:f803] Queen of Hearts
2012-07-16 13:14:53.565 PickACard[2685:f803] King of Hearts
2012-07-16 13:14:53.565 PickACard[2685:f803] Ace of Clubs
2012-07-16 13:14:53.566 PickACard[2685:f803] 2 of Clubs
```

*Figure 17.14 The **for in** loop playing card output*

Enumerating a Collection With a Block

To enumerate an **NSArray**, **NSMutableArray** or **NSSet** with a block, you use the **enumerateObjectsUsingBlock:** method.

To see this method in action, follow these steps:

1. Open the **PickACard** project if it's not already open.

2. Select the **PlayingCardBackViewController.m** file in the Project Navigator, and add the following code to the bottom of the **viewDidLoad** method:

```
[self.dealer.deck
    enumerateObjectsUsingBlock:
    ^(id obj, NSUInteger idx, BOOL *stop) {
        NSLog(@"%@",
        ((CardEntity *)obj).cardName);
    }
];
```

The **enumerateObjectsUsingBlock:** method loops through each item in the collection. For each object in the collection, it calls the block, passing these arguments:

- **obj** contains a reference to the current object.

- **idx** is the index of the current object in the collection.

- **stop** is a Boolean argument that you can set to **YES** to stop enumerating the collection.

3. Click Xcode's **Run** button to see this code work at run time. After the App appears in the Simulator, you will see a second collection output in the Console with Ace of Hearts listed first (Figure 17.15).

```
All Output ‡                                    Clear   [ ]  [ ]  [ ]
Enumerating with a block:
2012-07-16 13:14:53.598 PickACard[2685:f803] Ace of Hearts
2012-07-16 13:14:53.598 PickACard[2685:f803] 2 of Hearts
2012-07-16 13:14:53.599 PickACard[2685:f803] 3 of Hearts
2012-07-16 13:14:53.599 PickACard[2685:f803] 4 of Hearts
2012-07-16 13:14:53.599 PickACard[2685:f803] 5 of Hearts
2012-07-16 13:14:53.600 PickACard[2685:f803] 6 of Hearts
2012-07-16 13:14:53.600 PickACard[2685:f803] 7 of Hearts
2012-07-16 13:14:53.601 PickACard[2685:f803] 8 of Hearts
2012-07-16 13:14:53.601 PickACard[2685:f803] 9 of Hearts
2012-07-16 13:14:53.602 PickACard[2685:f803] 10 of Hearts
2012-07-16 13:14:53.602 PickACard[2685:f803] Jack of Hearts
2012-07-16 13:14:53.602 PickACard[2685:f803] Queen of Hearts
2012-07-16 13:14:53.603 PickACard[2685:f803] King of Hearts
2012-07-16 13:14:53.603 PickACard[2685:f803] Ace of Clubs
2012-07-16 13:14:53.603 PickACard[2685:f803] 2 of Clubs
```

Figure 17.15 The block enumerates the playing cards.

As already mentioned, if you are enumerating a small list of items, there's no real advantage to using blocks—in fact, it's preferable to use the for in looping statement instead.

Enumerating Objects in Reverse Order With a Block

If you need to enumerate the objects in a collection in reverse order (last to first), then you can use the **enumerateObjectsWithOptions:usingBlock:** method. Just pass **NSEnumerationReverse** as the first argument, and then pass the block as the second argument.

To see this method in action:

1. Open the **PickACard** project if it's not already open.

2. Select the **PlayingCardBackViewController.m** implementation file in the Project Navigator and add the following code to the bottom of the **viewDidLoad** method:

```
// Simple enumeration with a block, reverse order
NSLog(@"\n\rEnumerating with a block, reverse order:");

[self.dealer.deck
    enumerateObjectsWithOptions:
    NSEnumerationReverse
    usingBlock:
    ^(id obj, NSUInteger idx, BOOL *stop) {
        NSLog(@"%@",
```

337

```
        ((CardEntity *)obj).cardName);
    }
  ];
```

3. Click Xcode's **Run** button to see the output of this enumeration at run
    time. The cards will be displayed in reverse order with Ace of Spades listed
    first as shown in Figure 17.16.

```
All Output ⬍                                    Clear  ▢ ▮ ▢
Enumerating with a block, reverse order:
2012-07-16 13:45:46.240 PickACard[2796:f803] Ace of Spades
2012-07-16 13:45:46.241 PickACard[2796:f803] 2 of Spades
2012-07-16 13:45:46.241 PickACard[2796:f803] 3 of Spades
2012-07-16 13:45:46.242 PickACard[2796:f803] 4 of Spades
2012-07-16 13:45:46.242 PickACard[2796:f803] 5 of Spades
2012-07-16 13:45:46.242 PickACard[2796:f803] 6 of Spades
2012-07-16 13:45:46.243 PickACard[2796:f803] 7 of Spades
2012-07-16 13:45:46.243 PickACard[2796:f803] 8 of Spades
2012-07-16 13:45:46.243 PickACard[2796:f803] 9 of Spades
2012-07-16 13:45:46.244 PickACard[2796:f803] 10 of Spades
2012-07-16 13:45:46.244 PickACard[2796:f803] Jack of Spades
2012-07-16 13:45:46.244 PickACard[2796:f803] Queen of Spades
```

Figure 17.16 The block enumerates in reverse order.

Improve Performance by Enumerating Objects Concurrently

If you have a large number of objects to enumerate, you can request that your
enumeration be run concurrently (simultaneously) on multiple threads of
execution. To do this, use the
enumerateObjectsWithOptions:usingBlock: method and pass
NSEnumerationConcurrent as the first argument, and a block as the
second argument.

When you enumerate a collection concurrently, the order in which objects in
the collection are processed is not guaranteed. You should only use this option
if it makes sense to process objects in the collection in random order.

To see the concurrency option in action:

1. Open the **PickACard** project if it's not already open.

2. Select the **PlayingCardBackViewController.m** file in the Project
    Navigator and add the following code to the bottom of the **viewDidLoad**
    method:

```
NSLog(@"\n\rEnumerating with a block, concurrently:");

[self.dealer.deck
    enumerateObjectsWithOptions:
    NSEnumerationConcurrent
    usingBlock:
    ^(id obj, NSUInteger idx, BOOL *stop) {
        NSLog(@"%@",
        ((CardEntity *)obj).cardName);
    }
];
```

3. Click Xcode's **Run** button to see how this works at run time. After the App appears in Simulator, you will see items listed in the Console in somewhat random order (Figure 17.17).

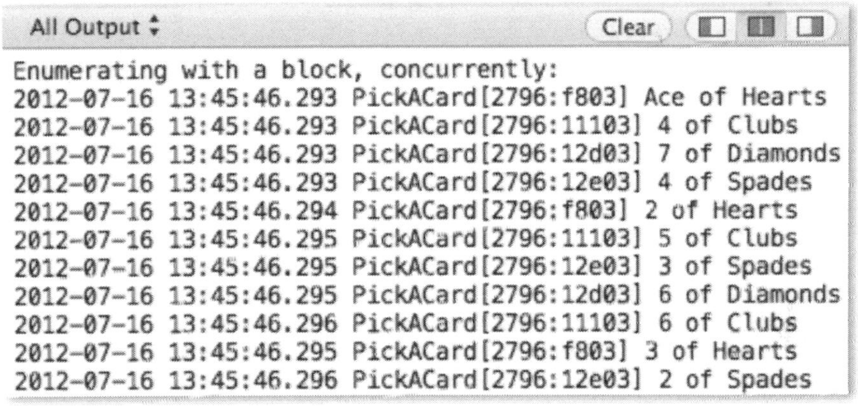

Figure 17.17 Enumerating items concurrently

You can see a basic pattern to which items are processed at a particular time, but there are no guarantees about the order in which items are processed. In fact, if you run the App again, you will see the items processed in a slightly different order.

Adding Flexibility With Algorithm Blocks

As mentioned at the beginning of this section, another reason you may want to use blocks for enumerating a collection is the flexibility it provides in using alternate algorithms.

To see an example of this:

1. Open the **PickACard** project if it's not already open.

2. In the Project Navigator, expand the **Business Layer** group and select the **Dealer.m** implementation file. Scroll towards the bottom of the code file to see the **shuffleDeckUsingAlgorithmBlock:** method:

```
- (void)shuffleDeckUsingAlgorithmBlock:
    (void (^)(NSMutableArray * deck,
    NSUInteger index))algorithm
{
    // Make a copy of the current deck
    NSMutableArray *shuffledDeck =
        [[NSMutableArray alloc]
        initWithArray:self.deck];

    // Enumerate the cards in the deck and
    // pass the deck and current card to
    // the shuffling algorithm
    [self.deck enumerateObjectsUsingBlock:
     ^(id obj, NSUInteger index, BOOL *stop)
        {
        algorithm(shuffledDeck, index);
        }
     ];

    // Set shuffled deck as current deck
    self.deck = shuffledDeck;
}
```

This method accepts a block argument, where the block returns nothing (**void**) and accepts an **NSMutableArray** and **NSUInteger** arguments:

```
(void (^)(NSMutableArray * deck,
    NSUInteger index))algorithm
```

The first line of code in this method creates a copy of the current deck of cards. Next, it sends an **enumerateObjectsUsingBlock:** message to the deck, passing along the algorithm block:

```
[self.deck enumerateObjectsUsingBlock:
    ^(id obj, NSUInteger index, BOOL *stop)
        {
        algorithm(shuffledDeck, index);
        }
    ];
```

For each item in the collection, the **algorithm** block is passed a reference to the deck of cards, and the index of the current card. It's up to the block to shuffle the cards in the deck based on this information.

3. If you look a little lower in the code file, you will see the **shuffleDeck** method:

```
- (void)shuffleDeck
{
    [self shuffleDeckUsingAlgorithmBlock:
     ^ (NSMutableArray * deck,
        NSUInteger index)
    {
        // Get a random number from 1-52
        int r = arc4random() % deck.count;
        // Exchange object at current index
        // with object at random index
        [deck exchangeObjectAtIndex:index
         withObjectAtIndex:r];
    }
    ];
}
```

This method calls the **shuffleDeckUsingAlgorithm:** and passes a block containing a common card-shuffling algorithm known as the Fisher-Yates shuffle.

If you pass a **shuffleDeck** message to the Dealer object, it passes a default shuffling algorithm to the **shuffleDeckUsingAlgorithmBlock:** method. The class is also extremely flexible because you can also pass your own shuffling algorithm to this method by calling it directly.

4. To see how the shuffling works at run time, select the **PlayingCardBackViewController.m** implementation file in the Project Navigator. Add the following code to the **viewDidLoad** method:

```
NSLog(@"\n\rEnumerating a shuffled deck:");

[self.dealer shuffleDeck];
for (CardEntity *card in self.dealer.deck) {
    NSLog(@"%@", card.cardName);
}
```

5. Click Xcode's **Run** button to see the output of the shuffled deck (Figure 17.18).

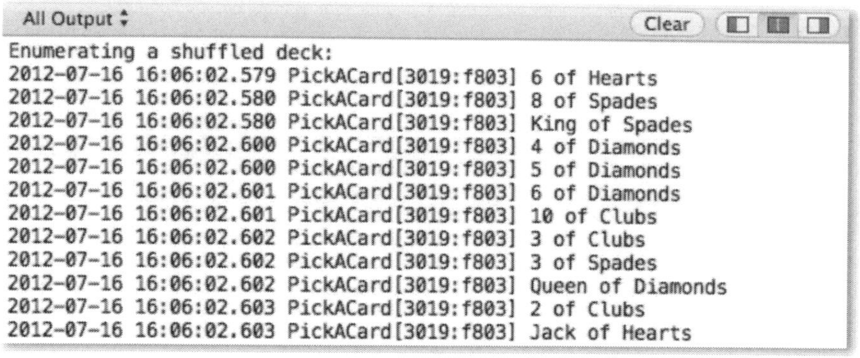

Figure 17.18 Cards in a shuffled deck in random order

The order in which the shuffled cards appear will be different than shown in Figure 17.18 because the order of shuffled cards is random.

Using Blocks to Enumerate a Dictionary

Enumerating a dictionary using a block can provide extra performance and convenience. For example, here is a standard **for in** loop that enumerates a dictionary:

```
NSString *key;
NSString *name;
for (key in self.players) {
        name = [self.players objectForKey:key];
        NSLog(@"%@:%@", key, name);
}
```

The **for in** loop enumerates the keys in the players dictionary. Within the loop, you must pass an objectForKey: message to get the object value associated with the key.

In contrast, the following code uses the **NSDictionary enumerateKeysAndObjectsUsingBlock:** method:

```
[self.players
        enumerateKeysAndObjectsUsingBlock:
        ^(id key, id obj, BOOL *stop) {
            NSLog(@"%@:%@", key, obj);
        }
];
```

The **enumerateKeysAndObjectsUsingBlock:** method passes both the current item's **key** as well as the object (**obj**) associated with the key, which avoids the need for the **objectForKey:** message. Notice this method also passes a **stop** argument to the block, which you can set to **YES** when you want to stop the enumeration loop.

Summary

Here are the key points in this chapter.

Selectors

- In Objective-C, the term *selector* has two meanings:

  1. When you pass a message to an object, the name of the method is known as the *selector*.

  2. *Selector* also refers to a unique identifier that replaces the method name when a project is compiled.

- You use the **@selector** directive to get the selector for a particular method. For example:

```
SEL done = @selector(done:);
```

- You can send a **performSelector:** message to an object to request that it invoke the selector. For example:

```
[myObject performSelector:save];
```

- To return a value from one of the **performSelector:** methods, store the result into a variable from the **performSelector:** message call. For example:

```
Calculator *result = [self
performSelector:getCalculator];
```

Target-Action Design Pattern

- The place you most often use selectors is in conjunction with the Target-Action design pattern.

- In the Target-Action design pattern, an object holds two pieces of information for sending a message:

  1. A *target*, which is the receiver of the message.

2.   An *action*, which is the method to be invoked.

Blocks

- A block is a self-contained chunk of code usually small in size that can be passed around as an object.

- Blocks can be executed:

  1.   As a callback when an operation has finished, or in response to the occurrence of an event.

  2.   Concurrently (simultaneously) on multiple threads of execution.

  3.   Over items in a collection.

- Blocks are *closures*, meaning they close around variables that are in scope at the time the block is declared.

- You can declare blocks inline or declare a block variable that holds a reference to a block then use that variable to pass the block around like an object.

- You can enumerate a collection using a block, but you should typically only use this functionality when working with large collections, enumerating the contents of a dictionary, or when you need to plug in different algorithms.

Exercise 17.1

In this exercise, you will use what you have learned about blocks to pass a block to a method.

1.   The **PickACard** project contains a **Dealer** class with a **shuffleDeckUsingAlgorithmBlock:** method.

     Add code to the **viewDidLoad** method of the **PlayingCardBackViewController.m** file that passes an **openNewDeck:** message to the Dealer object.

2.   Next, pass a message with a block argument to the Dealer object's **shuffleDeckUsingAlgorithmBlock:** method. In the block argument use the following sorting algorithm that reverses the order of the deck of cards:

```
// Sort deck in reverse order
if (index < 26) {
    int r = (52 - index) - 1;
    [deck exchangeObjectAtIndex:index
        withObjectAtIndex:r];
}
```

3. Add code to the **viewDidLoad** method that tests if the shuffling algorithm worked.

Solution Movie 17.1

To see a video providing the solution for this exercise, go to the following link in your web browser.

http://www.iOSAppsForNonProgrammers.com/B2M171.html

Conclusion

Now that you have the basics of Objective-C under your belt, where do you go from here?

Where Do You Go From Here?

Now that you have climbed the Objective-C learning curve, what are your next steps in learning to create iOS Apps for the iPhone, iPad, and iPod touch?

One of your next steps is learning more about Xcode. In this book, we have just scratched the surface of Xcode's capabilities. There is much to learn in laying out the user interface, writing code that responds to user interaction, testing your code, and making full use of the iPhone and iPad Simulators.

To get this knowledge quickly, and learn how to create some great sample Apps in the process, I recommend that you check out our third book in this series, _iOS App Development for Non-Programmers: Book 3 - Navigating Xcode_. Not only will you learn a lot about Xcode, you will also learn much about creating iOS Apps as you follow step-by-step instructions in each chapter.

When you create Apps for yourself or others, it's best to create a prototype first so you can get feedback from people representing your target audience. This saves a tremendous amount of time that will otherwise be spent reworking your App when you put it in front of users for the first time. Xcode is a great prototyping tool and you should learn how to use it in this way before building your first App. If you haven't already read our first book in this series, _iOS App Development for Non-Programmers - Book 1: Diving In_, I highly recommend you check it out for great tips and practical information on creating App prototypes.

Early on, you should also learn about creating a proper architecture for your iOS Apps. This includes learning design patterns that ensure the Apps you create are easy to maintain as you release subsequent versions with new features.

You will also need to learn (among other things):

- Managing lists of data with table views

- Application navigation

- Storing and retrieving data on an iOS device as well as on the web using web services and iCloud

- Getting user location and working with maps

- Interacting with other Apps

- Working with media such as images and video

- Making your App multi-lingual

- Making your App accessible to the visually-impaired

- Getting your App ready for the App store

This book is one of the first in a series of books written specifically for non-programmers. All of the topics listed here are covered in upcoming books in this series.

Ask Questions on Our Forum!

To get answers to your questions and engage with others like yourself, check out our forum:

http://iOSAppsForNonProgrammers.com/forum

Training Classes

I regularly teach hands-on training classes (with small class sizes) where you can learn more about iOS App development in a friendly, in-person environment. For more information, check out our web site:

www.iOSAppsForNonProgrammers.com/training.html

Appendices

The appendices in this section of the book provide quick access to information on Objective-C compiler errors and warnings, data types, operators, and string format specifiers.

Appendices:

Appendix A: Compiler Errors & Warnings

(What on earth does *that* mean?)

This appendix contains a list of compiler errors and warnings that new Objective-C developers often encounter, but have difficulty understanding.

Interface type cannot be statically allocated

You usually get this error when you forget to include an asterisk before a variable name that is an object pointer:

```
UILabel label = [[UILabel alloc] init];
```

To correct this problem, just add an asterisk before the variable name:

```
UILabel *label = [[UILabel alloc] init];
```

Missing sentinel in method dispatch

You usually get this warning when you forget to put a **nil** at the end of your argument list when calling methods such as NSArray's **initWithObjects**:

```
NSArray *choices = [[NSArray alloc]
                    initWithObjects:
                    @"Upper Case",
                    @"Lower Case",
                    @"Capitalized"];
```

To correct this problem, just add a **nil** to the end of the list:

```
NSArray *choices = [[NSArray alloc]
                    initWithObjects:
                    @"Upper Case",
                    @"Lower Case",
                    @"Capitalized",
                    nil];
```

Missing @end

You usually get this error when you accidentally delete a method's closing curly brace. For example:

```
- (void)viewDidAppear:(BOOL)animated
{
```

```
    [super viewDidAppear:animated];
```

To fix this, all you have to do is put the curly brace back!

```
- (void)viewDidAppear:(BOOL)animated
{
    [super viewDidAppear:animated];
}
```

Expected ';' after method prototype

You usually get this error in a class header file method declaration if you forget to put a colon (not a semicolon) before a parameter. For example, there is a colon missing after **addToTotal:**, the method name:

```
(double) addToTotal(double)value;
```

To fix the problem, just add a colon before the parameter:

```
    - (double) addToTotal:(double)value;
```

Control reaches end of non-void function

You get this warning when you have declared that a method returns a value, but you have left out the **return** statement in the method. For example, this code specifies the method returns a value of type **double**:

```
- (double) divideIntoTotal:(double)value
{

}
```

To fix this warning, just add a **return** statement that returns a value of the correct type:

```
- (double) divideIntoTotal:(double)value
{
        self.total /= value;
        return self.total;
}
```

Property access result unused – getters should not be used for side effects

If you try to call a method that takes no arguments using dot notation (rather than passing a message), you will get this warning. For example:

```
self.clear;
```

To fix this warning, change the code to pass a message instead:

```
[self clear];
```

Initializer Element Is Not a Compile-Time Constant

You usually get this compiler error if you place code that initializes an instance variable code outside of a class method. For example, the following code initializes the **devices** array above the **@implementation** declaration, and outside of a method:

```
NSArray *devices = [[NSArray alloc]
                    initWithObjects:@"iPod Touch"
                    @"iPhone",
                    @"iPad", nil];

@implementation Calculator
```

To fix the problem, declare the instance variable without initializing it:

```
NSArray *devices;
```

Then, initialize the instance variable elsewhere, such as in a view controller's **viewDidLoad** method:

```
- (void)viewDidLoad
{
    [super viewDidLoad];

    devices = [[NSArray alloc]
            initWithObjects:@"iPod Touch"
            @"iPhone",
            @"iPad", nil];
}
```

Missing Context for Property Implementation Declaration

You typically get this compiler error if you try to synthesize a property outside of a class implementation. For example, the following code tries to synthesize the **dealer** property before the **@implementation** declaration that marks the beginning of the class:

```
@synthesize dealer = _dealer;

@implementation PlayingCardBackViewController
```

To fix the problem, just move the **@synthesize** declaration after the **@implementation** declaration and before the **@end** declaration:

```
@implementation PlayingCardBackViewController

@synthesize dealer = _dealer;
```

Appendix B: Basic Data Types

Objective-C's basic data types are simple, *scalar* types that contain only a single value.

Data type	Description
BOOL	Boolean value that can be YES or NO, true or false, one (1) or zero (0)
char	A single character, such as the letter 'x'
int	An integer, or whole number (a number without a decimal point), that holds values from -2,147,483,648 to 2,147,483,647
short	A short integer that holds values from -32,768 to 32,767
long	A long integer in iOS holds the same range of values as a regular **int**, but you can use **long** as a prefix for other numeric types to increase their range (**long long**, holds values from -9,223,372,036,854,775,808 to 9,223,372,036,854,775,807).
float	A floating point number (values containing decimal points) ranging in value from -3.4E+38 to 3.4E+38 (E+38 means move the decimal point 38 places to the right)
double	Stores floating point numbers larger than **float** from -1.7E+308 to 1.7E+308
unsigned	You can use the **unsigned** prefix with **char**, **int**, **short**, **long**, and **long long** to create unsigned numbers (no negative numbers).

Appendix C: Objective-C Operators

Operator	Description	Example
=	Assignment	a = b;
+	Addition	a = b + c;
-	Subtraction	a = b - c;
*	Multiplication	a = b * c;
/	Division	a = b / c;
%	Modulus (the remainder that results from integer division)	a = b % c;
+=	Addition and assignment	a += b;
-=	Subtraction and assignment	a -= b;
*=	Multiplication and assignment	a *= b;
/=	Division and assignment	a /= b;
%=	Modulus and assignment	a = %= b;
++	Increment	a++;
--	Decrement	a--;
==	Equal to	a == b;
!=	Not equal to	a != b;
<	Less than	a < b;
>	Greater than	a > b;
<=	Less than or equal to	a <= b;
>=	Greater than or equal to	a >= b;
&&	Logical AND	a > b && a < c
||	Logical OR	a < b || a > c
!	NOT	!a
?:	Conditional operator	a = b ? c : d;
()	Cast	a = (b)c;

Bit Operators

Bit operations operate on integer values at the level of individual bits of information. You rarely use these in Objective-C programming, but they are listed for the sake of completeness.

Operator	Description	Example
&	Bitwise AND	a = b & c;
|	Bitwise Inclusive OR	a = b | c;
^	Bitwise Exclusive OR	
~	Ones complement	a = ~b;
<<	Left Shift	a = a << 2;
>>	Right Shift	a = a >> 4;

Appendix D: String Format Specifiers

This appendix contains a list of the more commonly used *format specifiers*.
For a complete list, see Apple's *String Format Specifiers* help topic from
which this table is derived.

Specifier	Description
%@	String
%d %D %i	Signed integer (**int**)
%u %U	Unsigned integer (**unsigned int**)
%f	**double** floating point number
%F	**double** floating point number, printed in decimal notation
%hi	Signed **short** integer
%hu	Unsigned **short** integer
%qi	Signed **long long** integer
%qu	Unsigned **long long** integer
%x	Unsigned integer (**unsigned int**) displayed in hexadecimal using the digits 0-9 and lowercase a-f
%qx	Unsigned **long long** integer displayed in hexadecimal using the digits 0-9 and lowercase a-f
%qX	Unsigned **long long** integer displayed in hexadecimal using the digits 0-9 and uppercase A-F
%o,%O	Unsigned integer (**unsigned int**), printed in octal
%e	**double** floating point number, printed in scientific notation using a lowercase e to introduce the exponent
%E	**double** floating point number, printed in scientific notation using an uppercase E to introduce the exponent
%g	**double** floating point number, printed in the style of %e if the exponent is less than -4 or greater than or equal to the precision, otherwise, in the style of %f
%G	**double** floating point number, printed in the style of %E if the exponent is less than -4 or greater than or equal to the precision, otherwise, in the style of %f
%c	**unsigned char**
%C	**unichar**
%%	'%' character

Glossary

Accessor methods   Accessor methods are the combination of the getter and setter methods used to retrieve and store values for a property, usually getting and setting the value to an associated instance variable.

Action   In the Target-Action design pattern, the action is the method to be invoked.

Animation   An animation is a smooth transition from one user-interface state to another. The user tapping a button that causes one view to slide out and another view to slide in is an example of an animation.

App   An App is a relatively small software application designed to perform one or more related tasks. In the context of this book, an App is specifically a software application that runs on an iPhone, iPod Touch or iPad.

ARC   See Automatic Reference Counting

Argument   An argument is a piece of data that is passed to an object in a message call.

You often see the words *argument* and *parameter* used interchangeably, but there is a subtle difference. An *argument* is a piece of data that you pass to a method. A *parameter* is a part of the method declaration that dictates the argument(s) to be passed to the method. In short, arguments appear in message calls, parameters appear in method declarations.

Atomic   By default, Objective-C properties are atomic, meaning they are guaranteed to retrieve or set the correct value in environments that have multiple threads of execution.

Attribute   Attributes describe the characteristics of an object. Xcode's Attributes Inspector allows you to view and change the attributes of user-interface objects.

For every object *attribute* you see in Xcode's Attribute Inspector, there is a corresponding *property* in the class definition.

An object's attributes are defined as properties in the class blueprint from which the object was created. Each attribute has a default value, also specified in the class. After an object has been created, you can change the value of its attributes. You can change an attribute on one object without affecting any other objects.

In this context, attributes and properties are similar. In Xcode, an object has attributes; in Objective-C, the class on which an object is based has properties.

Automatic Reference Counting   Starting in iOS 5, Apple introduced Automatic Reference Counting, or ARC, which deals specifically with memory management in your App. Before ARC was introduced, you had to manually insert retain messages in your code to increment your object's retain count, and release messages to decrement your object's retain count. When an object's retain count reaches zero, it is released from memory. Not sending the proper retain and release messages was a constant cause of *memory leaks* in iOS Apps.

With Automatic Reference Counting, the compiler inserts retain and release messages in the compiled code for you based on the context of how your object is used.

Bit operations   Bit operations operate at the level of individual bits of information. You rarely use these in Objective-C programming. Check out *Appendix C: Objective-C Operators* for a list of bitwise operations.

Block   A block is a self-contained chunk of code, usually small in size that can be passed around as an object. In fact, blocks are full-fledged Objective-C objects.

Boxing   When you convert a scalar data type to an object, it's known as **boxing**. For example, the following code converts (boxes) a scalar integer value to an **NSNumber** object.

```
NSNumber *number = [NSNumber numberWithInt:myInt];
```

Breakpoint   A breakpoint is a debugging feature in Xcode that allows you to temporarily pause an App and examine the value of variables, properties, and so on.

Business Object   Business objects contain the core business logic of your App. They often represent real-world entities such as a customer, invoice, product, or payment.

Camel case   Camel case is a term used to describe the capitalization style of symbols such as method and parameter names. A camel-cased name always begins with a lowercase letter, and then the first letter of each word in a compound word is uppercased (like a camel's head and its humps). For example, the method names **areYouOld** and **amIOld** are both camel cased.

Case sensitive   Objective-C is case sensitive, which means you must type the uppercase and lowercase letters exactly as the language expects, or you will encounter errors when you try to compile your code.

Cast   See **Explicit conversion**

Category   A category is an advanced feature of Objective-C that allows you to extend a class without creating a subclass. You can even extend the Cocoa Touch Framework classes.

Class   A class is like a blueprint for an object. You create an object from a class.

Class diagram   A class diagram is a formal representation of a class. It lists both the properties and methods of the class.

Class extension   In Objective-C, a class extension allows you to declare methods that are hidden from the public interface of the class. Class extensions are similar to categories except:

- They are usually found in the implementation (.m) file *of the class that they are extending*.

- There is no name listed between the parentheses.

- They allow you to declare *required* methods.

Class header file   The class header file declares the class's *public interface* to other classes.

Class implementation file   A class implementation file has a .m extension and contains the actual code for the properties and methods declared in the public interface. It also declares private variables and methods.

Class method   Class methods are methods that belong to the class itself, meaning that you pass the message to the class directly without creating an instance of the class.

Closure   You often hear the term closure in a discussion of Objective-C blocks. This term describes the ability of a block to close around variables that are in scope at the time the block is declared.

Cocoa Touch Framework   The Cocoa Touch Framework is a set of many smaller frameworks (which contain sets of classes) each focusing on a set of core functionality that provides access to important services such as multi-touch gestures, user-interface controls, saving and retrieving data, user location, maps, camera, and compass.

Code Completion   Code Completion is Xcode's way of helping you write code. Based on the characters you type, it provides its best guess as to what you need to complete a code statement.

Collection   A collection is a grouping of one or more related objects. Cocoa Touch Framework collection classes such as **NSArray**, **NSDictionary**, and **NSSet** allow you to group multiple items together into a single collection.

Comment   A comment is text that is added to a code file to provide an explanation of the functionality of a particular section of code. Comments are not code and are therefore not executed.

Compiler   A compiler is a software program that interprets, or converts the Objective-C code that you write into machine code, which an iOS device can actually execute.

Compound assignment operators   A compound assignment operator is an operator that performs two operations. For example, the += operator adds the specified value and then stores the result back into a variable or property. The -= operator performs subtraction, *= performs multiplication, and /= performs division, each storing the resulting value back into a variable or property.

Compound comparison   A compound comparison allows you to perform multiple tests in a single *condition*. For example, in the following code, one check is performed to determine if **iq** is less than **20**, and a second check is performed to determine if **iq** is greater than **140**.

```
if (iq < 20 || iq > 140) {

      // statements to be executed
}
```

Condition   A condition is an expression that is checked to determine if it is true or false. For example, in the following **if** statement, the condition in parentheses is checked, and if (**age > 100**) evaluates to **true**, the **NSLog** statement is executed.

```
if (age > 100) {
      NSLog(@"You are old!");
}
```

Constant   Constants are values that do not change after they are declared. Sometimes constants are stand-alone, but they are often grouped together with other related constants in an *enumeration*.

Core logic   The core logic is the code in an App required to perform actions when a user-interface object is touched or when any other processing takes place automatically. Whenever an App "does something," it requires code to execute a set of instructions.

Data   Data is the information and preferences maintained by an App. This can be as simple as storing the user's zip code or as complex as storing large amounts of data such as thousands of pictures and songs.

Designated initializer   The designated initializer for a class is the *initializer* method that guarantees all instance variables are initialized.

It's a convention in the Cocoa Touch Framework that the designated initializer is usually the one with the most arguments (or said another way, the method that allows the most freedom to determine the character of the new instance). Ultimately, the only way to determine the true designated initializer is to read the documentation for the class.

Discoverability   Discoverability is a measure of how easy is it to discover, or find the code that you need to perform a particular task.

Dot notation   Dot notation refers to a technique of accessing an object's properties by typing a dot, or period after the object name. For example, notice the dot after the **textField** object reference and before the **placeholder** property:

```
textField.placeholder = @"First Name";
```

Encapsulation   Encapsulation is an object-oriented programming term that refers to hiding unnecessary information within a class. When you design your classes, you don't want to expose more information to the outside world than is necessary.

Enumeration   An enumeration is a group of related constants. Enumerations and their member names are Pascal cased and typically begin with a suffix that describes what type they are. For example, in the **UITextBorderStyle** enumeration, each member of the enumeration begins with the prefix "UITextBorderStyle":

- UITextBorderStyleBezel

- UITextBorderStyleLine

- UITextBorderStyleNone

- UITextBorderStyleRoundedRect

Explicit conversion   An explicit conversion, also known as a *cast*, is a conversion from one data type to another that you perform manually in code.

To perform an explicit conversion, you simply place the data type you want to convert to in parentheses directly before the value to be converted. For example, the following code explicitly converts a **double**, or floating point number to an **NSInteger**:

```
NSInteger i = (NSInteger) 1.567f;
```

Fast enumeration   Fast enumeration is another name for Objective-C's **for in** loop that is used to enumerate a collection of objects.

Format specifier   A format specifier is a special set of characters within a string that begins with a percent sign (%) and is followed by one or more characters that specify how to format the following argument, which is inserted into the string.

For example, in the following statement:

```
NSLog(@"Sum: %f", sum);
```

The **f** in the format specifier tells **NSLog** that the second argument is a **double**, or floating point number, which is converted, formatted and then inserted into the string.

For more information, see *Appendix D: String Format Specifiers.*

Forward declaration   A forward declaration is the declaration of an identifier (usually a class) for which a complete definition has not been supplied. In Objective-C, the use of the **@class** directive is known as a forward declaration that provides minimal information about a class. In fact, it only indicates that the class you are referencing is a class!

Frame   A **frame** is a rectangle that specifies a user-interface object's position on the user interface (in x and y coordinates) as well as its width and height.

Function   A function is a lot like a method; it groups together one or more lines of code that perform a specific task. However, unlike a method, a function is not attached to an object or a class. It's stand-alone, or "free floating."

Getter   A getter is one of the two methods associated with a property. It *gets* the value of the property, usually from an associated instance variable.

Header file   See **Class header file**

High-level language   Objective-C is a high-level language, meaning it is closer to human language than the actual code an iOS device executes when it is running your App.

Immutable   An immutable object is one that can't be changed after it is created. For example, after you initialize an **NSArray**, you can't change the array—you can't add an item, remove an item, or change an item.

Implementation file   See **Class implementation file**

Implicit conversion   The Objective-C compiler performs an implicit conversion from one data type to another that it considers "safe." *Implicit* means the conversion is performed automatically.

Index   When used in the context of an Objective-C collection, an index is a number that references an item by its position in the collection.

Inheritance   Inheritance is a basic principle of object-oriented programming. It refers to the concept that a class can be based on, or inherit its attributes (properties) and behavior (methods) from, another class.

Initializer   An initializer is a method that is used to set, or initialize the values of instance variables in a newly created object. Initializer methods should always begin with an "init" prefix.

Instance   An object created from a class is referred to as an instance of the class.

Instance method   Instance methods are methods called on instances of an object—meaning you create an object from a class, and then pass a message to the object.

Instance variable   In Objective-C, an instance variable is a variable declared at the class level and is accessible by all methods within the class. Also known as an **ivar**.

Instance-variable visibility   An instance variable's visibility refers to the ability of other classes to "see" or access the variable. In Objective-C there are three levels of visibility:

- **public** – Any class can access the instance variable (don't use this one!)

- **protected** – The class in which the instance variable is declared can access it, as well as subclasses of the class in which it is declared.

- **private** – The class in which the instance variable is declared is the only class that can access it—subclasses cannot access it. Make an ivar private if you don't want other classes changing the value of the ivar.

Instantiate   The term instantiate refers to the act of creating an instance of a class. The process of instantiation creates an object from a class definition.

iOS See **Operating System**

Ivar   See **Instance variable**

Key-value coding   Key-value coding (KVC) is an advanced feature of Objective-C that allows you to access an object's properties indirectly by using a string containing the property name rather than directly by using the property accessor methods.

For example, the following code sends a **valueForKey:** message to the **customer** object, passing the object's **firstName** property as a string:

```
NSString *firstName = [customer valueForKey:@"firstName"];
```

Literal   A **literal** is a notation representing a fixed value. Here is an example of a string literal:

```
NSString *myString = @"Objective-C";
```

The "at" (@) sign indicates the beginning of the string literal.

Local variable   Variables declared within a method are known as local variables because they can only be accessed locally from within the method in which they are declared.

Localize   The term localize is used in iOS and other software platforms to describe the process of translating and adapting your App to different cultures, countries, regions, or groups of people.

Machine code   Machine code is an instruction set consisting of bits of data (ones and zeroes) specific to a particular processor. The compiler generates machine code from the Objective-C code that you write.

Memory leak   A memory leak is a situation whereby an App continually eats up memory until all memory allocated to the App is eventually consumed.

Message   A message is the method and associated arguments sent to an object to be executed.

Message call   A message call is the act of sending a message to an object.

Method   The behavior of an object, or the actions that it can perform, are defined in the class blueprint as methods. A method is comprised of one or more (usually more) lines of code grouped together to perform a specific task.

Method signature   A method signature is the name of the method and the number of and type of its parameters, not including the return type.

Mutable   A mutable object is one that can be changed after it is created. For example, the **NSMutableArray**, **NSMutableDictionary** and **NSMutableSet** classes are collections that can be changed (items can be added, removed, and edited) after the collection is created.

Nonatomic   You can declare that an Objective-C property is nonatomic, meaning there is no guarantee to retrieve or set the correct value in environments that have multiple threads of execution. This makes nonatomic properties considerably faster than atomic properties.

Object   Software objects are similar to real-world objects. They have both attributes and behaviors. Apps have user-interface objects such as text fields, sliders, web views, and labels, as well as *business objects* that contain the App's core logic and represent real-world entities such as a Customer, Address, Album, Song, and Calculator.

In Objective-C you create objects at run time from classes, which act like blueprints.

Operating system   On an iOS device, iOS is the operating system. It is the software provided by Apple that manages the device hardware and provides the core functionality for all Apps running on the device.

Override   You can override a method inherited from a superclass by creating a method with the same signature in the subclass. Overriding allows you to extend an inherited method or completely change its implementation.

Parameter   A parameter is a part of the method declaration that dictates the argument(s) to be passed to the method. For example, the following method has a parameter of type **double** that is named **value**:

```
(double) addToTotal:(double)value;
```

You often see the words *argument* and *parameter* used interchangeably, but there is a subtle difference. An *argument* is a piece of data that you pass to a method. A *parameter* is a part of the method declaration that dictates the argument(s) to be passed to the method. In short, arguments appear in message calls, parameters appear in method declarations.

Pascal case   Pascal case is a term used to describe the capitalization style of symbols such as class names. A Pascal cased symbol always begins with an uppercase letter, and then the first letter of each word in a compound word is capitalized—for example, **InvoiceDetail** and **PatientHistory**.

Pointer   A pointer is a reference to an object's location in memory. A pointer is like a book index which points to a specific page where information can be found.

Polymorphism   Polymorphism is one of the core principles of object-oriented programming. This term refers to the ability of a class to take many different forms. Polymorphism allows you to declare a variable of a particular type, and then store a reference to an object of that type or *any of its subclasses* in that variable.

For example, you can declare a variable of type **UIControl**, and then store a reference to any class that is a subclass of **UIControl**:

```
UIControl* control;
control = [[UITextField alloc] init];
control = [[UIButton alloc] init];
control = [[UISwitch alloc] init];
```

Polymorphism allows you to write more generic code that works with families of objects rather than writing code for a specific class.

Processor   A processor is a central processing unit, or CPU. It is the hardware within a device that carries out programming instructions. For example, the iPhone 4 and iPad use the Apple A4 processor, the iPhone 4s and iPad 2 use the newer Apple A5 processor, and the new iPad uses the A5x processor.

Programmatically   When you perform an action in code, it is considered to be done **programmatically**, or in the program's code.

For example, if you add a user-interface control to a view by writing code (rather than dragging and dropping it on a view at design time), you are doing it programmatically.

Property   A property is the part of a class definition that describes a class's attributes, or characteristics. A property defined in a class corresponds to an object attribute in Xcode, which can be viewed using the Attributes

Inspector.

Protocol   A protocol is an advanced feature of Objective-C that allow you to define a standard set of behavior that other classes can implement.

For example, the **UIPickerViewDataSource** protocol declares methods required by an object that wants to act as a data source for the picker view, and the **UIPickerViewDelegate** protocol declares methods required by an object that wants to act as a delegate for the picker view.

Protocols are equivalent to *interfaces* in languages such as Java and C#.

Public interface   A class's public interface describes the properties and methods that can be accessed by other classes. It is defined in the *class header file*. This public interface is what allows Xcode to pop up a list of available properties and methods in its Code Completion list.

Receiver   The object that you send a message to is known as a receiver.

Run time   Run time is when an App is running in the Simulator or on an iOS device.

Scalar values   Scalar refers to primitive data types that contain only a single value, such as Boolean, integer, and double.

Selector

1. In a message call, the selector is the name of the method to be invoked.

2. Selector also refers to a unique identifier that replaces the method name when a project is compiled.

Setter   A setter is one of the two methods associated with a property. It *sets* the value of the property, usually by storing it to an associated instance variable.

Signature   See **Method signature**

Statement   In Objective-C, a statement is a line of code that ends in a semicolon. Note that a statement can span multiple physical lines in a source code file, but is still considered a single statement.

Structure   Although not really a collection, Objective-C structures allow you to group values together as a single unit.

For example, the following code declares a structure named **SATScores** that has three members of type integer named **writing**, **math**, and **reading**:

```
struct SATScores
{
        int writing;
        int math;
        int reading;
};
typedef struct SATScores SATScores;
```

Subclass In an inheritance relationship, a subclass is a class that is derived from another class (its superclass), and is sometimes referred to as a "child class." In Objective-C, a class can have zero, one, or many subclasses.

Superclass In an inheritance relationship, the superclass is a class from which other classes are derived, and is sometimes referred to as a "parent class." In Objective-C, a class can only have one superclass.

Target In the Target-Action design pattern, the target is the receiver of the message.

Target-Action design pattern In the Target-Action design pattern, an object holds two pieces of information for sending a message:

1. A **target**, which is the receiver of the message and

2. An **action**, which is the method to be invoked.

Type inference Type inference refers to a compiler's ability to examine a value in the context in which it is used and infer, or figure out, the type of the value. Type inference is used to infer the return value of Objective-C blocks.

Typedef A typedef statement lets you assign a friendly name to an existing type such as a structure or enumeration. For example, the following typedef statement allows you to use the **DeviceFamily** enumeration without using the **enum** keyword:

```
typedef enum {
        DeviceFamilyiPhone,
```

```
        DeviceFamilyiPod,
        DeviceFamilyiPad,
        DeviceFamilyAppleTV
} DeviceFamily;
```

UI   UI is an acronym for **User Interface**.

Unit testing   Unit testing is a method by which units of code are tested to make sure they work properly. With unit testing, you create classes in a separate project that contain code that tests your App.

URL   A URL (*uniform resource locator*) is a character string that references an Internet resource or a local file on the device. Typically, a URL is a web address that points to a resource such as a web site, HTML page, image, or video—such as **http://www.apple.com**.

User Interface   The user interface is the part of the App that the user sees and interacts with by touch. It includes buttons, text fields, lists, and, as is the case with many games, the entire touch-screen surface.

Variable   A variable is a place in memory where you can store and retrieve information. It's called a variable because you can change the information that you store in it. You can store one piece of information in a variable and then, later on, store another piece of information in the same variable.

View   A view contains one screen of information on an iOS device.

View controller   Every view in an iOS App has a view controller that works behind the scenes in conjunction with the view.

It has properties that (among other things)

• Indicate if the user can edit items in the view,

• Report the orientation of the user interface (portrait or landscape), and

• Allow you to access user-interface elements.

It has methods that

• Allow you to navigate to other views,

- Specify the interface orientations that the view supports, and

- Indicate when the associated view is loaded and unloaded from the screen.

View controller objects are based on the Cocoa Touch Framework's **UIViewController** class or one of its subclasses.

About the Author

So, I was supposed to be a hardware guy.

While I was in college majoring in electronic engineering, I worked at a small company as I paid my way through school. Brian, the head of the software department, would tell me on a regular basis "You know, I think you're a software guy!"

Hardware guys typically do *not* want to be software guys, so I just ignored it as good-natured harassment. Then one day I decided to get him off my back by giving it a try.

As they say, the rest is history. I fell in love with writing software, and the honeymoon is definitely not over!

I learned that writing software is a *very* creative process. In just a matter of hours, I could conceive an idea, create a software design and have it up and running on a computer.

The first software I wrote was a tutorial program that helped new computer users understand how a computer works (this was not long after the birth of the PC). I came up with the idea after watching new computer users give up on themselves before they started.

Since then, I've devoted my teaching career to making difficult concepts easy to understand. So, when Apple released the iPhone and a platform for building Apps, I immediately started teaching classes to empower others to join this software revolution and share in the fun. Maybe you'll find you're a software "guy" too. — Kevin

More Books in This Series by Kevin McNeish

1. *Book 1: Diving In*

2. *Book 2: Flying With Objective-C*

3. *Book 3: Navigating Xcode*

4. *More books coming soon!*

Questions and Comments for the Author

Email me at kevin@iOSAppsForNonProgrammers.com.

Rate and Recommend This Book

If you have enjoyed this book and think it's worth telling others about, please leave your comments and rating for this book and tell your friends. Thanks!

Made in the USA
San Bernardino, CA
21 July 2013